MYRTLE BEACH

MYRTLE BEACH

A History, 1900–1980

Barbara F. Stokes

The University of South Carolina Press

© 2007 University of South Carolina

Published by the University of South Carolina Press
Columbia, South Carolina 29208

www.sc.edu/uscpress

Manufactured in the United States of America

16 15 14 13 12 11 10 09 08   10 9 8 7 6 5 4 3 2

Library of Congress Cataloging-in-Publication Data

Stokes, Barbara F., 1950–
   Myrtle Beach : a history, 1900-1980 / Barbara F. Stokes.
      p. cm.
   Includes bibliographical references and index.
   ISBN-13: 978-1-57003-697-2 (cloth : alk. paper)
   ISBN-10: 1-57003-697-7 (cloth : alk. paper)
     1. Myrtle Beach (S.C.)—History—20th century. 2. Seaside resorts—South
Carolina—Myrtle Beach—History—20th century. 3. Summer resorts—South
Carolina—Myrtle Beach—History—20th century. 4. Tourism—South Carolina—
Myrtle Beach—History—20th century. 5. Myrtle Beach (S.C.)—Economic
conditons—20th century. 6. Myrtle Beach (S.C.)—Biography. 7. Myrtle Beach
(S.C.)—Social life and customs—20th century. I. Title.
   F279.M93S76 2007
   975.7'87—dc22   2007026240

This book was printed on Glatfelter Natures, a recycled paper with 30 percent
postconsumer waste content.

To my children, Lacey and Jonathan, who are always my source of inspiration and awe

Contents

Illustrations

Preface

Myrtle Beach, South Carolina, represents many different things to those whose families have lived there for generations; to those transplants who were beckoned by the ocean, the mild climate, and the easygoing ways of the South; and to those who return year after year for recreation and rest. This place also has a heritage that few have fully come to appreciate. Pieces of it are captured in colorful photographs and postcards, in memoirs, and in written and oral traditions. This history was not written to supplant any of the local histories that have gone before but rather to complement them with thoroughly researched events; economic, social, political, and cultural trends; and documented facts.

Some may question why the time period of 1900 to 1980 was chosen. When Jenifer Powers and I were first commissioned by the Chapin Foundation of Myrtle Beach and the Chapin Memorial Library to research Myrtle Beach's history, we had to set priorities in order to bring some order to the research project. The 1980 "end" date was a crossroads period of sorts. Myrtle Beach at that time was struggling to deal with challenges associated with rapid growth and development, changes related to land use, environmental protection, and quality-of-life issues. The city was emerging from an adolescent state, seeking to redefine itself in more modern, contemporary terms as a mature, national resort. Many of those issues related to development and identity are still at the forefront of community debate. Dealing with these issues and events accurately and objectively would require more than just a chapter or two; it would also require a shift to a more modern current perspective. I believe that the modern period in Myrtle Beach's history since 1980 deserves its own detailed analysis. This was simply not the vehicle for doing so.

This book could not begin to tell all the stories of Myrtle Beach. Its main objective was to research, analyze, and capture for future generations how the sand of the Grand Strand was transformed into a national resort through the vision and hard work of many individuals, businesses, and institutions.

My objective was to produce an accurate representation of Myrtle Beach's people, places, events, and issues. There are many more stories to tell. This book, I hope, lays a solid foundation for future historians, researchers, and those who love Myrtle Beach and South Carolina.

Acknowledgments

This book is truly the product of many, many people who love Myrtle Beach and who appreciate the importance and value of a community's history. What began simply as a graduate assistantship research project, while I was attending the University of South Carolina, evolved three years later into this manuscript, plus a museum exhibit chronicling Hurricane Hazel's fiftieth anniversary, two videos, a collection of oral histories, historic photographs, postcards and ephemera, and a trove of research for the Chapin Memorial Library's archives—plus many, many warm memories and friendships gained along the way.

The entire project owes a debt of gratitude to the board of advisers of the Chapin Foundation of Myrtle Beach and its executive director, Cookie Sprouse, without whom it would never have been born. Her belief in this project and her friendship are sincerely appreciated. In addition the able leadership, patience, and friendship of Cathy Wiggins, executive director of Chapin Memorial Library, cannot be underestimated. Gale Chestnut, Ellen Richardson, and the rest of the library's staff were always ready to help with my endless questions. Other city employees who must be acknowledged are Mark Kruea in Public Information and the staff of the Planning Department, who continually try to maintain some balance between progress and historic preservation.

Very special thanks go to my partner in the early days of the project, Jenifer Powers, who was instrumental in researching the early history of Horry County and Myrtle Beach, conducting countless interviews, and writing several sections of the early manuscript. Her collaboration and brainstorming as the project took shape were invaluable to its success. Sarah Bryan deserves many kudos also for her excellent work in the Myrtle Beach Oral History Project, interviews that were important to the overall story. Her friendship is also much appreciated. My endless thanks to Susan McMillan, who never seemed to tire of wrestling with me on names, dates, places, and sequence of events. Her knowledge and her heart for Horry County made my job much easier.

The research assistance of Walter Hill at the Horry County Museum, Sallie Clarkson at Coastal Carolina University's Kimbel Library, and the able staff members at the South Caroliniana Library at the University of South Carolina, the Horry County Library System, the South Carolina Department of Archives and History, and the State Department of Parks, Recreation and Tourism actually made the process of scouring for primary and secondary sources an exciting journey. Many thanks go also to the many people who reviewed early drafts and shared their knowledge and insights.

Others to whom I am deeply grateful are Dr. Robert Weyeneth and Dr. Connie Schulz in the Public History Program at the University of South Carolina. They instilled in me a scholarly discipline and technique, as well as a hunger for uncovering the people behind a place and the value of heritage. My years spent under their tutelage will remain among some of my favorites.

To the many warm people who love Myrtle Beach and wanted to share their stories, I thank you all for your assistance. Last but certainly not least are my friends and family who stood behind me in this great adventure, especially my parents and my children. Without their support none of this would have been possible. I am most grateful to all.

One

From the Earliest Inhabitants to the Dawn of the Twentieth Century

Sixty miles of unbroken beach mark the Grand Strand's coastline, sand that has seen more footprints from seabirds and sea turtles than from human beings over the centuries. This stretch of sand, along a crescent-shaped inlet known as Long Bay, did not easily submit to change at the hands of human beings. Transformation was slow, yet inevitable.

There is evidence that early man existed in the area about fourteen thousand years ago, but not in any great density. European explorers from England, France, and Spain appeared in the fifteenth and sixteenth centuries, but populated settlements along the upper South Carolina coast were not evident for another two hundred years. They were located around Little River on the north end of the coast and along the Waccamaw River, the coastal swashes, and inland around what would become the county seat, Conway. The main reasons for scattered settlement of the Long Bay area were that poor soil would not support large rice and indigo plantations of the time and that suitable river ports, such as those found at Little River and the Waccamaw Neck, did not exist to support the docking of ships and boats. The beach was also largely inaccessible by land because it was surrounded by rivers, swamps, and marshes. The beach was a quiet and lonely place.

Travelers, however, skirted the coast for centuries, principally along Kings Highway, an early Indian trail that connected the colonies. The tradition of hospitality for these coastal travelers began in the 1700s as several taverns were recorded along Kings Highway. In fact, two of the Grand Strand's earliest celebrated "tourists" were the botanist and naturalist John

Bartram in 1760 and the first president of the United States, George Washington, in 1791. Bartram and his son William are credited with identifying and cultivating more than two hundred native American plants through their travels in the Southeast.

The Earliest Americans on the Grand Strand

Most of what historians and scientists know about the lifestyles of the prehistoric peoples who lived on Horry County's coast was discovered in the second half of the twentieth century, with the first organized research conducted in 1972.[1] Evidence indicates that the area had been occupied, in at least temporary fashion, for the previous fourteen thousand years, although the majority of discovered sites are scattered and date to the woodland period, 2500 B.C.–A.D. 1500.[2] Modern humans are believed to have come to the Grand Strand approximately fourteen thousand years ago as the remains of large animals that these people hunted were found at a construction site on Surfside Beach.[3] However, excavation equipment damaged the site too extensively to leave any data about the living conditions of the people.

Early man in the area would have maintained a hunter-gatherer lifestyle with seasonal campsites that shifted locations in order to make the best use of the limited food resources offered by the land. Although archaeological deposits indicate increasing numbers of people subsisting in the area between ten thousand and four thousand years ago, they did not create any population density that has been discovered along what became the South Carolina coast.

Archaeologists know that approximately fourteen thousand years ago early man was using the area's marine resources. Piles of shells from mussels, oysters, and clams help to identify these sites. Unfortunately, other than the shells and pottery left behind by these people, little evidence of their presence exists. The scattered campsites in the area indicate a simple lifestyle, in sharp contrast to the lives of the Mississippian peoples who lived farther inland. This would include small bands moving about the landscape and forming periodic large gatherings for trade, to find marriage partners, and to perform religious ceremonies.

Indians in the area from the archaic period through the woodland period would not have lived in settled towns along the coast because the land simply would not have supported their way of life. Towns were a marker of Mississippian culture, whose influence extended into South Carolina but did not touch the coast in a significant way. A few pottery shards found at a late Mississippian farmstead near Little River Neck are the only evidence of that culture along the coast.[4]

In general, the amount of archaeological work done along the strand is inadequate to discover the life patterns of the Native American peoples who occupied this area before the arrival of Europeans. The discovery of ceramics, the most abundant artifacts found, has provided little other than information about the continuity and change in pottery styles over time. Life patterns have to be inferred from what is learned at other coastal sites in the region, but this is a poor method to learn about an area that "clearly has its own, unique identity," according to the archaeologist Carl Steen.[5]

Earliest Explorations

Early European explorers to the Grand Strand area may have included John Cabot from England as early as 1498. Giovanni da Verrazano, under the French flag, sailed as far south as Long Bay (present-day Grand Strand) in 1524. The explorations in South Carolina by the Spanish, led by Lucas Vázquez de Ayllón, are more widely recognized. In 1521 Ayllón landed and made contact with the Native Americans in South Carolina, several of whom he kidnapped to take to the Caribbean islands as slaves. Ayllón returned to the area in 1526, founding San Miguel de Gualdape somewhere on the South Carolina coast. This colony failed after only a few months.[6] The French and Spanish attempted settlements in the Port Royal Sound area but failed.

Colonial Settlement

The first permanent English settlement in South Carolina was Charleston, founded in 1670. The European population of colonial South Carolina included English, Scottish, Irish, Welsh, German, Dutch, French, Swedish, and Jewish peoples. Among these groups were several subsets, such as the English from Old and New England, as well as people from the West Indies.[7] Early on, settlers carved out rice and indigo plantations along the rivers leading to coastal trading centers such as Charleston. They settled along rivers because the lands there were fertile and the waterways provided the best transportation routes, the dense swamps of the upper South Carolina coast being virtually impassable. Many of these plantation owners amassed great amounts of property and wealth, which their families maintained until the Civil War.

The noted folklorist Henry Glassie stated that the lifestyle that developed in the southern colonies was more an extension of the Caribbean lifestyle than that of the mid-Atlantic or New England region.[8] The climate and topography of the land and many early settlers mimicking their agricultural experiences from the Caribbean islands made the growth of the plantation system in South Carolina almost a foregone conclusion. This, in turn, led to the disproportional African and Caribbean slave populations in the coastal regions as a large labor force was required to produce high-cash crops such as rice and indigo.

The same settlement patterns, however, did not hold true in the northern part of Georgetown District, which became Horry District in 1801. In colonial times only a few scattered settlements existed there, although land grants in the area date as early as the 1730s. Kingston was one of the towns that the Lords Proprietors of South Carolina founded as an inland settlement to help protect the profitable settlements and plantation areas to the south from the Spanish, Indians, and slave rebellions.

Most of the early families in Horry came from Virginia and North Carolina, which included a sizable Scots-Irish population.[9] For the most part, the people of Horry were an independent, self-sufficient lot who farmed their own land and provided for themselves, rather than being dependent on Charleston for goods or slaves for labor.

A few families found arable land away from rivers such as the Waccamaw and natural harbors such as at Little River. The Withers family established an indigo plantation along most of Long Bay, today's beachfront for Myrtle Beach and surrounding communities. Although Francis Withers had prosperous plantations further south, it is speculated that he acquired grants for the property in Long Bay because he sought refuge from British mariners. Land grant records show that Withers was in the area by 1765.[10] James Henry Rice Jr., a South Carolina naturalist and author, wrote that "on the rolling strand of Horry, just back of the scrub that fixes the naked sand dunes, on a bold bluff overlooking a swash, stood another plantation house of the Withers family. Across the highway, to the northwest, there is a large field, extending right up to the edge of the scrub. This field was planted in indigo before the Revolution by James Withers, father of Francis Withers."[11]

The indigo boom in South Carolina began about 1740 when Eliza Lucas Pinckney refined a process of using indigo plants to produce dye. Between 1756 and 1757 indigo exports from South Carolina rose from 232,100 to 894,500 pounds per year. In 1775 some 1.1 million pounds were exported from South Carolina, with a modern value of about $30 million. Yet South Carolina's dependence on governmental bounties in order to preserve indigo's prosperity proved to be dangerous. Although indigo continued to be produced during the Revolution, after the Treaty of Paris in 1763 it was no longer protected by bounties and tariffs. Thus, Carolina indigo had to compete on the open market. Until the mid-1790s indigo continued to sell well because Britain needed it for its textile industry. However, indigo competition from India, the loss of the bounty, and the 1793 invention of the cotton gin caused indigo to be almost completely phased out of South Carolina agribusiness by 1798.[12]

Today all that is left of the Withers estate is Withers Cemetery, located at First Avenue and Collins Street, near the former site of the family home. It is maintained by First Baptist Church of Myrtle Beach and holds the graves of early families whose descendants still live in the area and whose names include Todd, Owens, Benton, and Stalvey, among others. The first post office in this area was named Withers, South Carolina, in 1888. This became Myrtle Beach Post Office in 1901.

Other early Grand Strand settlers included the Vaught family, who settled farther north on the coast in the general area of modern-day Restaurant Row on U.S. Highway 17. John Vaught migrated from Germany to Charleston in 1751 and after the Revolutionary War settled in Horry County. Four generations of his family would live in Vaught, South Carolina, which had its own post office in 1888.[13] John Allston was first granted the land that became known as Minor's Island and is today Cherry Grove. William Gause obtained a grant in 1737 to 250 acres of land that encompassed what is now known as Gause's Swash, or White Point Swash, near Windy Hill Beach in North Myrtle Beach.[14] He farmed the area and also started a tavern for travelers along Kings Highway.

Jeremiah Vereen was a third-generation American who settled on the Horry County strand near Singleton Swash in the early 1700s. His son, also named Jeremiah, was born there in 1745. He served under General Francis Marion during the Revolutionary War and was host to George Washington on his southern tour in 1791. A descendant of the original Jeremiah named Charles (born 1757) married the widowed Mary Withers from Withers Swash.[15]

The Revolutionary Era, 1776–1785

Still part of Georgetown District during the American Revolution, the swamps, bays, and beaches of the upper South Carolina coastal area played a significant role in the southern campaigns of the war. A prominent figure from the area was Peter Horry. His family fled France and settled in South Carolina after the Edict of Nantes was revoked in 1685. By Horry's death in 1815 he had established three plantations in Georgetown District, growing rice and indigo with slave labor. During the Revolutionary War he served in several campaigns, including the Battle of Camden against the British Lord Cornwallis. He perhaps was best known for his role as a colonel under the command of Brigadier General Francis Marion, nicknamed the "Swamp Fox" by the British because of his elusive and daring strikes. Marion and his forces brought valuable relief to the northern revolutionary forces by drawing many British regiments away from that front and continually hampered Cornwallis's efforts to secure the South during the war. Hiding out in the swamps and remote plantations of North and South Carolina, Marion destroyed British supply lines, captured troops, and routed military victories.

The only significant battle in the Grand Strand area was at Bear Bluff, which is located on the Waccamaw River near Nixonville. Here two detachments of Whigs, or Patriots, from Kingston and Little River trapped a group of Tories, who were forced to flee. Another activity in the area was the 1776 great encampment on Little River Neck of nine thousand revolutionary troops, who were on their way to Charleston to fight the Tories.[16]

The Years 1786–1860

Hoping to prevent sectionalism from dividing the new nation, President George Washington toured the New England states in 1789 and the South in 1791, which included stops on the Grand Strand. His journal indicates that his entourage spent four days in April traveling from Wilmington, North Carolina, to Georgetown. He was entertained by families that still have connections in the area, including the Vereens, the Flaggs, the Allstons, and the Pawleys. The president wrote about having breakfast at William Gause's tavern; staying overnight at the home of Jeremiah Vereen, who also ferried the president and his party across what is known today as Singleton Swash; lodging with Dr. Henry Flagg near what is today Brookgreen Gardens; and visiting with Captain William Allston at Clifton Plantation in Georgetown County.

In 1801 Horry District (it became Horry County in 1868) was carved from Georgetown District and named in honor of its local hero, Peter Horry. Kingston became the capital of the district. The town's name would be changed to Conwayborough (and later shortened to Conway in 1883) in honor of another revolutionary hero, General Robert Conway. In the 1800 U.S. Census 2,606 people, of which 708 were slaves, were counted in Horry County. The highest percentage of slaves, 40 percent, was recorded in 1820. Thereafter blacks made up 30 percent of the population. A surge of immigration gave the area one of the highest population gains in the state after 1840, and this would not be matched again until after the Civil War. By 1860 almost 8,000 people lived in Horry District, compared to more than 21,000 in Georgetown County. Most settled near the towns of Conwayborough and Little River, but river crossings and crossroads villages such as Socastee and Galivants Ferry attracted country stores and taverns that served the isolated farms scattered throughout the area.

The county was in many ways "an underdeveloped eastern frontier of South Carolina," according to the author Bruno Gujer. Rather than rice, the richest natural resource available to Horryites was its forests, which fueled the growth of turpentine distillers and other naval-stores production. Salt flats along the coast provided another source of income. Horry District was also set apart from its southern neighbors in politics. In the 1832 elections the great issue of the day, nullification, was debated even in isolated Horry County. Unionists dominated the district, making it stand out in opposition to the other planter-dominated tidewater districts. When the Civil War broke out, however, Horryites volunteered for service in the Confederate army in record numbers.[17]

The Civil War Years, 1861–1865

The coastal beaches along Long Bay were fortunate to avoid the devastating battles of the Civil War, although several significant events did occur there in the latter part of the war. The coastlines of Horry and Georgetown counties were the sites of skirmishes in 1863 due to Confederate fortifications on the Santee River and Winyah Bay, located at the mouth of the Waccamaw River near Georgetown. These outposts restrained the federal raids upstream, but minor clashes continued to occur on the strand. Most of the encounters occurred north of Winyah Bay and involved Confederate blockade-runners trying to break the hold that Union ships had on the coast. One of the skirmishes occurred on December 5, 1863, at Murrells Inlet, where a blockade-runner's ship was being outfitted. The U.S. brig *Perry* fired on the ship and then sent two boats ashore at Magnolia Beach (modern-day Litchfield Beach) to set fire to her. A detachment of the Twenty-first Georgia Cavalry attacked the landing crew, capturing three officers and twelve men. Federal forces then launched a punitive strike at Murrells Inlet on December 30, which included six vessels, one hundred marines, and four howitzers. They intended to capture the Confederate cavalry unit and destroy the blockade-runner and anything associated with the saltworks. They succeeded in demolishing the Confederate ship and its cargo of turpentine on January 1, 1864.[18]

Union sailors continued up the coast and in April destroyed saltworks at Singleton Swash and Withers Swash. Peter Vaught, whose family owned property in the Windy Hill area, built and operated saltworks at Singleton Swash during the war. Salt was a profitable item to manufacture. The price varied, generally ranging from four to six dollars per bushel during the war. The federal commanding officer described the saltworks as being four separate works, each containing "12 large pans, the water being raised from the beach by horsepower, leading into a cistern large enough to contain 100,000 gallons, built of timber, planked and caulked on the inside"; it also included "about thirty buildings, three of them large warehouses built of heavy logs, containing about two thousand bushels of salt and large quantities of rice, corn, and bacon."[19] Today evidence indicates that the small tidewater lagoon on the eleventh fairway of the Dunes Club at Myrtle Beach was the site of a large saltwater storage tank for a saltworks. Nearby, along the banks of the Singleton Swash marsh, outcroppings of old brickwork for sections of the saltworks are visible. After the destruction of the saltworks at Singleton Swash, the Union ship set sail. By 9:00 A.M. the next morning, it arrived at Withers Swash, where the soldiers went ashore and destroyed a saltworks at a house owned by a Mr. Chilson.[20]

The other Civil War site of significance is Fort Randall, which was located at Tilghman Point on Little River. The outline of the earthworks of the fort is all that is left of the structure. U.S. Navy forces led by Commander William B. Cushing stormed the position on January 5, 1863, but the Confederate soldiers had already fled.

Horry County suffered less than many other parts of the South at the war's end but still felt the economic impacts of its conclusion. The county was not directly in the path of U.S. general William T. Sherman's march of destruction through the South, and the area, which was composed mostly of self-supporting farmers, had not been dependent on slave labor. However, the war stymied production of naval stores, one of the county's main industries, as timber was needed for war efforts and transportation of the large barrels of turpentine became difficult. After the war, the naval-stores industry, as well as other antebellum industries along the Atlantic coast, regained momentum, and turpentine production intensified with railroads providing access to new markets. From approximately 1870 to 1900 one of the principal businesses of Conway-based Burroughs & Collins, the company that would lead the development of Myrtle Beach in the next century, was the manufacture of naval stores for the ship-building trade.[21]

Naval Stores in Horry County

Peak production of South Carolina naval stores occurred in 1882–83, with most coming from Horry County. "Naval stores" refer to the group of commodities that come from timber, such as tar, pitch, rosin, and turpentine. Tar was used on ships' rigging, and pitch was used for caulking boat seams, for general waterproofing, and in medicines for animals and humans. Today these products from slash and longleaf pine trees include inks, adhesives, perfumes, and other consumer products. The industry in South Carolina dates back to about 1705, when the British Parliament authorized bounties on naval stores. These bounties had a significant impact on South Carolina's economy, which produced more naval stores for the British Empire than any other colony by 1720. However, after 1728, when the bounty was revised to require naval stores to be produced by the Swedish method, using green pine trees, South Carolinians turned to a more cost-effective, profitable crop —rice. Pine products once again regained their economic prominence as demand and prices increased in the 1840s and 1850s.[22]

Unfortunately the process of extracting naval-store products from the longleaf pine had not changed since colonial times, and this primitive technique took a terrible toll on the forests. It severely damaged the trees from which the resin came, making them susceptible to wind and disease, and the scarred and deadened trees caught fire easily and burned furiously when ignited. Decades of this practice drove the industry out of its base in the Carolinas to the south and west where railroads were opening access to vast new pine forests.

At the end of the 1880s, which had been a prosperous time for those connected with naval stores, Conway and Horry County's economy was in a state of transition, with rice, cotton, and naval stores facing a grim economic future.[23] With the depression in 1893 and a hurricane that heavily damaged the coastal pine forests that same year, the naval-stores industry was on the decline, which in turn affected the tightening of credit in the region. By 1900 the center of the turpentine industry had moved to southern Georgia and Florida, and Burroughs & Collins had largely shifted from the turpentine business to timber production and truck farming, making the most use of their vast acreage along the strand. They also began buying the land of debt-ridden landowners hurt by the decline of the naval stores.

An event of economic and historic significance for the area was the advent of the railroad, which further diminished the inaccessibility of the Horry County coast. With the connection of Conway by rail via the Wilmington, Chadbourn and Conway Railroad in 1887, the new rail line first opened Horry County's isolated market to the north in Wilmington and to the west in Marion. The Grand Strand was poised to move into the twentieth century.

Two

Transformation of the Sand

*A*s the residents of Horry County moved into the twentieth century, they were generally upbeat about the future. The New South philosophy of the early 1900s, which espoused progress and modernization without sacrifice of racial, political, or cultural continuity, was evident in activities of the Conway Chamber of Commerce and the editorial stances of the *Horry Herald*. Civic leaders were also encouraged by improving tobacco prices and the growth of the infrastructure and banking in the county. The coming of the railroad had a lot to do with an optimistic outlook, even though at first glance that might not seem the case. The expanding rail lines to the south and west of the region opened access to relatively untouched timber supply, although they also helped contribute to the decline of the county's naval-products industry. The positive consequence of the advent of the railroad to Conway in 1887 was the opening of new markets in Wilmington, Marion, and other points north and west.

Seeking to get the highest value for its property in the face of a declining turpentine trade, Burroughs & Collins Company decided to market its vast coastal timber instead of the timber byproducts.[1] However, getting this timber to market required rail transportation because the Waccamaw and Pee Dee rivers and their adjacent swamps surrounded the strand. The state of South Carolina awarded a charter to Conway and Seashore Railroad in February 1899 allowing Burroughs & Collins to run a line from Conway to the Atlantic Ocean at or near Withers Swash, with an option of extending the line to Pawleys Island. In Conway it would connect with the Wilmington, Chadbourn and Conway Railroad. The first train ran from Conway to New Town, the name for the settlement that was to become Myrtle Beach, in May 1900.[2]

In 1900 Dogwood Neck and Socastee townships included clusters of farming communities, black and white, which would form the basis of the Myrtle Beach population in coming years. Two particular communities close to the beach were the Withers Swash area and Sandridge, a farming community situated approximately between modern-day Seventeenth Avenue South and Third Avenue North. Several generations of families, some with roots in the 1700s, populated this area, cementing the community's foundations. Descendants of many of these families still live in the Myrtle Beach area, and modern streets and landmarks carry their names: Bellamy, Bessent, Causey, Chestnut, Clardy, Cooper, Cox, Hemingway, Owens, Nance, Macklen, Stalvey, Todd, and many more. Relatives of some, such as the Stalveys, inhabited the area as early as the mid-1700s. Descendants of William J. Todd, who settled in Horry County in the late 1700s, are still active participants in Myrtle Beach political and civic life. Most of these family members stem from William T. Todd and Erasmus Todd, brothers born in 1846 and 1857, respectively, in Dogwood Neck. Other families migrated in the late 1800s with the jobs created by the timber and naval-stores industries. They maintained family farms in addition to other jobs they may have found. Their farms were mostly self-sustaining with large kitchen gardens, barns for the animals, workshops, blacksmith operations, smokehouses, beehives, fruit trees, grapevines, and more.[3]

The Burroughs & Collins commissary was built about 1901 to serve the visitors who came to the beach, as well as the farmers and laborers living in the area. It was located near the railroad depot and was dismantled in 1927, when Chapin Company opened. The identity of the man in the foreground is unknown. Courtesy of Horry County Museum

MYRTLE BEACH HOTEL, MYRTLE BEACH, S. C., HORRY CO.   Pub. by W. K. Hamilton, Conway, S. C.

Sea Side Inn, also called Myrtle Beach Hotel, opened in May 1901. Courtesy of Horry County Museum

Farming, though, could not provide all their needs, as many families did not own their land and were trapped by the vagaries of nature and economics in sharecropping. On the 1900 U.S. Census for Dogwood Neck Township (803 men, women, and children listed), the majority noted their occupation as farm laborers, which meant that they worked for Burroughs & Collins's farming interests or as sharecroppers for other landowners. William Edward Benton presents an example. He moved his family from near Shallotte, North Carolina, to the Pine Island area west of Myrtle Beach in 1907 in order to farm land owned by Burroughs & Collins. Cotton was his main crop until about 1917, when the boll weevil spread through the area, decimating cotton crops and forcing many farmers to switch to tobacco growing. Farmers faced a poor economy as prices went down and debts went up. Benton's sons left the farm in the early 1920s to find jobs in construction in the burgeoning town of Myrtle Beach.[4] One of those sons, Casper Benton, eventually formed his own general contracting company, C. L. Benton & Sons, which has been involved in Myrtle Beach's growth for generations.

New Town was officially renamed Myrtle Beach in November 1900 for the myrtle bushes that grew there abundantly.[5] Myrtle Beach Post Office was established in May 1901, replacing Withers Post Office, with George R. Sessions as the first postmaster. Its office was in the Burroughs & Collins commissary near the rail line.

For several summer seasons Myrtle Beach consisted only of Sea Side Inn, a bathhouse or crude pavilion, and small Burroughs & Collins company cottages. Even though Burroughs & Collins commissioned an engineer, F. B. Garrett, to lay out a plat for lots, the first one was not sold until 1909, due to fear of hurricanes and the high cost of bringing building materials to the beach.[6] The earliest cottages were owned by Anneas W. Barrett, Charles J. Epps, and Will A. Freeman, all of Conway.[7] Oceanfront lots sold for as little as twenty-five dollars, and anyone building a house costing at least five hundred dollars was promised a free lot. According to Edward Burroughs, "Early cottages were sturdy but roughly built. The main architectural features were a wide porch with a low hanging roof to cut the glare, family bedrooms on the south side to catch winds, a large dining room area, kitchen and servants' quarters. Most people didn't put in window screens because they rusted from one summer to the next. Outhouses were partitioned into two rooms—one for the family and one for servants. The water supply was usually a pitcher pump on the back porch, but some cottages had artesian wells."[8]

Burroughs & Collins was the driving force in all these developments. The company built a dance pavilion adjacent to Sea Side Inn in 1908, complete with electricity, as well as a boardwalk from the beach to the hotel. A crudely built beachfront shelter may have served as the first pavilion, built about 1902. The 1908 hotel pavilion, although described as a round building, was actually multisided, with each side containing an open window. The entire structure was circled with a covered porch. It had a red roof and gray walls with white trim to match the hotel.[9] In addition to these structures, the village contained the Burroughs & Collins commissary, which was originally built in 1901 to serve the company's timber and farm workers, as well as farmers in the surrounding area. Located near the railroad depot, it also served the needs of summer visitors, selling everything from horse collars, flowered chintz, canned foods, and chewing tobacco to candy and household essentials such as lanterns, stoves, and rocking chairs. By 1910 Myrtle Beach, with a population of about twenty-five, had two general merchandise stores, according to a Dun and Bradstreet report—the Burroughs & Collins store and W. T. Todd and Sons.

In March 1905 Burroughs & Collins organized the Myrtle Beach Development Company with capital stock of seventy-five thousand dollars and Franklin A. Burroughs, Benjamin G. Collins, and James E. Bryan Sr. as officers. The new company's objective was to purchase, improve, and sell real estate and to drain and clear the several thousand acres of swampland near Myrtle Beach. Some of the land had been cleared and made productive, but

Rail service to the beach from Conway improved considerably after the Atlantic Coast Line Railroad purchased the line and installed heavier rails in 1911. A road to the beach was still three years away. Courtesy of Horry County Museum

larger acreage was to be converted for farming.[10] It appears that this company's formation was a formality to comply with state regulations regarding land drainage and may never have been an active company. The small community was connected to Conway by telegraph, the railroad, and one telephone, which was located in Bryan's office.

None of these first vestiges of visitor accommodations, however, would have been possible without the railroad. Across the country, railroads were becoming important precursors to the development of previously inaccessible mountains and seacoasts. The railroads brought the visitors to nature's wonders, prompting its owners to build hotels and resorts to house the tourists. For example, in the 1870s the Northern Pacific Railroad worked behind the scenes to support Yellowstone's preservation as a national park because the company saw its potential as a destination market. To participate in that potential, the company also underwrote hotel development in the park area around 1886. The Great Northern Railway built two lodges and a series of chalets adjacent to Glacier National Park between 1911 and 1915.[11] Burroughs & Collins Company followed the example set by these major rail lines. It built and managed the beach's first hotel, Sea Side Inn, which opened on May 23, 1901.[12] Rates were two dollars per day for a room and three meals.

Trains were not the only means of transportation revolutionizing southern tourism. By 1904 several thousand Americans were taking annual vacations in their new automobiles. Henry Ford introduced the Model T in 1908, and although it was not the first automobile, it was the first to be mass-produced with assembly-line techniques, making it more affordable to the masses. The first American filling station opened in 1905 in St. Louis, and by 1910 sales of motorized vehicles skyrocketed with a total of more than 350,000 cars on the road in the United States.[13] In 1911 Horry County claimed 19 of the 5,355 cars that had been registered in South Carolina since 1906.[14] One of Myrtle Beach's earliest gas stations is thought to have been the Conway Oil Company station opened circa 1924 by Charles Dusenbury. He also had a garage for storing automobiles.[15]

In the earliest days of the beach's transformation, the only way to get there was by ferry and cart, both of which were quickly replaced by the train and the automobile. "The ferryboat [from Conway] came to Socastee and crossed at what was known as Peachtree Landing," recalled Edward Burroughs. "There was a road where the air base is now. That was the road we took to Myrtle Beach."[16] The train from Conway ran passengers to Myrtle Beach and back on Saturdays, Sundays, and Mondays during the summer season. The fare for a round-trip ticket was sixty cents; a child's ticket cost thirty cents. Another choice was to drive the dirt road from Conway to Myrtle Beach, built in 1914, but that road could be treacherous after hard rains, according to newspaper accounts. One said, "Miss Sadie Magill suffered a painful accident one day last week while riding in a touring car returning to Myrtle Beach where she was visiting Mr. and Mrs. Don Burroughs. Deep holes were cut in the road by the recent rains. The car running into one of these caused the springs to throw the young lady against the top [ceiling of the car] and injured her head and face in a way which was painful, but fortunately not of a permanent nature."[17]

That dirt road from Conway to Myrtle Beach had a difficult birth. Many in the county did not want to contribute tax dollars for it because they believed that such a road would serve only people of means—in other words, those with automobiles. Without public support, the county could not afford to build the road, the most difficult part of which was getting through the swamps outside Conway. At a community meeting in May 1912, Franklin A. Burroughs said that Burroughs & Collins would donate one-third of the cost, not to exceed twenty thousand dollars, to build the road from the new bridge to the beach. By the following summer the road was under construction.

South Carolina was not alone in wanting to develop its coastal resources during these early days of the twentieth century. "A pilgrimage of pleasure," as authors Lena Lencek and Gideon Bosker call it, was in full swing by the 1870s further north on the Atlantic coast at such resorts as Atlantic City and Cape May, New Jersey.[18] This development was spurred by the growth of extensive and inexpensive rail service, a growing middle class with disposable income, and a spreading social belief in the healthful benefits of the seashore.

Cape May, at the southern tip of New Jersey, was a pioneer of American seaside resorts. During the summer season in the late nineteenth century, more than three million visitors went there for up to two-week holidays. So-called "day trippers," or same-day-only visitors, contributed another eight million people. By 1900 Atlantic City boasted four hundred hotels, some with the capacity of as many as one thousand guests.[19] Miami Beach's development followed closely behind that of the New Jersey shore. Miami had little development until the 1870s, when an enterprising entrepreneur from New Jersey named Henry B. Lum visited the area and was inspired to set up a coconut-growing business there. With two friends from his home state, Lum bought up virtually all of what would one day become Miami Beach and went to work turning the beach into a coconut plantation. His farm venture failed, but in the meantime other investors were attracted to this coastal paradise. In 1905 Biscayne Bay was opened, yielding a new island roughly 7.5 square miles in area and with an 8-mile-long beach. By 1915 more than two hundred hotels and boardinghouses along the route of the Seaboard Air Line Railway dotted Florida's shores, with the largest number of accommodations located in Daytona Beach, Miami, St. Augustine, and St. Petersburg.[20] Many thought it was Horry County's turn to capitalize on its beach.

Even with all the activity and development in Myrtle Beach, Burroughs & Collins learned around 1911 that the company was "land rich but cash poor." The fiscally conservative management valued the security that ready cash provided.[21] To generate cash income, Franklin and Donald Burroughs decided to liquidate part of the company's landholdings to support planned development, and they put the word out for interested buyers. In 1912 an agent in Pinehurst, North Carolina, connected them with Simeon Brooks Chapin, who had a winter home and other business interests in Pinehurst and was considering investments in the region. A banker and stockbroker in New York City, Chapin had visited the Myrtle Beach area in 1911 on a hunting trip around freshwater lakes nearby. He expressed then that the beautiful ocean strand was second only to that in Daytona Beach, Florida, where he had taken his wife on their honeymoon in 1892. After surveying the property in question, Chapin expressed interest in investing. However, he was unable to convince two of his company representatives to relocate in order to manage the property and reluctantly decided not to invest after all. He made a personal trip to Conway rather than sending an impersonal telegram.[22]

Before he left Conway, however, Chapin decided to go into partnership with Burroughs & Collins, as the Burroughs brothers would be the best representatives to manage things from Horry County. The brothers agreed, and Myrtle Beach Farms Company was born. Chapin contributed capital for a one-half interest, and Burroughs & Collins put in almost sixty-five thousand acres in fifty-three tracts of coastal land. The deed, dated October 24, 1912, conveyed the land from Burroughs & Collins Company to Myrtle Beach Farms Company, although the former continued to operate as a separate company.[23] Another important outcome of this partnership was the formation of Chapin Company, which was preceded by Burroughs & Collins Company divesting itself of all mercantile stock around 1919 and engaging exclusively in real estate business. James E. Bryan bought that stock, presumably from the Myrtle Beach store.[24] The former Burroughs & Collins commissary in Myrtle Beach was torn down to make way for the construction of the new Chapin Company store, which opened in January 1928.[25]

While Simeon Chapin's investment in Myrtle Beach was a fortuitous turning point for the fledgling development, that area's growth was curbed by a weak local economy. The rest of the United States may have been experiencing an economic boom around 1920, but South Carolina was not. According to Dr. A. Goff Bedford, the period between 1918 and 1935 was the worst ever in Horry County, even though some growth was occurring along the coast.[26] The economic distress started about 1921 with the collapse of farm prices, including cotton and tobacco, as a result of overproduction, drought, and the loss of overseas markets after World War I. To make matters worse, the boll weevil hit South Carolina's cotton industry, decimating the crops, and state farmers produced less than one-third the number of bales produced in 1920. By the end of that decade, half of the state's farms were mortgaged and 70 percent of the farmers were living on credit. One industry that was doing well was the textile business, and many former farmers moved to mill towns to make a living. By 1925 South Carolina led the nation in cotton-goods production.[27]

Much of the rest of the United States was enjoying an economic boom in the industrial sector, as well as in improved average personal income and general standard of living. It was a decade of significant transportation changes. The air age and the automobile age were both in their infancy when the 1920s began. By the end of the decade, life without cars would be unimaginable for most Americans, and aviation was about to make the leap from an adventure to a commercial transportation system and strategic military force. Both forms of mobilization played parts in Myrtle Beach's transformation, but none more so than the automobile in the 1920s. As roads improved, cars brought visitors and new residents from around the region.

By the 1921 season, Sea Side Inn added a twenty-five-room annex to meet growing seasonal demand and expanded the dance pavilion. Myrtle Beach Farms Company divided forty acres into two hundred lots for residential sale, at a cost of $50 to $250 each, and built a new garage near the hotel for cars. Contractors and plumbers were busy installing waterworks and sewage connections at every cottage.[28]

In 1922 Myrtle Beach Farms added three thousand feet of boardwalk to connect the many new cottages. "The boardwalk stretched from the Pavilion, going north and south, to the last cottages on the beach. Each year it grew longer and longer, as more cottages were built. We spent hours taking walks, going all the way to each end. . . . That boardwalk seemed to be the cohesive core binding the community together," wrote Lucille Burroughs Godfrey.[29] Perhaps the most encouraging investment news in 1922 was that a group of men from Conway, Florence, and Marion were organizing Myrtle Beach Yacht Club, with membership limited to 125 persons. This corporation built a three-story clubhouse facing the ocean, with forty bedrooms with bathrooms, broad piazzas, a bathhouse, and other modern conveniences. Myrtle Beach Farms "donated" the two lots for a nominal amount, presumably because the club would enhance the development of the small town. A mortgage of seventeen thousand dollars from Myrtle Beach Farms to the club on the same date that the deed was filed probably covered materials and furnishings, a common practice used by Myrtle Beach Farms to assist new businesses. Plans were made for a 370-foot pier, the first in Myrtle Beach, that would run from the clubhouse to the ocean and would include a covered deck at one end.[30]

A new pavilion, a true predecessor to the modern-day Pavilion, was built in 1923, providing a central place not only for dancing but also for general entertainment. The main building housed a dance floor upstairs and on the lower level concessions, a bowling alley, and other amusements. There was also a midway with a Ferris wheel, carousels, and slides.[31] By the following year, both the Methodist and Baptist congregations had church buildings on the beach, and buses were running from Conway to Myrtle Beach. The bathhouse was enlarged, and a new barbershop and pressing club opened. However, as evidence of South Carolina's economic distress, Myrtle Beach Yacht Club gave up its members-only restriction because it had been operating at a loss since opening the previous year. The stockholders leased it to a manager, who operated it like any other hotel, filling its rooms with summer tourists and visiting conferences, such as those of the Red Cross, the Methodist Sunday School Training Institute, the Baptist Pee Dee Academy, the Presbyterian Sunday School Convention (from Greensboro, North Carolina), the South Carolina Bankers Association, and the South Carolina Conference in Social Work.

By the beginning of the 1925 season, the *Horry Herald* noted that "Myrtle Beach has already grown from a place of two or three houses, which were little more than shacks a little over 25 years ago[,] to several hundred homes of a better class."[32] In addition, some single and widowed females and married couples opened guest houses, laying the foundation for the accommodations industry in Myrtle Beach. In May 1923 the *Horry Herald* announced that one of the earliest, Burney Cottage, was open and ready for the summer with twelve rooms on the oceanfront "on the same side of the beach as the Yacht Club." Women who bought property in the early 1920s included Bessie and Margarete Sessions, Mrs. Maggie Cuttino, and Bessie Williams, among others.

Even with the steady growth of the community, however, its residents looked at the riches flowing into Florida and wondered, why not South Carolina? In June 1925 a group of about twenty South Carolinians took a tour of coastal Florida to see its development firsthand. They found that hundreds of millions of dollars in development were being pumped into Miami by private investors. "The amount of money being expended and the vast development being made in Florida are almost inconceivable," said Congressman Thomas McMillan of Charleston in the *Beaufort Gazette*.[33] The group concluded that South Carolina could duplicate the Florida experiment. "If we just had a George Merrick, the creator of Coral Gables, we could blossom. Perhaps we shall find him yet," another member of the group said. The editor of the *Beaufort Gazette* called for a united movement in South Carolina to bring more tourists and investments to its shore. The article noted that money was being spent in Florida for a transportation system, telephone companies, general stores, and other developments; complained about too much sectionalism among South Carolina counties; and placed a priority on getting U.S. Highway 17 (or Kings Highway) completed. By the late 1920s Myrtle Beach found its "George Merrick" in the person of John T. Woodside.

Franklin Gorham Burroughs

Born in December 1834 in Williamston, North Carolina, to Anthony and Ethelinda Cobb Burroughs, Franklin Gorham Burroughs came to Horry

County in 1857. It was not his destination, however. He was en route to Memphis, Tennessee, looking for greater opportunities than the Carolinas seemed to afford him. He stopped in Conway to visit a cousin, Jim Burroughs, who had a store there and a turpentine still. Franklin was an independent young man with a good eye for opportunity but not much money. He bid on some public works projects in Conway that included building the town gallows and a bridge. He became involved in Conway life and civic affairs, purchased property, partnered with Benjamin J. Singleton to manufacture naval stores, and set down roots.

In 1860 Burroughs volunteered as a private in the Brooks Rifle Guards, which became part of Company B of the Tenth Regiment of the South Carolina Volunteers. Singleton continued to operate the partnership during Burroughs's initial absence until 1863, when Burroughs bought Singleton's interest and closed it for the duration of the war.[34] In 1864 he was captured in the Battle of Nashville and held as a prisoner for the remainder of the war. He returned to Conway and met and married Adeline Cooper in 1866. They had eleven children, three of whom died in infancy. The surviving children were four girls (Ruth, Sara, Ella, and Lucille) and four boys (Franklin A., Donald M., Edwin, and Arthur M.).

Burroughs took on a new partner, William D. Gurganus, who died in 1870. Two Burroughs and Gurganus employees, Hampton Hart and Benjamin Grier Collins, bought Gurganus's share of the business. Hart left the company shortly after this to partner with John E. Tolar as commission merchants in New York City, and they later handled much of the naval-stores business for Horry County turpentine distillers. In the 1880s the Burroughs and Collins saw the potential of getting into the steamboat business and purchased its first steamboat in 1882. The emergence of affordable transportation via rail and automobile diminished the role of steamboats in the area, and the business closed in 1919, almost forty years later.

In 1895 Burroughs & Collins Company was incorporated after Collins bought Hart's shares with assets of eighty thousand acres of land. Its business interests included transportation (rail and steamboat); commissaries in Port Harrelson, Bayboro, Socastee, Grahamville, Pine Island, Myrtle Beach, Nixonville, Cool Spring, and Galivants Ferry; naval stores, farming, and milling businesses; and the purchase and sale of real estate.

Franklin Burroughs died in 1897, just a few years before he would have seen the fledgling town of Myrtle Beach begin to transform the Horry County coastal landscape. However, his company and his descendants would follow his example and leave an indelible mark on South Carolina's Grand Strand.

Simeon Brooks Chapin

Born in Milwaukee, Wisconsin, on May 31, 1865, Simeon Brooks Chapin built his fortune in the stock market. The fourth of five children of Emory David and Marietta Armour Chapin, Simeon was educated in the public schools in Milwaukee, moved to Chicago in 1878, and attended the Harvard School for Boys in Chicago. After the untimely death of his father, who had been a Chicago Board of Trade operator, Chapin went to work at the age of seventeen as a bank messenger for his uncles at Armour Bros. Banking Co. of Kansas City to help support his family. The following year, 1883, he moved to the Chicago office of Armour and Company, where he worked for the next nine years. In 1892 he began his own business as a banker and broker in Chicago, forming the second-oldest firm on the Chicago Stock Exchange. Also that year he married Elizabeth Mattocks of Chicago. In 1900 he paid the last of the debt left by his father due to business reversals, a total of about forty thousand dollars, even though most of the debts had been forgiven by the creditors at his father's death. By 1901 he formed S. B. Chapin and Co., one of the first trading houses with offices in Chicago and on Wall Street. In 1906 he moved the main offices of his company to New York, where his family made their permanent residence on Fifth Avenue in Manhattan. He and Elizabeth had four children, Marietta, Elizabeth, Simeon Jr., and Virginia.

Chapin had several other business interests in the South besides Myrtle Beach Farms Company, including Chapin Orchards in Pinehurst, North Carolina. In 1894 the family had a summer house in Lake Geneva, Wisconsin, where he was among the first summer residents. There he raised Brown Swiss cattle, for which he won many prizes. In addition to their New York home, the Chapins had a home in Pinehurst, North Carolina (built 1912), and Myrtle Beach (built 1936). Chapin was well known for his philanthropy, most of which was with churches, hospitals, and educational institutions. He also was one of the country's leading Protestant laymen of his time, serving as trustee of a variety of religious organizations, with special interest in religious education. Retiring from business in 1941, Chapin formed four charitable foundations in 1943 in communities where he had lived. The Chapin Foundation of Myrtle Beach, one of the four, by 2005 had contributed more than $15 million to churches, institutions, and hospitals in the city. Other foundations were the Chapin-May Foundation in Chicago (Alice Chapin May was Simeon's sister), the Chapin Foundation in Lake Geneva, and the Chapin Foundation of North Carolina in Pinehurst and Sanford. He died in 1945 in Pinehurst.

Benjamin Grier Collins

Born in Georgetown in October 1845 to Robert Hearn and Mary Jane Grier Collins, Benjamin Grier Collins was orphaned when he was eleven. His adoptive parents were poor but raised him with strong values. He joined the Confederate army when he was sixteen, and upon returning to South Carolina after the war, he went to work for Franklin G. Burroughs driving a turpentine wagon. About 1870 he and fellow employee Hampton Hart bought Burroughs's deceased partner's share of the business, and soon after that Collins also bought Hart's share. In 1895 the company was incorporated under the name Burroughs & Collins Company. In 1870 he married Burroughs's sister-in-law, Laura Jane Cooper, with whom he had eleven children. He was a lay preacher and a founding member and director of the Bank of Conway, which became the First National Bank of Conway in 1909. Collins sold his interest in Burroughs & Collins in 1906 to the Burroughs brothers in order to pursue his banking interests, but the company name was retained and continued to operate as such until 1990. Collins died in 1929 in Conway.

James Edward Bryan Sr.

The other pivotal partner in the early development of Myrtle Beach was James Edward Bryan Sr. Born in February 1876 in South Carolina, he began his professional career as a teacher in Bucksport but was working as a salesman in a Burroughs & Collins commissary in 1900. He went to work at the company's store in Myrtle Beach in 1902, supervising their timber and farming interests. He married Susan Stone of Little River the same year. Through the early formative stages of the new coastal town, James Bryan managed the Burroughs & Collins commissary and oversaw the operations of Sea Side Inn and the Pavilion. In general, to the people of Myrtle Beach and the surrounding area, he was known for building the community, providing jobs, helping people who needed help, and assisting new businesses.

While they lived at the beach year-round in the early years of their marriage, Susan Bryan set up a household in Conway for the winter months when children started arriving, and Bryan "commuted" between Myrtle Beach and Conway on the weekends. The Bryans had seven children: Elneda, James Jr., George W. "Buster," Leon, Emma Jay, Geraldine, and Susan. The family stayed in the Myrtle Beach cottage every summer until the late 1930s, when they built a home there and moved permanently. Affectionately known as "Mr. Jim," Bryan was the first president of Myrtle Beach Farms Company in 1912 and the first president of the Chapin Company in 1928. Bryan died in December 1937 in Myrtle Beach.

Three

Depression-Era Developments

*I*n October 1929 the stock market crashed and threw the United States into the worst economic depression of its history. Businesses failed, banks closed, and millions lost their jobs and their homes. Even in the depths of disillusion and collapse, this dark chapter in American history was also a time of building new systems of government and new institutions of public life. A relative stability could be found in places across the country. Myrtle Beach, South Carolina, was one of these places.

Far from being the case for all of South Carolina, Myrtle Beach underwent important, positive changes during the Great Depression and the New Deal period. These changes consolidated its transformation of the 1920s from an isolated coastal area to a regional tourist haven. Key individuals and aid from federal programs fostered this period of transition that was critical to the development of the infrastructure and institutions in the area. This development would allow for tremendous growth in the near future, and it was all the more remarkable because it took place during and because of the Depression.

For the South, the Depression actually began in the earlier 1920s. Already staggering under the collapse of agricultural prices, the region experienced economic problems that were only exacerbated by the 1929 stock market crash. The decade was a difficult one for South Carolina: cotton lost almost three-fourths of its value between 1920 and 1930, and annual per capita income dropped almost 40 percent between 1929 and 1933. During the 1920s twenty-five of the state's forty-six counties decreased in population as farmers and turpentine workers left the area looking for better opportunities. Within the state, they found nonagricultural jobs mainly in Myrtle Beach, Greenville, and Spartanburg. The population of Horry County grew by 22.7 percent, with greater growth found only in Greenville County (32.2 percent) and Spartanburg County (23.3 percent). Dogwood Neck Township, the location of Myrtle Beach, grew by almost 50 percent during the decade, from 827 in 1920 to 1,240 in 1930.[1]

Even with Myrtle Beach's growth, especially at the end of the decade, Burroughs & Collins Company was unsure that the area could live up to its potential. One significant impediment to its further growth was transportation access. Until the 1920s Horry County had a difficult time getting new roads built due to the conflict between people who lived in the towns (and consequently had more cars) and those in the country (who did not want to be taxed for roads they believed were unnecessary). Rural roads were largely the responsibility of county governments in South Carolina. Without public support for financing construction, Horry County could not afford to build a road to the beach. The first road between Conway and Myrtle Beach, by way of Socastee, was completed in 1914. It was financed with a donation of up to twenty thousand dollars from Burroughs & Collins, fifty thousand dollars from a road tax of three dollars on all able-bodied men between the ages of twenty-one and fifty-five, and thirty thousand dollars raised by the public.[2]

Pressure was mounting nationally for the federal government to provide better roads as the automobile was creating a transportation revolution by 1920. In 1916 Congress passed the Federal-Aid Road Act, under which each state would create a highway agency to carry out federal-aid projects. South Carolina organized its state highway department the next year, but this agency acted principally as the link between the federal government and the counties. The counties still had to support bond referendums to help pay for roads, which many Horry County citizens were loath to do. Development of major new roads in the coastal areas of South Carolina by the late 1920s was largely confined to the building of the Atlantic Coastal Highway.[3]

The turning point for South Carolina's highways came in 1929 with the passage of a $65 million state bond issue for roads.[4] A 1929 Atlantic Coastal Highway map indicates that this bond issue would include the hard-surfacing of Kings Highway from the North Carolina state line through Myrtle Beach to Georgetown.[5] That would not come soon enough for Burroughs & Collins. In January 1926 the company's board of directors retained Earle Sumner Draper, a landscape architect, to study the transportation issue. Draper reported that without adequate roads, prospects for a successful resort town at Myrtle Beach were slim. A month later the board voted to sell more than sixty-four thousand acres of land to Greenville textile magnate John T. Woodside for $950,000 ($100,000 down payment and $850,000 mortgaged). This included the majority of Myrtle Beach Farms

The Widespread Popularity of

Charming
MYRTLE BEACH
America's Finest Strand

IS INSURED BY Its Elaborate Program
Its Remarkable Opportunities
Its Logical Location

Beautiful Home Sites

It would be difficult to find a more charming location for your coastal resort home. Beautiful home sites facing or near the beach are available, while the development offers fishing, swimming, yachting, riding, driving, bathing, hunting (in season); and the plan contemplates golf, tennis, and other forms of recreation. The social life in all its ramifications has long since been established at Myrtle Beach. Thousands of visitors have seen Myrtle Beach in past years, and the development already enjoys a very extensive colony of permanent home owners.

America's Finest Strand

Twelve miles of broad, hard sea shore, backed by 104 square miles of picturesque coastal plains combine to make a natural setting for a delightful resort center at Myrtle Beach. The property involves many sparkling lakes, all bedecked with typical subtropical vegetation. The most fertile soil, natural resources, and a railroad and complete net work of highways and bridle paths insure the accessibility and the value of this property.

A Great Ideal

Myrtle Beach is being developed by well known South Carolinians—the Woodsides of Greenville,— not with a view to personal profit, but in line with their higher aims of service to mankind. The same determination, high ideals, inspiration and stability that has marked their very successful endeavors in the Piedmont section will permeate their development on the coast. The earnings at Myrtle Beach are designated for the development of the property and the service of mankind, instead of personal gain, a factor which alone speaks for the success of the undertaking.

Write or see our local representative in your city for literature and details

MYRTLE BEACH SALES COMPANY
F. J. PARHAM, Sales Director
MYRTLE BEACH, S. C.

Directors
John T. Woodside
J. D. Woodside   E. F. Woodside
R. I. Woodside   H. B. Springs
J. R. Ricketts

Officers
John T. Woodside, President
H. B. Springs
V.-Pres. and Executive Mgr.
J. R. Ricketts, Sec. and Treas.

Active Program This Summer

The program of development of Myrtle Beach will necessarily extend over a number of years, so great is its extent and so gigantic the undertaking. A hotel already is at the public's service, as well as a pavilion and other facilities, while churches, a club and private homes are already in use. Shortly, no doubt, a new and larger hotel will arise with pavilion, ballroom, casino, golf course, tennis courts, garage, stables and other necessary facilities. New streets are being opened and municipal facilities improved. In short the program involves the erection of a model resort city, as Carolina's own playground for the nation.

Opens June 15

Myrtle Beach is not new. It is already well known and popular. Under the new program, however, the sale of home sites will open on June 15. In keeping with the construction organization there has been formed a large sales organization with headquarters at Myrtle Beach. Lots will be offered beginning June 15 at a comparatively very low figure and on convenient terms. You are invited to visit the property. Spend your next vacation at Myrtle Beach. Reservations can be made now for lots in hotel and club section.

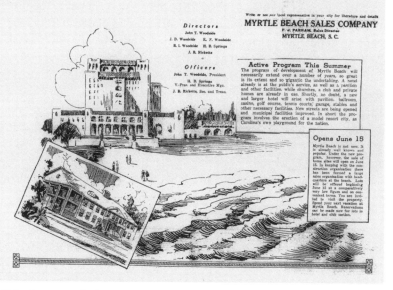

In 1926 John T. Woodside placed a series of ads promoting Myrtle Beach in newspapers around the region. He had purchased sixty-five thousand acres from Myrtle Beach Farms Company early that year. This ad appeared in the Horry Herald.

Company's property, except for about thirteen hundred acres comprising the Pavilion, surrounding property and its beachfront, as well as commercial property in the downtown area.[6]

John T. Woodside made his fortune in cotton mills, banking, insurance, and real estate in the Greenville area in the early 1900s. In 1924 he began branching out with hotels and resorts, his first venture being the Poinsett Hotel in Greenville, which was followed soon thereafter by Wildwood, a mountain retreat twenty-five miles outside of Greenville.[7] Encouraged by the success of these ventures, Woodside decided to expand his resort holdings to Horry County after reading a copy of James Henry Rice Jr.'s book *Glories of the Carolina Coast,* according to James Grist, editor of the *Yorkville Enquirer* (York, South Carolina) in the mid-1920s.[8] Rice wrote, "We cannot have a developed State until we reckon the coast among our assets; nor earn mankind's respect until we show that so rare and exquisite benefactions stir our hearts."[9]

Woodside asked Horry County native Holmes B. Springs Sr., an executive in two of his Greenville companies, about the area. Springs, a cousin of Franklin Burroughs's wife, Iola, put him in contact with Burroughs & Collins, and on February 10, 1926, Springs closed the deal for Woodside to purchase most of the assets of Myrtle Beach Farms Company. The purchase included a total of 64,488 acres with twelve miles of ocean frontage.[10] According to the *Horry Herald,* the property included nine freshwater lakes of 2 to 15 acres in size, as well as Myrtle Beach Farms, which employed 125 persons and had forty to fifty tenant homes, more than three hundred Hereford cattle, two hundred Duroc-Jersey hogs, 250 acres of Irish potatoes, 40 acres of string beans, 500 acres of corn, 100 acres of soybeans, and 5,000 acres of pastureland.[11] Due to the amount of property involved in this sale, payment was to be completed in six annual installments through 1932 at an interest rate of 6 percent. Woodside was sixty-one years old at this time, an age at which most men were retiring, but his energy and vision were infectious. Unfortunately his timing was not good.

Woodside had big plans for his new holdings on the coast. These plans embraced the natural environment and an early form of a master-planned development. According to Springs, "It is planned to lay out the entire property in such a way that it may be developed in sections and not interfere with the whole scheme of setting up a city. Landscape architects and engineers are to make all the necessary surveys to take care of every condition that might affect such a city in years to come. Complete plans are contemplated, taking care of all the public utilities including lights, water, power lines, sewerage and sewerage disposal where necessary. Sites for hotels, churches and schools, railroad terminals and other public institutions are

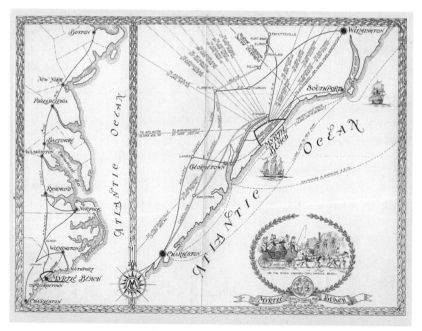

This map appeared in the May 15, 1927, issue of the Spur *in an article titled "Myrtle Beach, South Carolina, a Stupendous All-Year Resort in the Making," by John Vavasour Noel. Early promoters proclaimed that Myrtle Beach was midway between New York and Miami, omitting how difficult it still was in 1927 to reach the growing town.*

planned to locate as to best serve the entire area. A complete system of zoning."[12]

Myrtle Beach Estates, one of the new companies that Woodside formed to develop the coast, went to work immediately constructing an administration building. Its lower floor was for the company's offices, and the upper floors were hotel guest rooms. By December 1926, however, the demand for guest rooms was so high that the entire building was converted to a hotel and renamed Sea Side Inn.[13] The original Sea Side Inn, which was renamed the Carolina and later the Strand, was physically moved closer to the beach, the Pavilion, and the bathhouse. Renovations included new bathrooms in every room, a new kitchen and cafeteria dining room, and an enlarged lobby with entrances on the south side facing Eighth Avenue and on the north facing the quadrangle between the "new" Sea Side Inn and the ocean. The company also added four miles of boardwalk, set aside a fifteen-thousand-acre game preserve, and developed programs to ensure year-round visitors. It worked on better transportation access by opening an airport in August

1928 and encouraging Atlantic Coast Line Railroad to spend half a million dollars improving its line from Conway to Myrtle Beach.[14]

The *National Real Estate Journal,* quoting the *Greenville News* (Greenville, North Carolina), reported that as of October 1928 Myrtle Beach Estates was incorporated for $6 million and had holdings worth $8.5 million, backed by $15 million in investments in other Woodside interests. The company's principal near-term objectives were the sale of eight hundred lots at prices ranging from $500 to $7,000 in the "Hotel District," the area around the original community, and infrastructure development. Five salesmen were located in Myrtle Beach, and others were in offices in Columbia, Charleston, and Greenville, South Carolina; Wilmington, North Carolina; Atlanta, Georgia; New York City; and Jacksonville and Miami, Florida. Woodside even hired a fleet of seven-passenger Hudson sedans to transport potential investors from Columbia, Walterboro, and Conway to the beach.[15]

The company upgraded communications, installing a new telephone triple-trunk line from Myrtle Beach to Conway, with telephone service to several rooms in Sea Side Inn and connections between the hotel and other buildings in Myrtle Beach. There was a plan for a chamber of commerce to be located in the new administration building at the corner of East Broadway and Railroad Avenue facing west.[16] The company proposed having an exhibit or museum room in this building in which samples and specimens of the area's plant and animal life would be displayed. In February 1927 contracts for more than five hundred thousand dollars were approved, covering new waterworks; electric lights; concrete curbing, gutters, and sidewalks; street surfacing and lighting; and development of the Ocean Forest Golf Course and Country Club. The twenty-seven-hole golf course opened in 1927, and Ocean Forest Hotel, popularly called the "Million Dollar Hotel" because of its grandeur, was completed in late 1929.

Within four years the quiet summer village of Myrtle Beach was transformed into a resort town, with Woodside capital providing the foundation for the town's future growth. All of this activity kept many people employed for several years. Horry Benton, who remembered working on Ocean Forest Hotel and the golf course, said that most of the labor was done by local people and those from around Horry and Georgetown counties:

[Anyone] that wanted to work had a job because it took that many people. [For some,] it was hard to get here and most of them would come and stay five days and work. . . . When we was building the golf course, 'course we used labor to grade it by hand, mules and scoop and shovels and picks to take up the stumps and everything. . . . I would take the truck and before that Monday morning, I would go

The mule was a valuable contributor to the development of Myrtle Beach, used for farming, early road building, construction, and transportation. This 1936 photograph shows Lafayette Hotel in the background. Betty Hartnett Collection, courtesy of Chapin Memorial Library

down and get help between Socastee and Pawleys Island, back in those woods and pick up a lot of people to work. . . . I'd bring them up here on a Monday morning, have them here by the time to go to work. They would stay until Friday, and Saturday morning, they would get paid and I would take them back to their home. And that's the way the golf course was built. A lot of those people, the carpenters and better class of people than the laborers, lived close around. They didn't bring no labor from up north or anything like that."[17]

Woodside hired Robert White, the first president of the Professional Golfers' Association (1916–19), to design and build the Ocean Forest course. Casper Benton, Horry's older brother, worked for White, who sent Casper to New York City to learn how to build a golf course. Casper was a bit amused by this, his brother remembered, telling Horry that all his life he had fought grass on the farm, trying to kill it, and "[n]ow I'm going to go up there to learn how to grow grass." Horry Benton sowed the first seeds on the golf course "with a pair of mules with one of those wide seeders to mix them with some sand so all the seeds wouldn't pour out."[18]

In 1929, as Ocean Forest Hotel was being finished, Woodside announced his most ambitious project, Arcady, a sixteen-thousand-acre recreational hideaway for America's most prominent families, the likes of which few in South Carolina had seen. Woodside joined the architect Raymond Hood at

Ocean Forest Hotel, also billed as the Million Dollar Hotel, was built by John T. Woodside and celebrated its grand opening in February 1930, just months after the stock market crash of October 1929. It was razed in 1974. Myrtle Beach Postcard Collection, courtesy of Chapin Memorial Library

a Manhattan, New York, press conference to present renderings of Arcady.[19] Ocean Forest Hotel and the Ocean Forest Golf Course and Country Club were to be used by Arcady members until the 350-room main house and golf course were completed. The development would have four miles of beachfront and would be owned entirely by a membership group. Family membership certificates were similar to shares. The Arcady prospectus, dated February 5, 1929, stated that expectations were to sell the first 500-membership unit by December 30, 1930, or refund all units sold up to that date minus the 20 percent administration fee. The first 500 units cost $1,250 each.[20]

Arcady was intended for whole families and featured golf courses for men and women and special golf courses for mothers and children, indoor playrooms for children and camps for boys and girls nearby, as well as educational facilities so that children would not miss school during visits to the beach. In addition to the main house, the one-hundred-room beach house, which was to be close to the ocean, and the golf house with another one hundred rooms were planned. Joining Woodside in the project were the architect Raymond M. Hood of Raymond Hood, Godley and Fouilhoux of New York, noted for his design of the Tribune Tower in Chicago; and

Albert A. Ainsworth of New York, chairman of the executive committee, who was responsible for memberships and general project management.

Woodside was not the only builder in Myrtle Beach during this period. In 1928 Burroughs & Collins chartered the Chapin Company, to be led by James E. Bryan Sr. The new company assumed certain Myrtle Beach Farms assets of property, office and store fixtures, a post office, a delivery truck and an automobile, merchandise, a filling station building, inventory and equipment, two commercial buildings, and three cottages. This included a one-story, block-long, mission-style Chapin Company building, which opened in June 1927 on Main Street. Myrtle Beach Post Office, Delta Drug Store, and Winstead's Furniture Company moved into the Chapin Company building. Richard Hussey recalled that in the mid-1930s Chapin Company served as a "bank" of sorts: "They had the only safe in Myrtle Beach, and so they'd keep your money for you so you wouldn't have to go to Conway. My brother used to send me down—see, everybody walked everywhere they went—he used to send me down the street to put the money in the 'bank' for them. I remember Mr. Luke Ward, he was working in the office here at Myrtle Beach Farms. He and Buster Bryan, I used to see them all the time in there. If you wanted anything in Myrtle Beach, you went to Chapin to get it."[21]

Chapin Company became the center of commerce, according to Howell "Skeets" Bellamy Jr., and Myrtle Beach could not have grown without that company: "When the tourists left on Labor Day, it [the store] was there, and Chapin Company really looked after the people in the community for a long time. It was the bank, it provided credit to people that couldn't afford to buy groceries. A lot of folks subsisted on what they earned from June to September and Chapin Company carried them until the next summer season."[22] Bellamy's father, Howell V. Bellamy Sr., served as president of Chapin Company from 1955 until his death in 1975.

Woodside's investment and vision for the Grand Strand also helped stoke the flame of interest in surrounding beachfront property. In 1926 a group from Florence formed Ocean Drive Estates and prepared subdivision plats of the Ocean Drive area. Cherry Grove was growing, adding about a dozen cottages in 1924, and the Crescent Beach and Windy Hill developments began in 1930. In the 1920s "Doc" Allen Spivey's Horry Land and Improvement Company began buying land south of Myrtle Beach, which he would develop as Spivey Beach. Further south near Murrells Inlet, George J. Holliday bought a large tract that he planned to develop into Floral Beach (modern-day Surfside Beach). In early 1926, however, he sold it to Robert D. McClure of Columbia, who formed Floral Beach, Inc., intending to transform it into a resort "with a modern resort hotel, golf courses, dancing pavilions and other resort features."[23] Even further south, wealthy industrialists and others were buying former plantations in Georgetown County, many of which had reverted to swampland when rice production ended.

What would become Brookgreen Gardens, the nation's first sculpture garden, was part of one of these plantation purchases. A native of New York, Archer M. Huntington was the son of Collis P. Huntington, a founder of Central Pacific and Southern Pacific railways. Archer Huntington and his wife, the renowned sculptress Anna Hyatt Huntington, purchased four adjoining plantations in 1930: Brookgreen, Laurel Hill, Springfield, and the Oaks. Brookgreen was one of the most productive rice plantations in the South in the mid-1800s. Huntington's plan was to build a winter home and a public sculpture garden to display his wife's work, as well as that of other sculptors. The twenty-five-hundred-acre Huntington Beach State Park, where the Huntingtons' former home Atalaya is located, and nine-thousand-acre Brookgreen Gardens, which officially opened in 1932, were carved from that original purchase. Construction of Brookgreen Gardens and Atalaya provided welcome jobs for many in the area during the darkest years of the Depression. After the gardens opened to the public, many local women worked as tour guides and hostesses.[24]

The stock market crashed in October 1929. Four months later, on February 21, 1930, Ocean Forest Hotel celebrated its grand opening, a gala affair with visitors from all over the country. However, this was a bittersweet event for Woodside. His business empire was collapsing quickly, although few details are available as to exactly what transpired financially. Woodside was ousted as president of Woodside Cotton Mills in February 1931, a corporate takeover engineered by William Iselin and Company, Woodside's New York–based broker and banking house. Iselin Company officers Floyd Jefferson and Oliver Iselin headed Woodside Mills' new board of directors after this date. In his study of Woodside's career, James Dunlap says that the takeover by commission sales agents was not entirely unexpected: "Sales agents and machinery manufacturers in the Northeast wielded tremendous economic power over their Southern clients. Throughout his memoir, Woodside mentions going east to buy textile machinery or secure operating capital from cotton sales agents. Woodside routinely borrowed money from commission merchants."[25]

With his financial empire collapsing, Woodside took great hope from a December 1931 bill in Congress to establish the Reconstruction Finance Corporation (RFC). The new agency began operations in February 1932 with the objective of lending money to financial institutions and the railroads. Woodside traveled to Washington, D.C., in 1932 in order to persuade the RFC to lend money directly to cotton mills.[26] However, legislation to authorize the RFC and the Federal Reserve System to make working capital loans to businesses would not be passed until 1934, too late for Woodside, who by that time had lost his position and his wealth.

Documentation is not available as to what Woodside was doing between 1932 and 1933 or when he relinquished control of the Ocean Forest hotel and golf club. Newspaper reports indicate that the 1930 and 1931 seasons were busy with many tourists and conventions at the hotel. However, the hotel closed sometime in 1932 and remained so until May 1933, according to Horry Benton, who was a hotel watchman and an employee of Ocean Forest Country Club in 1933: "A long period of time that the Ocean Forest was closed. A year or more. Two watchmen lived there during that time. Robert White was in charge of the hotel and had to have a guard on site for insurance purposes."[27] Horry and his wife, Lucille, moved into the hotel, and in March 1933, while they were living there, their daughter was born. In May the hotel reopened and the family had to find another home.

On April 6, 1933, the *Horry Herald* announced that unsold portions of Myrtle Beach Estates were to be available at public auction the next month. Myrtle Beach Farms, which held the mortgage for the Woodside property, paid the tax lien of $270,000 ($60,000 of which was for the land under Ocean Forest Hotel) and regained its property with significant improvements. Myrtle Beach Farms then sold about forty-seven thousand acres of the total to P. O. Mead of Charleston for $100,000 to cover back taxes and set aside funds for future taxes. Eventually this inland tract was purchased by International Paper Company.[28]

Iselin and Company purchased the contents of Ocean Forest Hotel for $70,000 and reopened the hotel for the 1933 season. In 1940 Lawrence Barringer and John Stoddard purchased the hotel and a Mr. Carmichael of Charlotte, North Carolina, bought the golf course.[29] The hotel would have several more owners before it was razed in 1974. The golf club also changed ownership several times until it was sold to Frederick Miles in 1944, who renamed it Pine Lakes Golf Club. The Miles family owned it for more than fifty years, selling it to Burroughs & Chapin in 2001.[30]

The Woodside legacy was a foundation for future prosperity and an infrastructure that would have taken many more years for the town to gain on its own. This included improved water and sewer systems, paved streets and highways, new accommodations for tourists, and perhaps most important, exposure and publicity for Myrtle Beach that would bring tourists and investors to South Carolina's shores for years to come.

Outside of the physical development of Myrtle Beach, the Depression years were perhaps hardest on the farmers, sharecroppers, and tenant farmers in South Carolina. According to Bernard Baruch, a native South

Carolinian, owner of Hobcaw Barony in Georgetown County, and trusted adviser to Presidents Woodrow Wilson and Franklin Roosevelt and consultant to four other presidents on economic and international affairs, "I saw the effects of the Depression up close in South Carolina, where a decade of agricultural depression had preceded the ultimate collapse and made it even worse. At Hobcaw, the people were taken care of, but some farmers in the area were utterly impoverished. My neighbor, Tom Yawkey, owner of the Boston Red Sox, and I helped provide food for them. But private charity could not make a ripple in the ocean of destitution."[31] By October 1933 more than 23 percent of South Carolina's 1.74 million citizens were members of relief families. The predominantly rural counties of the Piedmont had a high rate of tenant farms dependent on cotton, which suffered during this period. Between 1929 and 1931 the cash value of the state's farm commodities fell more than 50 percent, from $149.7 million to $71.2 million. In 1932 rural poverty was so severe that 45 percent of South Carolina's farms carried delinquent taxes.[32]

Even so, tourists were still coming to the beach, and few persons in the area were on relief in 1930. Only thirteen people of the more than twelve hundred living in Dogwood Neck Township were reported on the unemployment schedule as without a job or able to work and looking for a job.[33] The summer of 1930 saw the South Carolina Bankers Association conference, a regional Kiwanis Club conference, a South Carolina State Senate meeting, the Southern Textile Association conference, and other meetings at Ocean Forest Hotel. A new miniature golf course opened at the corner of Kings Highway and Ninth Avenue. Women from Greenville, Cheraw, and Bennettsville announced new guest-house operations, and between fifteen thousand and twenty thousand were expected for July 4 festivities.

To make ends meet and accommodate a rapidly increasing tourist and resident population, many people, predominantly women, started boardinghouses or guest houses by 1930. Several women bought property in 1926 for such accommodations, hoping to capitalize on the excitement and interest generated by the Woodside investment. Women who purchased property in their names from Myrtle Beach Farms in 1925 and 1926 included Mrs. J. K. Stalvey, Sallie Sanders Barnwell, Mrs. Essie Rogers, Mary Louise Brown with Nan Brown and Mrs. Walker Brown Davis, Alva and Myrtle Johnson, Mrs. Clif Rankin, Elsie K. Farber, Mrs. William F. Hucks, Mrs. N. G. Gonzales, Mrs. Dot K. Monroe with C. J. Gasque, Mrs. R. B. McKorell, Mrs. Loulie H. Waters, Mrs. Lena J. Scurry, and Mary Platt.[34] Twenty households in Myrtle Beach on the 1930 U.S. Census had boarders, many of whom were young, in nonagricultural professions, and single. These lodgers listed occupations that included auto mechanic, public-school teacher, sign painter, civil engineer, surveyor, salesman, carpenter, general laborer, and others.[35] An active demand for guest houses also came from employees with the various construction crews working in the area. Myrtle Beach experienced an influx of international workers with the opening of Ocean Forest Hotel. Rudolph Woender, whose parents were from Austria and Canada, managed the grand hotel. He employed a houseman from Martinique; waiters from Switzerland, Germany, and Holland; an assistant manager from Ireland; and a dishwasher and chef from Italy, plus many others from around the United States.

The steady growth in population and tourism also stimulated commerce during this period. Mack's 5 & 10 Cent Store opened in 1933. Ben's Broadway Theatre, adjacent to it, opened in 1936. Clarence Macklen and C. L. Phillips began publishing the *Myrtle Beach News* in 1935. Delta Drug Store, at least two liquor stores, and a few restaurants, such as Seven Seas Grill and Ocean Front Tavern, were operating in the mid-1930s.

National recovery from the Depression did not begin in earnest until Franklin D. Roosevelt (FDR) was elected president in 1932. In FDR's first one hundred days in office, he pushed through many of his New Deal programs. Nearly two billion dollars in federal funds came to the South through New Deal programs largely designed to put people back to work, and they touched the lives of nearly every citizen in South Carolina due to the severity of the economic situation there.[36] Some of the most active

Youpon Dunes, built in 1936 by Simeon B. Chapin, cofounder of Myrtle Beach Farms Company, is shown shortly after completion. The house is located at 3202 N. Ocean Blvd. Note the height of the original sand dunes. Courtesy of Betty Hartnett Collection, Chapin Memorial Library

agencies in the state were the Agricultural Adjustment Administration, the Rural Electrification Administration, the Works Progress Administration (WPA), and the Civilian Conservation Corps (CCC). By the mid-1930s the economic situation in Horry County was improving, due in large part to the number of public and private construction projects under way and the continuous pilgrimage to the beach. Several families, such as that of Daniel W. Nance, sold their farms in the area and moved to Myrtle Beach to work on the construction projects or form their own companies. Myrtle Beach's Myrtle Heights–Oak Park Historic District, located on either side of North Ocean Boulevard between Thirty-second Avenue North and Forty-sixth Avenue North, was one of the neighborhoods developed during the early 1930s. This district contained homes of the founders of Myrtle Beach Farms Company: Simeon Chapin, James E. Bryan Sr., and Franklin A. Burroughs. In addition, two notable New Deal construction projects in the area were the Intracoastal Waterway and Myrtle Beach State Park, both of which celebrated major milestones in 1936.

Intracoastal Waterway

The Intracoastal Waterway extends from Maine to Florida along the Atlantic coast. The South Carolina section was one of the last segments to be completed. Since 1910, civic leadership in Conway had promoted a waterway from the Waccamaw River in Conway northward to Little River that could be used for barges, rafts, and small sailing craft transporting timber and turpentine. These products could then be shipped north from Little River. Planning by the U.S. Army Corps of Engineers began in 1930, but the Conway route was not to be. The final plans called for digging a straight cut through some of the highest land in the county from Little River to Socastee Creek, the longest manmade ditch in the entire length of the Intracoastal Waterway. Work was completed on the final cut of the waterway at Socastee in the spring of 1936. Local, county, state, and national dignitaries attended the celebration at the Socastee swing bridge in April 1936. Geraldine Bryan, daughter of James E. Bryan Sr., cut the white ribbon across the waterway, and a flotilla of yachts from Charleston made its way through this last section. Work, however, would continue for several more years to deepen it, employing hundreds of men from 1931 to 1937. Not only did it significantly contribute to the war effort during World War II by providing safe passage for defense cargoes along the Atlantic, but the waterway also drained about seven thousand acres in the area for farming and desirable development.

One of the young men who worked on the waterway was Philip Gray, who was twenty-one years old at the time. He wrote the following account in his memoir:

I learned there was a crew coming to Myrtle Beach late that year
[1937] to work on the Inland [sic] Waterway. The Inland Waterway
was dug in 1931–32, but they had a crew coming in 1937 to deepen
and widen it. I drove up to Myrtle Beach [Gray was working in
Georgetown at the time] and talked to the people at Walter S. Ray
Construction Company out of Pittsburgh, Pennsylvania, who had
the contract. They hired me to work along with their crew coming
in at $1.00 an hour. . . . When I first moved to Myrtle Beach I stayed
a few weeks at the Todlin Inn on the Boulevard, which did not have
good heat and no meals. I moved over to the Blue Sea Inn, which
was pretty much the same thing. And then in January I moved up
on Highway 17 to the Brunswick Guest House. Mrs. Swain operated
it. I had a room and she served meals, and I stayed there for some
time.

I went to work for the Walter S. Ray Company in December.
In early January the large Busaris Monagan draglines began to come
in disassembled, and there was quite a crew of us out at the Inland
Waterway at the Pine Island Bridge assembling these draglines, one
on each side of the Waterway. We worked there for several months.
In the meantime they brought a wooden barge in from Georgetown,
and they switched me down to the barge, which was going to be
transformed into a repair barge.

Mr. Cadwalder was the master mechanic there, and I worked with
him. We built the wooden barge up with a shed on it, built a crane
on it and fixed it up—put a lathe in it and got it fixed to repair the
machinery.

We finally got the barge finished—the work barge—and had everything we needed, and had a little gas-driven tow boat that would run
up and down the Waterway. A black man named Prince Washington
operated it, and he was a very good operator. On the repair barge were
Mr. Cadwalder, Jimmy Taylor, and myself, plus a couple of other men.
We had a lathe and welding equipment to maintain the equipment.
They had four small half-yard draglines building levees, and there
was a 12-yard dragline over on the west side of the Waterway, which
had a bucket large enough to drive a car into. On the other side there
were two six-yard draglines, plus a dredge brought in from Wilmington to do part of the Waterway up next to the Windy Hill section,
where the banks were so low you couldn't get the draglines in there.

I worked on the Waterway all during 1938 and most of 1939. It
was quite an experience working there on different draglines and the
dredge. They had a drill barge they had brought in to drill into the

coquina rock and blast it out with dynamite. It was quite unnerving
to me to work around that barge with all the blasting going on.[37]

Myrtle Beach State Park

The South Carolina State Park system, and most notably Myrtle Beach State
Park, owes much to the New Deal. The results of devastating forestry practices and erosion of farmlands, coupled with a need to put young men to
work in the early 1930s, led to national and statewide policies of conservation and park development and the creation of the Civilian Conservation Corps (CCC). South Carolina had no state parks until 1933, when the
South Carolina General Assembly enacted a law authorizing the State Commission of Forestry to develop such a system. A combination of local initia-
tives and federal involvement, including an embrace of the CCC, led to
many state parks. Cheraw State Park was the first property in the system in
1934 when the community purchased 706 acres for a state park. Sixteen
parks were acquired and built by the CCC in the 1930s, and Myrtle Beach
State Park was the first to open, on July 1, 1936.[38] In Myrtle Beach's case,
the public did not purchase and donate the land to the state; a private concern, Myrtle Beach Farms Company, made the exchange.

Recruits for the CCC were young men between the ages of seventeen
and twenty-eight who were unmarried, unemployed, physically fit, and U.S.

*Game room in the Myrtle Beach State Park bathhouse, late 1930s. Myrtle Beach
State Park Collection, courtesy of Chapin Memorial Library*

The centerpiece of Myrtle Beach State Park was its Greek-revival-style bathhouse, built in 1936 by the Civilian Conservation Corps. The building was demolished in 1967, but the wings were restored as a small country store and a picnic shelter. Myrtle Beach State Park Collection, courtesy of Chapin Memorial Library

citizens. Some exceptions were made for war veterans and older men with forest experience.[39] Each man was paid thirty dollars a month, from which the sum of twenty-two dollars was sent to his family. Six-month terms of enrollment were renewable. Preference was given to eligible young men whose families were on public aid.[40]

Both Myrtle Beach Farms and the state of South Carolina were advancing individual goals. Myrtle Beach Farms wanted to increase tourism, which would in turn increase their land sales and profits. The state wanted to expand its fledgling park system and preserve its natural resources. Taking advantage of the labor available from CCC employees and the technical and professional assistance from the National Park Service served both objectives. Myrtle Beach Farms donated 320 acres of land, with beachfront, to the South Carolina Forestry Commission for the park. The CCC constructed all of the facilities available at the park, including rental cabins, caretakers' cottages, picnic shelters, and a bathhouse. Holmes B. Springs Sr., acting as agent for Myrtle Beach Farms Company, worked directly with state forester Homer A. Smith, who agreed with the company's objectives: "I also think the existence of a State Park near Myrtle Beach would be of considerable value to the Farms Corporation," as this would attract more tourists and potential property owners.[41]

Springs began working on the possibility of a state park in 1934, and negotiations appear to have taken longer than anticipated by either Springs or the state. Springs pushed Smith to ensure that government inspections were carried out in time to qualify the project for CCC aid in the next fiscal period.[42] Smith countered to Springs that in order for this park to qualify as a CCC project and to have a camp located on the property to carry out the work, they would have to submit the proposal as one on private cooperators' land. This led Myrtle Beach Farms to propose selling the land to the state for two cents an acre. Since priority for CCC labor was given to projects on federal- or state-owned lands, privately owned land camps had a difficult time competing with projects on state-owned lands. In the end, Myrtle Beach Farms simply donated the land to the state.[43]

This was by no means the end of the obstacles confronting the park, however, before it finally opened in July 1936. What would actually be built in the park was a subject of debate between Smith and Orin M. Bullock, who was the National Park Service regional inspector in Richmond, Virginia. Smith insisted that rental cabins be constructed at the park. Bullock was concerned that this would infringe on the domain of Myrtle Beach Farms and other local property owners. Smith assured him that, for the park, the CCC would build only a few cabins that would not be competitive with the local market. To crystallize his point, Smith reminded him to "bear in mind that the real purpose behind State Parks is to give to those people of the lower income bracket an opportunity to enjoy the pleasures of a resort place without running up against commercial prices." The construction of campgrounds, picnic shelters, and cabins run by the state would ensure this opportunity. Further, Smith pointed out the future maintenance needs of the park and asserted, "It is the cabins which can underwrite the financing of the entire program."[44]

The centerpiece of CCC construction at Myrtle Beach State Park was a large bathhouse. The memorable building in a Greek-revival style had a central hall that was used as a two-story concessions and recreation area. The large wings flanking the hall were devoted to changing areas and showers for the bathers. The second story of the wings formed a walkway with covered shelters at either end to provide scenic views of the ocean. Manicured lawns surrounded the structure. The bathhouse was designed to serve two thousand park visitors a day.[45]

Myrtle Beach State Park opened to visitors on July 1, 1936, but did not celebrate its formal dedication until the following summer.[46] On June 17, 1937, South Carolina governor Olin Johnston was the keynote speaker at the ceremonies, followed by representatives of the South Carolina Forestry

Commission and the National Park Service. Activities included a demonstration of lifesaving and "novelty" contests judged by Mrs. Robert Stackhouse and Mrs. T. P. Pearson of Myrtle Beach, such as the girl with the reddest hair (Elsie Beard of Myrtle Beach); the largest family present (the twelve-member Wright Shuley family of Socastee); the oldest man and woman present; the person with the most freckles (June Hora of Murrells Inlet); the tallest man; and the people coming from the longest distance (New Jersey).[47]

While no one can deny that the years on either side of the Great Depression were difficult ones in South Carolina, Myrtle Beach did not experience the destitution and hardship felt by many other places in the state. The foundation for growth and business activity fueled by John T. Woodside's investment in the 1920s, federal-aid projects that built the infrastructure for the burgeoning community, and growth of tourism by an expanding middle class helped Myrtle Beach survive the Depression as a relative oasis of stability.

Myrtle Beach's Grand Hotel, the Ocean Forest

The world's grand hotels, both large and small, have an ageless tradition of honoring the value of aesthetics, comfort, quality, and luxury in a setting of natural beauty. Myrtle Beach, South Carolina, had its own grand hotel, which is now only a page in history and an indelible memory for those who knew her.

Ocean Forest Hotel, built by John T. Woodside in 1929, was meant to position Myrtle Beach as a tourist destination for the growing middle and upper classes of the late 1920s, and as a precursor to the opulent sixteen-thousand-acre Arcady development he proposed to build. Construction started in 1928 on the "Million Dollar Hotel," as it was soon dubbed. Designed by Stanhope S. Johnson and R. O. Brannon of Lynchburg, Virginia, the steel and poured-concrete Ocean Forest was to be a landmark as well as a destination. Its ten stories, flanked like a wedding cake by two five-story wings, and more than two hundred guest rooms sat twenty-nine feet above sea level behind the high-tide line surrounded by ancient sand dunes and pine forests.[48] The hotel was advertised as fireproof and storm-resistant. It survived the direct hit of Category 4 Hurricane Hazel in 1954 virtually unscathed. Only a wrecking ball and explosives in 1974 could bring it down.

Its opulence included Czechoslovakian chandeliers, Italian marble floors, elevators, indoor and outdoor swimming pools, an arcade of shops, stables, tennis courts, and dining rooms. The exterior was painted white so that the magnificent hotel would shine like a beacon in the afternoon sun along the shoreline. In fact, a beacon was designed to top the hotel's cupola, and for early aviators the hotel was a landmark on the beach.

The grand opening celebration was held on February 21, 1930, and the invitees were among the financial, commercial, industrial, and social elite of the eastern seaboard. After the formal opening, the hotel welcomed the general public. The Ocean Forest was the scene of many a romance during the 1940s and 1950s as young couples danced under the stars on the Marine Patio to big bands of the day such as those of Tommy Dorsey, Guy Lombardo, and Count Basie. In 1954 Jane Barry Haynes, who was an actress and director in North Carolina, arrived in Myrtle Beach to direct the summer-stock theater in the Ocean Forest, one of the first theaters-in-the-round in the Southeast.

Conventions and meetings filled the hotel from the opening season, but the facility was closed for a period after Woodside lost his Myrtle Beach assets during the Depression. After reopening in 1933 under new management and ownership, the Ocean Forest reportedly continued to operate successfully until about the 1960s, when modernizations were sorely needed. One tentative buyer with an option, Landcroft Corporation of Baltimore, proposed converting the hotel into a retirement home, which many opposed as the hotel provided much-needed convention capabilities. That deal fell through. The opening of the city's convention center in 1967 probably helped speed the demise of the Ocean Forest since conventions and meetings were a significant portion of the center's trade. A decline in revenue naturally followed, and the recession of the 1970s made the economic picture even more grim for all in the hospitality industry. The last owners were the late Niles "Sonny" Stevens and Dexter Stuckey, who purchased the hotel and twelve acres surrounding it in August 1973. Stories abound as to why the hotel did not survive the wrecking ball on Friday, September 13, 1974:

Insurers were forcing the owners to close unless they upgraded wiring and plumbing, although demolition experts who crawled through the building reported that the hotel could have been upgraded at a reasonable price.

The owners wanted to modernize the hotel, but the job became too costly.

The owners tried to find a buyer for the hotel and a national chain was interested, but the deal fell through.

The owners bought it strictly for the land and had always intended to tear the hotel down.

Customers did not like the small rooms and lack of air-conditioning in the main hotel, but both features supposedly could have been upgraded.

New annexes in the 1970s contained more-modern rooms.

Room rates in the 1970s did not justify the cost of remodeling.

With a depressed economy, the owners needed to find a way to make the property profitable again, which meant demolishing the hotel in order to build in its place a new hotel that would be bigger and cheaper to operate and would generate more income.

Memories of Ocean Forest Hotel live on in homes of people who bought pieces of the hotel at the demolition sale, in photographs, and in fond reminiscences. In addition, the "footprint" of Myrtle Beach's grand hotel is still visible in the unique street layout on which the Ocean Forest sat, even though condominiums were soon built on the property. Between Fifty-second Avenue North and Sixty-first Avenue North on North Ocean Boulevard, drive to the tip of the "V" that is created by Poinsett Road and Calhoun Road and you will be at the former location of the circular drive that carried people from all over the country to the door of the grand Ocean Forest Hotel.

The Federal Writers' Project and the Grand Strand Area

Many worthy projects came out of the New Deal years, but perhaps one of the most historically significant was the Federal Writers' Project of the Works Progress Administration (WPA). This project put unemployed professionals to work collecting stories, writing guides to states' histories, and chronicling historic structures, among many other activities. One of the results of this project was the Slave Narrative Collection, a group of autobiographical accounts of former slaves that today stands as one of the most enduring and noteworthy achievements of the WPA. Compiled in seventeen states between 1936 and 1938, the collection, which is housed at the Library of Congress, consists of more than two thousand interviews with former slaves, most of them first-person accounts. More than 280 former slaves were interviewed in South Carolina, many of them by Murrells Inlet native Genevieve Willcox Chandler.[49]

Although the project writers were advised to record the interviews, which had to be transcribed by hand, in Standard English, some were able to capture the true rhythms and cadence of the Gullah dialect. Few were better at this than Chandler. She is credited with having collected twelve hundred pages of memories, stories, and folktales from the Gullah culture.

While many of the former slaves were reluctant to share disturbing tales of slave life with white interviewers, Chandler, because she lived among many of them all her life, was able to get open and frank interviews with information that most would not have been able to collect. Another reason she was accepted was because her brother Dr. Dick Willcox, who was known affectionately as "Bubba Dick," was loved by his black patients because he would take care of black people when other white doctors would not. The mention of his name opened doors in more than one instance. Genevieve "Sister" Chandler Peterkin, who often accompanied her mother and the photographer Bayard Wooten on their rural adventures, shared this story:

When Ms. Wooten was with us, she had a driver named Smitty.

. . . We were in her car that day and it bogged down on those sandy roads in the Freewoods [near Burgess]. It was so down in the rut that there was no possibility of a child and two women, with him driving the car, to push it up. So Mama said we were just going to have to find some men to help us get it out. Across a savannah, which were open spaces, it was probably about a mile across this area, we saw smoke coming out of a chimney. So Mama said we should go to that house because somebody would be home if a fire's going. We walked over there and Ms. Wooten had a bandanna tied around her head and I think we all probably looked like tramps. As we came up in the yard, there was a rather large black woman who was seated on the porch of her little house and she had a long skirt on, as most of them did in those days, and she was sitting with her hands kind of stuck under her skirt. The thing I noticed immediately was that her face showed fear of us and I'd never seen that when going with Mama to any black person's home—a look like she feared us coming into her yard—and then I could also see fear and anger. Mama called "Auntie, aren't you at home?" Everyone called old black women Auntie at that time. She said, "Yes'm" and her face changed a little bit but not much. And then Mama said, "Do you know Dr. Dick?" She said "Yes'm," and Mama said, "Well I'm Miss Ginny, his sister." Well, she jumped up and dropped this ax she had tucked under her skirt. She said, "Lordy, Miss Ginny, I been take you for gypsy. The gypsies come through here and take everything we got. They'll take the clothes off the line, the quilts off the bed, the chicken off the yard. They take everything we got, and I thought I was going to kill gypsies today."[50]

Four

~~~~~~

War Comes to the Beach

*W*orld Wars I and II may have been fought on foreign shores, but their impact was clearly felt on the home front. In Myrtle Beach making sacrifices and facing hardship were part of its residents' heritage, whether due to war, drought, boll weevils, hurricanes, or economic depression, and they took the war years in stride. During World War I about 10 percent of Dogwood Neck's population registered for the draft. Tourism was dramatically curtailed during World War II when gasoline and tires were rationed by the government. The wars also brought the beginning of a rediscovery of the South. Soldiers from around the country trained in South Carolina during both wars. Thousands went through Myrtle Beach Army Air Force Base during World War II, and many of them returned to the area to visit or put down roots later.

World War I and the Postwar Years

In 1917 the United States was entering heated battlegrounds not only in Europe but also in intense ideological struggles at home with woman suffrage and racial unrest. South Carolina was wrestling with its own issues. The state was coping with population shifts and economic changes created by the growth of the textile industry and the resulting move of people from the family farms to the mill towns. Between 1895 and 1907 upstate South Carolina businessmen built 61 new textile mills and expanded older ones. By 1910 the state had 167 mills and ranked second only to Massachusetts as a leading textile-producing state.[1] These mills and other industries attracted families struggling to make a living on the family farms as they dealt with low prices for overproduced commodities, greater competition, and the economic vise of sharecropping and tenant farming.

U.S. Census figures for Dogwood Neck Township in Horry County indicate a shift in population away from independent and tenant farming to agribusiness, with some people leaving the district altogether, between 1910 and 1920. The total population of the district dropped in that decade, from 943 persons in 1910 to 827 in 1920. This decrease can be explained not only by the World War I draft but also by the difficulty small farmers had making a living during this decade. Many gave up farming completely and moved to mill towns to work. By 1930, however, the Dogwood Neck population increased almost 50 percent to 1,240, about half of whom were now listed as residents in the newly enumerated Myrtle Beach.[2]

At the same time the Progressive movement was being felt in communities all around South Carolina, as advocates sought to reform society and politics as well as modernize and diversify the economy. The boosterism of this movement spilled over into South Carolina's overwhelming support for the entrance of the United States into World War I on April 6, 1917. Six days after the declaration of war on Germany, the people of Conway and the surrounding area participated in a parade extending from the Burroughs School down to the public square, where several leading citizens delivered stirring patriotic speeches and schoolchildren sang national anthems.[3] More than three hundred thousand black and white South Carolinian men registered for the draft, with more than fifty-four thousand of them actually drafted.[4]

In 1917 Myrtle Beach was a sleepy coastal village of about two hundred people, the majority of whom worked for Myrtle Beach Farms Company or were otherwise employed as farmers, fishermen, or workers in the timber business or in jobs related to the summer tourist season. Despite the war, the 1917 summer season began in June with a dance and lawn party at the opening of Sea Side Inn. About three hundred people attended. On the July 4 weekend hotel management organized a moonlight bathing party and a baseball game between teams from Marion and Conway. A live orchestra played most nights during the season, and between seventeen hundred and eighteen hundred people visited that summer.[5]

Area residents and visitors also contributed to the war effort. In July 1917 local women organized an Allies Festival, which was held at the Myrtle Beach Pavilion. The evening included the singing of "new Allies' war songs," amateur and professional singing performances, card games, a children's party, and dancing to a live band. Proceeds from refreshment and souvenir sales went to the "war relief work."[6]

The U.S. home front during the war was organized around the National Council of Defense, which was federated through the state down to each county and its school districts. Representatives from churches, schools, banks, manufacturing, professional and agricultural interests, women's organizations, and the press were included. In Horry County the chairman of the county Council of Defense was Franklin A. Burroughs. Representing Myrtle Beach on the county council was Dr. Edgar Stalvey. George W. King led the local council for Myrtle Beach School. The Myrtle Beach Council had sixty-six members, including two wives of servicemen. As the *Horry Herald* reported, "We feel peculiarly blessed in having among our members two very brave young women. Mrs. Moore, whose husband is 'over there[,]' and Mrs. Malone, whose husband is also in the service. They have given us examples of our splendid American womanhood."[7] The women apparently worked in the Atlantic Coast Line office on behalf of the Myrtle Beach Council.

In a June 27, 1917, letter from the South Carolina Council of Defense to the county councils, Chairman David R. Coker said, "The most important work immediately before the council of defense is informing and arousing all people as to the situation which the war has thrust upon us. An efficient and prompt successful prosecution of the war will be impossible unless the whole nation stands solidly behind the government. A Negro committee composed of leading colored citizens should be waged [*sic*] among the colored race as vigorously as among the white. The council of defense will be used as the mouthpiece of the government and the information of the government as to the state of affairs in the country."[8]

Raising funds for the war effort was a major role of the council. In the first Liberty War Bonds campaign at the beginning of the war, Horry County quickly organized and exceeded its $25,000 goal by 40 percent. By the following summer the council was even more highly organized for the War Savings Stamps campaign. This time the county's goal was $600,000, which was then broken down by allotments to school districts based on approximately $2 per person living in that district, a major sum for struggling farmers and merchants. Myrtle Beach School was reported to have 71 students enrolled and an estimated population of 262.7. The school's goal for 1918 was to raise $5,254 for war efforts. Within two weeks residents pledged more than $1,000. Myrtle Beach Colored School had 31 children enrolled and an estimated population of 114.7. Its 1918 goal was $2,294. By June 1918 residents of Myrtle Beach had invested $359.60 in War Savings Stamps and $150 in Liberty Bonds and had donated $400 to the Red Cross. Nonparticipation in any of these efforts was socially unacceptable and discouraged. On a per capita basis South Carolina's financial support of the war effort was among the highest in the nation.[9]

The Myrtle Beach community also aided and benefited from the war effort through its agribusiness. According to Emma J. Bryan Epps, daughter of James E. Bryan Sr., who was president of Myrtle Beach Farms Company during this period, one of the farm's major crops during World War I was Irish potatoes. "That war was fought almost entirely in trenches," she recalls, "and they would send the soldiers out there, and would somehow have to stay through battle for two or three days at a time. Well, they could cook those potatoes and put them in the soldiers' mess kits because they would keep safely for them to eat. . . . And Myrtle Beach Farms grew many hundreds of acres of Irish potatoes during the First World War."[10] Prices for agricultural crops soared after 1917, benefiting everyone from landowners and merchants to tenants and sharecroppers. In 1919 a pound of cotton cost 35¢ and a pound of tobacco was 88¢. The healthy prices were due to a lack of foreign competition during the war, which resulted in market expansion. Prosperity did not last long, however; prices collapsed by 1920, with cotton plummeting from a high of 41¢ a bale in April 1920 to 13.5¢ that December.[11]

The war also brought an increasing federal presence to South Carolina, as well as dollars and jobs, with the U.S. Army establishing training centers at Camp Jackson in Columbia, Camp Sevier in Greenville, and Camp Wadsworth in Spartanburg. These particular camps also held small contingents of prisoners of war who were seamen and enemy aliens (each camp contained fewer than one hundred men).[12]

Another effect of the Council of Defense efforts was the inauguration of daylight saving time in March 1918 as part of a home-front effort to save energy, both electrical and human, for war production by taking advantage of the longer hours of daylight between April and October. The conservation of food rather than rationing, as would be done in World War II, was also promoted by the council. In October 1917 more than two hundred Horry County teachers and school trustees met in Conway to pledge support in the food conservation campaign. According to Lawence D. Magrath, of Horry County Trust Company and secretary of the Horry County Council of Defense, "We appeared before a meeting of over 200 of the school teachers and trustees today here at Conway and had them pledge their support and support of their schools in the Food Conservation campaign. We feel sure that every home that has a child in school will sign a Hoover Pledge Card."[13] One of the major staples for conservation was wheat. Public eating places and clubs observed two wheatless days per week. Victory bread recipes using substitutes for wheat were widely circulated, and the tending of victory gardens was encouraged.

As part of its campaign to rally everyone around the flag in support of the war effort, the National Council of Defense suggested to all state councils that Independence Day, the Fourth of July, be "everywhere suitably celebrated this year on a high plane of national patriotism." Independence Day, while recognized as a holiday, had not been celebrated in much of the white South with such national patriotism since before the Civil War. In Conway on July 4, 1918, a segregated parade formed at 6:00 P.M. to march to the courthouse. Of special note were the decorated cars in the parade, especially the one decorated in white with large red crosses on the body representing the Red Cross. At the courthouse speakers read the Declaration of Independence and the proclamation of the president regarding the observance of the day, and the Council of Defense awarded Horry County with an honor flag for exceeding its quota in the third liberty loan program.[14]

Horry County, with the rest of the nation, celebrated in November 1918 when the war was over. Emma J. Bryan Epps remembered, "The first memory that I have [is] that I came running in the house. Mama [said], 'What is it? What is it?' [It] was everything in Conway that had a whistle, and everything that had a bell was ringing. Just this massive noise of bells and whistles. And it was the end—they had signed the armistice at the end of World War I. And how happy we were that war was over."[15]

The intervening years between the wars brought significant changes to Myrtle Beach. The increasing disposable income of the middle class in the 1920s and relatively inexpensive transportation provided by the railroads and its new competitor, the automobile, made the summer resort vacation an American institution. Business and community leaders in Conway and Myrtle Beach, filled with the Progressive boosterism of the period, were taking advantage of these new trends, seeking ways to make their area more attractive to business investment and growth. Within a month after the conclusion of World War I, a statewide movement for better roads began, and efforts were made to improve educational opportunities and speed the introduction of electricity and telephones to more homes and businesses.

By early 1922 the Conway Chamber of Commerce had produced a promotional brochure that hailed the town's and the county's "attractions and points of excellence," with the objective of bringing large statewide conventions to the county. Of significance was the chamber's invitation to and acceptance by the South Carolina Press Association to hold its annual conference in Myrtle Beach in June 1922. The early 1920s were a time of sustained growth and expansion, with new construction of cottages, guest houses, Myrtle Beach Yacht Club, thousands of feet of boardwalk expansion, twenty-five new rooms at Sea Side Inn, and an expanded Pavilion. Major investment in Myrtle Beach in 1926 by the Woodside brothers, even though stopped in its tracks by the Great Depression, brought national attention to the area and laid the foundation for continued investment in later years. In 1930 Myrtle Beach had grown to almost seven hundred residents, many of whom moved there to participate in the new construction or find work at Ocean Forest Country Club, Ocean Forest Hotel, or the many new boardinghouses. While the Depression years slowed growth, a certain stability sustained the area as federal, state, and local entities built infrastructures, such as the Intracoastal Waterway, that would support later development. By 1940 Myrtle Beach's population had more than doubled to approximately sixteen hundred, according to the U.S. Census.

World War II

World War II affected Horry County and Myrtle Beach long before the attack on Pearl Harbor, with the state, county, and city organizing early in the war and preparing for the worst. In August 1940 Governor Burnet R. Maybank created the South Carolina Council of Defense, modeled after the World War I councils, to mobilize the home front in the war effort. Within six months county councils were organized. Paul Quattlebaum, state senator representing Horry County from 1935 to 1944, was the chairman of the Horry County Council of Defense, and Bunyon B. Benfield, former Myrtle Beach city councilman and owner of the Gloria and Broadway theaters, was chairman of the Myrtle Beach Council of Defense. Oliver C. Callaway, who was chief of the Myrtle Beach fire department and would serve as Myrtle Beach mayor from 1943 to 1947, was commander of the Citizens Defense Corps for the county. In addition to representatives from Conway, Loris, and Aynor, Myrtle Beach mayor Wilford L. Harrelson and resident Joseph W. Little served on the corps.[16] The council was instrumental in organizing three evacuation districts in the state, of which Horry County was one. A plan was established for moving people in these districts away from the coast in case of an attack. The evacuation plan indicated that the Horry County district had a total of 357,504 whites and 453,997 blacks. In case of evacuation, the whites would move to designated reception areas in Chester, Lancaster, and York counties, which had room for 816,254 whites, while the blacks would go to Lancaster County, where room was available for only 272,085 persons.[17] The report does not explain where the remaining blacks would go.

Perhaps one of the greatest impacts of the war on Myrtle Beach was its discovery by the military, a relationship that community leaders actively pursued. Since John T. Woodside's first air strip in the late 1920s, a municipal airport was viewed as an important ingredient in making Myrtle Beach more accessible to tourists, investors, and other interests. Ten years later Myrtle Beach's first two mayors developed a larger, more effective airfield that eventually transformed the farms and forests south of Myrtle Beach into a national military installation.

This certificate was awarded to J. E. "Poddy" Bryan III in 1942 as part of a World War II scrap-metal salvage campaign. What the certificate does not mention was that it was for a defunct tractor from Myrtle Beach Farms, of which his father was president. His daughter, Sarah, said he was embarrassed about the award but did enjoy the roll of movie tickets he won. Courtesy of Sarah Bryan

During his first administration Dr. Wilford L. Harrelson purchased the original portion of the airport tract on the Myrtle Beach–Conway Highway (present-day Highway 15) and developed it under the engineer T. Max Jordan in cooperation with the newly organized Myrtle Beach Chamber of Commerce and the South Carolina Aeronautics Commission. The actual construction of the airport began during Ben Graham's administration with the assistance of the Works Progress Administration and the Civil Aeronautics Administration. Graham and others, such as Holmes B. Springs Sr., however, envisioned even greater potential for the airport beyond accessibility.[18] In 1940 President Franklin D. Roosevelt signed the National Defense Act, and several people saw an opportunity to turn the forest and the largely vacant sections of beaches into a range for bombing and gunnery practice. The National Defense Act authorized a $300 million budget, six

Myrtle Beach Air Force Base celebrated its 25,000th visitor in July 1965. The base, which was open from 1940 to 1947 and 1956 to 1993, played an important role in Myrtle Beach's economy and development. Mark Garner Collection, courtesy of Chapin Memorial Library

thousand airplanes to be built for the U.S. Army Air Corps and an increase in air corps personnel to more than three thousand officers and forty-five thousand enlisted troops.[19]

Myrtle Beach was not the only community seeking a piece of the mobilization pie; others around the country were vying for government military projects. However, the South became the great training ground for the nation's military forces as a result of the work of southern legislators, whose favor Roosevelt needed; a largely unorganized labor pool; and municipalities clamoring for the economic boon of having a military installation in their midst. Myrtle Beach got its share of the defense budget by late 1941. The U.S. government commandeered the Myrtle Beach airport, seizing through lease and sale nearly one hundred thousand acres of pine forest and farmland in Horry and Georgetown counties to serve as bombing and gunnery ranges under the Second War Powers Act.

In total, the military installations at Myrtle Beach, Conway, and George-town operated on more than ninety-seven thousand acres in nine tracts, three of which were owned and six of which were leased by the United States government. The Myrtle Beach tract contained the base and quarters for the troops, the landing field, and five air-to-ground gunnery and bomb-ing ranges. The base, the center of training for combat teams, completed thousands of gunnery and bombing training missions. Targets used for gun-nery practice were set up all along the sand dunes from the state park to Garden City. "After the war, we picked up machine gun shells like tourists pick up seashells off the beach," said Mary Emily Platt Jackson.[21]

Some significant events occurred at the Myrtle Beach base during the war. For example, in May 1943 a detachment of the Royal Netherlands Military Flying School flew in to Myrtle Beach. The "Flying Dutchmen" performed incredible feats with their B-25s. The men who flew with Lieu-tenant Colonel James Doolittle on the first raid on Tokyo received some of their training at Myrtle Beach. A 75-millimeter cannon that had been in-stalled on a B-25 aircraft got its first real test at the field. President Frank-lin D. Roosevelt visited the base on April 23, 1944, during a month-long visit at Bernard Baruch's Hobcaw Barony plantation.[22]

The U.S. government also leased a tract of land in the Windy Hill beach area, about twelve miles north of Myrtle Beach. Fort Bragg's antiaircraft artillery unit, with more than four thousand officers and men, began rotat-ing through the site for three-week periods beginning in May 1941. The site was used as a firing range and a camp for the army's 345th Brigade. A leased property in the Murrells Inlet area provided docking facilities for crash and target boats and quarters for those crews.

For the residents of Myrtle Beach, World War II was in their backyard by early 1942. Continual reminders included the roar of airplanes overhead from the air base and its bombing ranges, the rumbling of trucks moving prisoners of war (POWs) from their camps to their work sites around Myr-tle Beach, and the debris that washed ashore from battles at sea. "Certainly another memory that was important to me was being a kid during World War II, because my mom's [guest] house at that time was commandeered by the Air Force for young pilots in training," recalled Sigmund Abeles, whose mother, Henrietta, opened Paul's Guest House at 506 Kings Highway in 1936. In 1942 he was eight years old. "I was mascot to many of those people. They would put their big, heavy, leather and wool flight jackets on me, and they would put those flight helmets on me, and I would be dwarfed by them around in the hallway. It was all kind of neat, except that two of those pilots, two of those incredibly young pilots, got killed in training. And my mother was devastated. She'd gotten to know them; she was surrogate mom for them. She had to pack their stuff and write letters to their parents about what lovely young men they were."[23]

Many townspeople's lives crossed paths with the soldiers who were training at the Myrtle Beach base and then flying off to parts unknown to fight. Athalia Stalvey Ramsey was one of them. The widow of Jasper Ramsey, who owned Nu-Way Laundry and other businesses during this period, she remembered cleaning the uniforms of some of those soldiers who were part of Doolittle's Raiders over Tokyo. A colonel from the base brought in the uniforms and asked that they be done by the next afternoon because they were leaving early the following morning. "That meant all of those in the dry-cleaning department had to work just about all night. There was nowhere else to take them [the uniforms]." Ramsey was already at work at Nu-Way when the aviators flew out. "It was after nine o'clock and they took off, and they came right over the laundry, and they dipped their wings. We stood outside the door and watched them."[24]

As those in London did, residents of Myrtle Beach had to observe blackout conditions, but not because of air raids. By August 1942 the Horry County Council of Defense conducted practice blackouts and drills in Myrtle Beach because of the constant threat from Germans patrolling the Atlantic coast. German submarines sank ships all along the coast, with the Outer Banks of North Carolina being a favorite hunting ground. Recreational fishing was closed during the war as no private boats were allowed to take parties offshore. Onshore blackout requirements included painting the upper half of car headlights black, using only low beams at night, and never turning a car directly toward the ocean.[25] Many nights the residents of Myrtle Beach could look out to sea and observe the light of an explosion or a burning ship. It was only when the debris washed ashore that they might have an idea if the ship was ally or enemy.

In addition to the area's blackout conditions, the coast was patrolled by the United States Coast Guard.[26] All coastal patrols were done at first on foot and later on horseback. In Myrtle Beach patrols were done on foot with dogs. Through the local Council of Defense, private citizens were also used in the vigilance against invasion. As a student at Myrtle Beach High School, Genevieve Peterkin of Murrells Inlet recalled helping with lookout duty in a tower at the beach during her study-hall hours: "I learned all the shapes of the German planes and the Japanese planes, and, of course, the American planes, and thank goodness we never saw a plane that wasn't ours."[27]

Many areas also used picket patrol boats to monitor the myriad inlets, bays, and remote islands along the coastline. Local residents heard constant rumors that the Germans would invade at any moment, that a German submarine would surface before their very eyes, or that someone would infiltrate local defenses. Most were unsubstantiated but nonetheless kept everyone alert. One rumor stated that ticket stubs for a Charleston movie theater were found in the pockets of captured German sailors. Another rumor was that Archer and Anna Huntington, who had purchased more than six thousand acres south of Murrells Inlet in 1930, were collaborating with the Germans. The suspicions were fueled by gossip because of the Huntingtons' wealth and extensive worldwide travels at a time when most people were suffering in the Depression. Some believed that a refueling operation for German submarines was located at the Huntington estate along the Waccamaw River. In reality, the Huntingtons lived in the North for the duration of the war. The U.S. Army Air Corps used their home, Atalaya, as a radar station, even fitting the outer walls with machine guns to counter any trouble. The men stationed there also patrolled the beaches and assisted the 455th Bomber Squadron stationed at Myrtle Beach.[28]

People continued to come to the beach despite the activities there related to the war. The April 19, 1942, issue of the *Myrtle Beach News* reported a healthy demand for reservations for the upcoming summer season: "In view of the increasing number of people who are coming to the beach, there is every indicator that they are overcoming the apprehension as to the safety of the beach this summer with regard to the war situation. . . . It is understood that the concessions will be operated as usual and that the pavilion will be open for dancing and other amusement, with a system of shaded lights to meet Army and Navy requirements. An Army officer of years of experience . . . stated there would be a very remote possibility of the enemy bombing Myrtle Beach proper because it would hardly be reasonable to assume that a $75,000 or $100,000 plane would come 4,000 miles with a $1,000 bomb and drop it on Myrtle Beach."

Another local impact was the draft of men into military service, which drained certain industries of needed labor. The United States Selective Service, which Holmes B. Springs Jr. managed for South Carolina, had to start from scratch in setting up county boards to organize the draft. Between 1940 and 1945, 503,542 persons from the state answered the call to serve; 59 percent of these were white and 41 percent were black. Of the total number of registrants receiving medical examinations, 41 percent were rejected because of problems ranging from illiteracy to heart, hernia, or other medical-related problems. The national rejection rate was 28 percent. Horry County's rejection rate was 42 percent. Serving on the Horry County Selective Service Board No. 44 from Myrtle Beach was Thomas M. Jordan. Drs. M. Henderson Rourk and William A. Rourk served the board as examining physicians, and Carl C. Pridgen, president of the Myrtle Beach Depository, was on the reemployment committee.[29]

Prisoners of war during World War II. The German soldiers were used in forestry and agricultural industries and for routine labor at Myrtle Beach Army Air Base. These men are standing in front of a produce packinghouse they built for Trask Farms. Ruth Gore Collection, courtesy of Chapin Memorial Library

The shortage of labor in agricultural and forestry industries caused by men and women going to war was alleviated somewhat by POWs. German POW camps were prevalent in the United States during World War II. From 1942 to 1946 South Carolina had twenty permanent camps and eight temporary camps, and these held 11,645 soldiers at their peak. The POW population in the United States, which included Germans, Italians, and Japanese, crested at almost 426,000 in 1945. South Carolina's policies regarding treatment, privileges, food, clothing, and work performed by the POWs were consistent with military policy at all U.S. camps. Supplying POWs to fill labor needs in a community, jobs for which they received wages paid by the private employers, was common. Enlisted men received eighty cents a day for working and an additional ten cents per day in coupons for the purchase of canteen items such as toothpaste and razor blades. German POWs were first brought to South Carolina in 1943 to harvest peanuts, as manpower had been drastically decreased due to the military draft and enlistment. Before long, peach and tobacco growers and the timber industry were clamoring for camps in their areas. In total, Myrtle Beach's camp had about six hundred prisoners, who were used primarily at the Myrtle Beach Army Air Base to perform routine maintenance work but also in the forestry and agricultural industries.[30] June Hora, who was a secretary at the Myrtle Beach base during the war, remembered POWs who cleaned the officers' club: "One man used to bring fresh flowers for the table. Such nice young boys."[31]

As a Jewish boy growing up in Myrtle Beach, however, Sigmund Abeles was afraid of the POWs because of his mother's, aunts', and uncles' reactions to learning about the Nazi concentration camps. He said, "I grew up with fear [that] if I got caught they'd kill me because they were determined to kill all the Jews. And so I was really scared when those trucks would go by my house with the German prisoners of war. They would say, 'Heil, Hitler,' and all that stuff when they saw you."[32]

The small camp at Myrtle Beach opened in June 1944 and operated for almost two years. It was first located on the city's north end between Seventy-first Avenue and Seventy-ninth Avenue North, a wooded area along Cane Patch Swash from the beach to U.S. Highway 17. Later this temporary camp was dismantled and the POWs relocated to barracks, which they helped build, on the Myrtle Beach Air Base. Edouard Pattee of the International YMCA inspected many of these facilities and wrote of the "lovely" setting at the Myrtle Beach camp: "I could not help but think of a Boys Summer Camp in which I used to spend my vacation; same beautiful trees, same seclusion, same quietness of the woods, and similar barracks, too."[33]

Rationing hit Myrtle Beach hard, as it did everywhere, but the biggest impact to the town came from gasoline rationing. Ration coupons were distributed on a monthly basis from the local center of the Office of Price Administration (OPA). Scarce consumer goods in wartime, such as tires, automobiles, sugar, gasoline, fuel oil, and certain foods, were rationed soon after the United States entered the war. "We had rationing in the grocery department [of the Chapin Company]," remembered Harold Clardy, retired president of the Chapin Company. Fresh meat and sugar were among the grocery items that were hard to come by. He recalled people lining up to get their portions of the rationed foods and that some places would not allow blacks to get in the lines even if they had coupons. Chapin Company, he said, never denied blacks their right to line up with everyone else to buy their portions.[34]

June Hora recalled that gas rationing was difficult even on residents. She was on the Myrtle Beach High School basketball team and had to hitch rides to and from the school for games and practices. Most drivers were given the lowest priority for ration stamps, designated by an "A" sticker placed on the windshield, which allotted three gallons a week. A "B" sticker was for six to eight gallons a week, and a select few, mostly doctors and government officials, received "C" stickers for unlimited gas. Add to that the fact that tires were virtually impossible to get until the war was over, and it becomes clear why the tourism trade slowed considerably in the war years.[35] In addition, the OPA was authorized by the federal government to establish ceiling prices for most commodities in order to prevent wartime inflation. This included ceilings on residential rents. In addition to selling war bonds, the Myrtle Beach community participated in scrap metal and newspaper drives. "During the war years, we were given one movie ticket for each ten pounds of scrap metal that we turned in," said Sigmund Abeles. "My best buddy, Poddy Bryan, whose father was president of Myrtle Beach Farms, was given a huge, heavy defunct tractor to turn in and was given a full roll of movie tickets . . . so movies on Saturday were practically an assured freebie when one was on the good side of 'P' Bryan, which I always was."[36]

While the war slowed tourism in Myrtle Beach, business did not stop completely. This was largely due to services and products required by personnel at the air base. Atlantic Beach provided temporary housing for black soldiers who were building the base. Guest houses, such as that of Henrietta Abeles, were host to servicemen needing housing. Soldiers on leave sought entertainment venues that the town had to offer, such as moviegoing, dancing, swimming, and bowling. Many dates between local young women and soldiers ended up in marriage proposals while they were dancing on the Marine Patio at Ocean Forest Hotel or at the Pavilion. Carpenters, brickmasons, plumbers, and other building tradesmen found work as the air base took shape and expanded to fulfill its role in the war effort. The Meher Center north of Myrtle Beach was under development during the war years, and since lumber was difficult to get for buildings, Elizabeth Chapin Patterson would hire local workmen who had trucks and other equipment to move old, surplus buildings she found around the county. The base closed down in late 1947, and the airfield and tower were turned over to the city of Myrtle Beach. In total, about $4.75 billion went into military installations and related housing in the southern states. In 1944, as a result of military bases and other projects, government payrolls accounted for about 25 percent of salaries and wages in the South.[37]

When World War II ended, the United States rapidly demobilized, resulting in armed forces being cut from a wartime strength of 12 million to 1.5 million by early 1947. The annual military budget was reduced to about $10 million in 1947 from a high of more than $90 million during the war.[38] As part of this reduction in forces and budget, the Myrtle Beach base was deactivated in November 1947 and the land was returned to the town of Myrtle Beach for an airport.

Within a few years, however, the American military and its supporters were beginning to stir once again, especially with the involvement of the United States in the Korean conflict and cold war concern over the spread of Communism and the threat of nuclear war. The latter concerns were the principal reasons for rebuilding American defenses and weaponry and gave birth to the military-industrial complex. The air force gained power as the branch of the armed forces charged with nuclear-weapon delivery, if such an alternative were required. More money was being poured into building bombers and missiles out of fear that the Communists were moving ahead of the United States in the arms race.[39] National defense, especially from the air, was taking center stage once again.

Although the Myrtle Beach base was not officially reopened until 1956, political and civic leaders in Myrtle Beach began working behind the scenes to attract the air force as early as 1951, an activity that was as economically practical and advantageous as it was ideological. A delegation of Myrtle Beach leadership met with air force officials in Washington, D.C., in late 1950 and early 1951 in an effort to encourage the reopening of the base. "While nothing official had been released up to yesterday [January 25, 1951] it now appears that the city has an opportunity to do its bit toward assisting in the overall defense plan of the country during the present expansion of the armed forces," according to the *Myrtle Beach Sun*.[40] The newspaper article indicated that this was not the city's first meeting with the military. In addition, Myrtle Beach was one of many cities vying for air force bases to be built around the country. In February 1951 E. A. Anthony, the Myrtle Beach airport manager, represented Myrtle Beach in Dayton, Ohio, at a meeting called by the U.S. Air Force's Air Material Command. The purpose of the conference was to discuss various phases of the air force's expanding pilot-training program. About six hundred representatives from cities across the country attended.[41]

By January 1952 the city of Myrtle Beach was notified that the air force was considering reactivating the former base for a light bomber group and that an air force inspection team would be visiting the site as well as other prospective base sites in the Carolinas, Texas, and Pennsylvania.[42] The Myrtle Beach base was ultimately chosen later the same year, but congressional appropriations for its mobilization were not approved and reactivation was delayed for two years. The first air force unit, the 727th Tactical Control Squadron from Shaw Air Force Base in Sumter, was transferred to Myrtle Beach in September 1954, just weeks before Hurricane Hazel blew into town. The squadron was to play an important role in keeping radio communications open during the height of the hurricane. Within the next year crews began clearing ground and building new facilities and buildings.

Personnel were flowing in by the hundreds, and furnishings and supplies were coming in right behind them.

The grand opening of the base was held December 7, 1956, the anniversary of the Japanese bombing of Pearl Harbor. The significance of this date was not lost on U.S. airmen and those familiar with aviation history. The Tactical Air Command fighter wing stationed at Myrtle Beach, which was part of the Ninth Air Force, received the official designation as 354th Fighter/Day wing. General E. J. Timberlake, commander of the Ninth Air Force, officiated at the ceremony. Guests included General Otto P. Weyland, commander of the Tactical Air Command; Bernard Baruch; Senator Strom Thurmond; and several Medal of Honor winners who led the original 354th in its combat tour in the European theater.[43] The newly reactivated 354th was now to be working with one of the most advanced fighter planes of the new aviation era, the North American F-100-D Super Sabre. Colonel Frances S. Gabreski, the base's first commander and the top living air ace in the nation, landed the first of these supersonic jets at the opening ceremonies. Ever mindful of the role that the base would play during the cold war, Gabreski stated, "We at Myrtle Beach consider it a high privilege to carry on the hallowed tradition of one of history's outstanding fighter organizations. It not only offers a privilege but also a responsibility to uphold that tradition in the accomplishment of our present-day mission here. We must earn the right to call ourselves the 354th by maintaining our pilots and planes in readiness to meet, if necessary, threats to peace similar to those met so gallantly by the Pioneer Mustangs thirteen years ago."[44]

Myrtle Beach welcomed the base in grand fashion, letting all Horry County schools out early so that children could attend the opening. The chamber of commerce recommended that all businesses close for the opening so that staff could attend, American flags were displayed in front of all businesses, posters were hung throughout the town, and colorful parking meter covers added to a festive atmosphere. The famed Thunderbird team, the world's first supersonic aerial demonstration team, performed; the base's tactical aircraft did a flyover; and the air force gave tours to the public, in addition to many other events.

In the years to follow, a massive complex took shape. The Capeheart Housing project contained more than $15 million worth of housing for married officers, married enlisted men, and bachelor officers. Two dormitory buildings, a mess hall, a chapel, a hospital, two automotive repair shops, an aviation fuel and lubricant underground system, more than fourteen miles of roads to connect the facilities, and a new hangar were built. Water, sewage, and electricity facilities were doubled. All this construction meant jobs for the Grand Strand and money flowing into the economy, in addition to that being attracted by a booming tourist trade.

The growth of the base had its growing pains, however. Housing in the late 1950s was a constant challenge. The base's Capeheart project, which provided homes for eight hundred families in the beginning, was not available until the summer of 1958. In the meantime, almost twelve hundred married personnel were assigned to the base in June 1957, the majority of whom were living with their families in the local area. By the time the new housing project was completed, the base population had far exceeded Capeheart's capacity, growing to about sixteen hundred. Myrtle Beach's available rental apartments and houses, normally vacant during the off-season in order to be available for summer tourists, were needed for the military families as the base grew beyond its own housing capacities. Landlords were faced with the dilemma of having their rental properties tied up in one- and two-year leases and having nothing available for summer visitors. The answer: new construction, both public and private. Construction on the housing project alone provided jobs for more than eight hundred skilled and unskilled workers.

Squadrons from Myrtle Beach played a part in several of the major global tensions of this period, including the Vietnam War. The base's mission of fighter-day training was converted to fighter-bomber training in 1958. Between 1958 and 1966 one or more squadrons were constantly deployed overseas.[45] In July 1958 U.S. forces, including two fighters from Myrtle Beach, were sent to stand by during a rebellion against the president of Lebanon. Eighteen F-100 jets from Myrtle Beach were stationed in Germany during the 1961 crisis over the Berlin Wall construction. Three fighter squadrons were deployed to Florida during the Cuban missile crisis in 1962. In the 1965 Dominican Republic crisis, when President Lyndon B. Johnson sent in American troops to quash an overexaggerated coup, the Myrtle Beach base sent more than four hundred personnel and eighteen aircraft. The first Myrtle Beach aircraft was deployed to South Vietnam in August 1966, and the conflict drained the base of all but one unit. The 354th would be reassigned to South Korea from 1968 to 1970 but were returned to Myrtle Beach in the mid-1970s and remained there until the base closed in 1993.

Between 1960 and 1985 the population associated with the base (active-duty personnel, civil servants, and military dependents) would increase by about 36 percent. In 1960 the base's budget was $4.7 million, which included civilian salaries but not military salaries. In 1961 about 2,800 officers and airmen were assigned to Myrtle Beach and 460 civilian workers were employed there. The base's total population was 7,100, or about one-third of the entire permanent population in the Grand Strand region. By 1968 the complex had grown to include 601 buildings, with 330 acres of paving and 98 miles of utility systems, having a value of $38 million. Nearly $1 million in new base construction was still planned. In addition to construction's contribution to the local economy, the base spent more than $4 million with local businesses in 1968; more than $1 million was spent in the first quarter of fiscal 1967–68 alone.

In 1985 Myrtle Beach Air Force Base was Horry County's largest employer, with its payroll making up 25 percent of the total county payroll. Its population, which included almost 3,500 personnel on active duty, 495 civil servants, and more than 5,200 dependents, totaled more than 11,200. The base not only came to affect economic growth for the Grand Strand and the county but also impacted schools, churches, and the social structure, with thousands of retiring airmen deciding to live their senior years in Myrtle Beach. It brought the first taste of racial integration to the community, which created conflicts in the beginning, especially as related to housing and recreational amenities. Myrtle Beach and its residents, however, ultimately benefited from the base's presence over its tenure there.

The war years, as well as the years before and after them, were ones of change as well as continuity for the area. The principal change was in the physical and psychological makeup of the Myrtle Beach community. Agribusiness there between 1910 and 1920 was slowly supplanting the small farmer, and the timber industry, which had been prevalent in the late 1800s and early 1900s, was dramatically weakened by the movement of markets further south. However, in the 1920s enthusiastic investment in and promotion of the beach tripled the population as scores of new skilled labor, business, and service jobs were added as a growing town took root, attracting former farmers into the business community. The population more than doubled from 677 in 1930 to 1,600 on the 1940 federal census. By 1944 and the end of the war, the unofficial population count was 2,500, directly attributable to the air base personnel. The combination of beach resort and military base enhanced the prospects for increased tourism and residential migration, along with all the attendant services those people would need. The population was more than 3,300 by 1950, and Myrtle Beach growth has not slowed since then.

Five

Natural and Environmental History of the Grand Strand

The state of Rhode Island could fit within Horry County. The largest in South Carolina, the county boasts more than sixty miles of beach, half the size of the longest sand beach in the United States. A unique part of South Carolina lowcountry in large part because of its geography and natural resources. The region's beautiful sandy beach and mild climate have been attracting people for more than one hundred years. And, according to developers and tourism experts, that attraction is not expected to wane any time soon, thanks to Mother Nature. Horry is one of the one hundred fastest-growing counties in the United States.[1]

The coastal geography of Horry County is divided into outer and inner plains that rise in terraces from sea level to as high as two hundred feet, the results of the ebb and flow of ancient seas.[2] Several rivers and marshes are part of these plains. The Grand Strand area, characterized by a crescent-shaped bay stretching from the North Carolina border to Pawleys Island, is surrounded by water on three sides—the Atlantic Ocean on the east, the Waccamaw River to the south, and the Intracoastal Waterway to the west. Because of the area's many rivers and swamps, the early inhabitants of Horry were somewhat isolated from the outside world. This geographic isolation, as well as the county residents' somewhat contrary attitude before the Civil War toward the political passions of the time, earned the county the nickname "Independent Republic of Horry."

The geology of the Grand Strand consists of layers of unconsolidated sediments (sand, gravel, coquina shells, peat) and limestone over piedmont igneous and metamorphic rocks. The sediment has been laid down over the last one million years and ranges in depth from about thirty feet below sea level at the coastline to approximately ten feet about fifteen miles inland. The layering occurred as the sea level rose and fell over time.[3] During the height of the most recent (Wisconsin) glacial age, approximately twelve thousand years ago, the ocean was eighty to two hundred feet lower than it is today, which would have put Myrtle Beach up to sixty miles from the seashore.[4] Near Myrtle Beach the sedimentary formations are known by the names Pee Dee and Black Bear, the latter of which was exposed as Hurl Rocks on the beach south of Twenty-first Avenue South. Hurl Rocks, between one and two million years old, were the only exposed native rocks on the South Carolina coast before they were covered by sand in the beach renourishment programs of the late twentieth century. The Pee Dee and Black Bear sedimentary formations also contain a series of aquifers that served as Myrtle Beach's water supply until the 1980s. The area's rapid population increase starting in the 1950s resulted in the steady lowering of the aquifer. Deeper aquifers cannot be used for water supply as access is cost-prohibitive.

Barrier islands line the Atlantic coast from North Carolina to Georgia. Both north and south of the Grand Strand these islands are fully formed (the Outer Banks of North Carolina and the sea islands of South Carolina and Georgia). However, along the Grand Strand these islands merge with the coastline and create its magnificent beaches, which are up to two hundred feet wide in places. Three high, sandy beach barriers exist in eastern Horry County. Myrtle Beach rests on the appropriately named Myrtle Beach Barrier and the Talbot Terrace, a high ridge of sandy soil between Kings Highway and the ocean that is not a barrier but rather an ancient dune. The Myrtle Beach Barrier extends thirty-four miles from Little River to Winyah Bay. The renowned freshwater lakes of the area, which are separated from the ocean only by dunes and the beach, form where the barrier "indents." In addition, the gullies in the barrier create riverlike forms known as swashes, which are basically tidal streams.[5]

The notable Carolina bays, located north of U.S. Highway 501 and west of the Intracoastal Waterway, are not marine features but rather elliptical depressions composed of peaty soils. They are aligned in a southeast/northeast direction, are edged by sandy rims, contain thick vegetation, and are considered to form a type of isolated freshwater wetland. The depression of a bay fills with rainwater, usually in winter and spring, and dries in the summer months. The Carolina bays constitute one of only four such concentrations in the world. The others are found in north-central

Alaska, the southern Kalahari in Botswana, the Netherlands, and northeastern Bolivia.[6]

The origins of the Carolina bays have long been debated, but they captured the public's imagination after being photographed from the air during the 1930s. "It is easy to imagine the wonder expressed by the locals at the sight of the magnitude and symmetry of the Carolina bays viewed from aerial photographs," George A. Howard noted in a 1997 paper. "These were structures that for generations had been regarded only as a peculiar nuisance."[7] Howard stated that the debate over origin is divided between those who propose that terrestrial mechanisms operating together formed the bays, and those who conclude that a single encounter with a space-borne object, such as a meteor, best accounts for their unusual characteristics. Research regarding the meteor theory has been inconclusive as field surveys have been unable to locate any meteoritic material or other features traditionally associated with meteor strikes.

The theory that was more widely accepted in 1997 was espoused by Douglas A. Johnson, who envisioned a vast series of artesian springs from which water flowed after traveling under great pressure underground from the mountains to the coastal plain. These springs would have eroded the marl and unconsolidated sediments through which they flowed, resulting in a pool of surface water that would become steadily more elongated in response to the migrating source. Johnson then theorized that a steady and consistent wind from the northwest, which would further scallop out the water body, created the elliptical depressions we see today. In more modern times most of these bays have been drained or otherwise altered. Fortunately twenty-three Carolina bays in Horry County are protected within the Lewis Ocean Bay Heritage Preserve, the largest number of undisturbed Carolina bays in South Carolina. The Heritage Preserve is part of the Heritage Trust Program of the South Carolina Department of Natural Resources.

One of the major geological hazards for the Grand Strand area is erosion. The South Carolina Office of Coastal Resources management has determined that the ocean is advancing onto the beach 0.68 inches per year on average. Local and state laws work to counteract this retreat through certain controls on development and through beach renourishment. Since the 1970s the latter has been a cooperative effort between local, state, and federal governments.

Plants and Vegetation

Few of the original dunes exist on the Grand Strand as a result of devastating storms or pressures from development. Along the oceanfront these dunes were generally ten to twenty feet high, with sand ridges of approximately thirty feet in height. The sand dunes are once again secured by scrub, but within recent memory they have migrated a few hundred feet.[8] The most spectacular feature of the beach vegetation, according to James Fussell, is the sea oats.[9] Tempe Oehler remembered when, as a child in the 1930s, she could "walk down to the Pavilion from our house in summertime and could pick enough blackberries for my mother to make a blackberry cobbler or blackberry dumplings. Because the blackberries grew wild along the shore, you know. Lots of sand dunes, lots of sea oats, which are gone."[10] The dunes and their natural vegetation have changed greatly in recent decades. Instead of blackberry brambles, stunted red cedar and bayberry can be found, providing a sharp contrast to the white sands of the dunes.[11]

The Grand Strand has few salt marshes because of the limited number of inlets. The most extensive marshes are found in the Murrells Inlet area and Little River. Within Myrtle Beach the largest marsh community is around Withers Swash. Myrtle Beach State Park and Meher Spiritual Center have some of the last, relatively intact examples of maritime forests in the area.

Longleaf pine and wiregrass were largely decimated during the late 1800s during the boom days of the naval-stores industries and timber farming days. Oak/hickory, mixed pine, hardwood, and oak-gum have been harvested since the late nineteenth century. However, a stand of cypress trees that are more than one hundred years old is protected by the Waccamaw Heritage Trust Preserve. Several varieties of gum trees can be found in the Carolina bays. The wetlands also support several unique floral species, including the endangered Venus's-fly trap.

Wildlife

Urban sprawl has reduced or destroyed the habitats of many forms of wildlife that once occupied the Horry County coast. The red-cockaded woodpecker and loggerhead turtles have lost nesting habitats and are now federally protected. Because of construction and clearing of the land, migrating birds have a difficult time finding food supplies in Grand Strand areas where they once stopped. But coastal South Carolina still maintains biological diversity, especially in its wetlands areas. Many varieties of birds, fish, shellfish, ducks, reptiles, and mammals still make the Grand Strand area their home. From chickadees, mourning doves, and wrens to herons, pelicans, and bald eagles, birdwatching is nature's gift to humanity. Black bears and alligators still can be found in the area. Beavers, opossums, and many species of toads, frogs, salamanders, butterflies, and dragonflies add to the richness of the beauty of the area.[12]

City of Myrtle Beach Parks and Recreation Department

With recreation and tourism being the economic engine for Grand Strand prosperity, enhancing and protecting the area's natural resources has become a local priority since the late 1940s. As the Grand Strand has grown in population, so too has the demand for more park facilities and recreation services. The City of Myrtle Beach Parks and Recreation Department evolved from a South Carolina General Assembly act in 1947, when it began operating at the county level. A commission, headed by James E. Bryan Jr., was in charge of the ten-mil assessment, which funded a part-time director, Ray Dean, a local schoolteacher, to manage its activities. At that time the extent of the programs offered included after-school activities, mainly sports. All of this changed in 1954 as the school districts were being realigned statewide and the Myrtle Beach district was integrated into the Horry County system.

In 1951 when Frank Beckham joined the commission as the first full-time director, the city had only one park, Chapin Memorial Park. In 1954 the city transformed the commission into a city department, which occupied the first floor of Chapin Memorial Library until 1969, when it moved into its own building. During this period the department developed five parks, added lighting for four ball fields, and built a city-owned ball field. The department also took over supervision of the beach patrol during the summer season. As the city's boundaries expanded and population and number of tourists increased, the recreation department became integral not only to providing recreational options for residents but also to enhancing the experience for visitors, many of whom came to Myrtle Beach to stay a week or more. Beckham served as director of parks and recreation until his death in 1987.

Myrtle Beach State Park

Seeking to protect the natural environment and also attract more visitors seems like a paradox, but by the 1930s South Carolina was trying to do both. In 1933 the South Carolina General Assembly enacted a law authorizing the South Carolina Forestry Commission to develop a state park system.[13] Myrtle Beach Farms Company donated 320 acres in August 1934 to the state for the park, realizing its added value to tourism and outdoor recreation. On July 1, 1936, Myrtle Beach State Park was the first in the system to open. Within two months more than 42,000 people used the park, and by the time it was formally dedicated in June 1937, five cabins, picnic shelters, a bathhouse, a recreational building, trails, and twenty campsites with trailers had been built. For the fiscal year 1939–40 almost 100,000 visitors passed through its gates, and by the next year Myrtle Beach State Park had the highest attendance among all the state parks. This number-one position was repeated in the 1970–71 fiscal year (1.39 million visitors) and in the 1975–76 fiscal year (1.4 million visitors).[14]

The park was closed from 1942 to 1945 when the U.S. Army Air Force took over the facility for use as a coastal defense post.[15] In the summer of 1950 a 640-foot fishing pier was added to the park's amenities with the assistance of Spring Mills, which also built the swimming pool in 1957. The latter remained a popular attraction at the park, even with the ocean nearby, into the 1980s, when it was closed.[16]

Myrtle Beach State Park saw many changes in the 1960s. After approximately thirty years of memorable service, the bathhouse that the CCC built in the late 1930s was torn down in 1967 because of maintenance problems. The wings were saved and turned into a small country store to serve the growing needs of campers as camping became more popular on the Grand Strand and for use as picnic shelters. Typically park attendance has grown each year, with the exception of sharp drops between 1963 and 1965 due to the state's fight against federally mandated desegregation of the parks (see chapter 13, "African American Community"). Throughout the 1960s and 1970s the camping facilities at the park were continually expanded with the growth of tourism in the area. Between 1970 and 1983 the number of campsites grew from 150 to 350. In some instances campers moved into new sites as soon as sites could be cleared, sometimes literally waiting in the drive as the park workers finished preparations. In 1975 a public parking fee of one dollar per car was introduced to ease overcrowding in the picnic areas, causing a verbal uproar but no downturn in visitors.[17]

Public campgrounds began competing with private ones in the 1960s as major tracts of land were converted for trailer and camper hookups. Several trends merged during the late 1950s and early 1960s to fuel the popularity of such camping, such as improved highway systems, increased leisure time and income, and establishment of new travel-trailer companies, such as Winnebago Industries in 1960. Jack Nelson started one of the first private campgrounds north of Myrtle Beach in 1960, Lake Arrowhead Family Campground, with 250 sites. In 1959, on the south end of the Grand Strand, Carl and Marian Perry opened Camp Beachwood, a small, 125-site camp, to handle the overflow of campers from Myrtle Beach State Park; it was located west of the state park across U.S. Highway 17. Perry moved his campground business to oceanfront property in 1962, where it still existed in 2006 as Lakewood Camping Resort. A bit farther south, Nelson and Mary Emily Jackson opened Ocean Lakes Campground in 1970. Over the next ten years several other campgrounds opened, bringing more than 1,500 campsites to the south end of the Grand Strand alone.

Brookgreen Gardens and Huntington Beach State Park

The nation's first public sculpture garden sits within a magnificent natural setting, in a vision that only great financial resources could have made possible. In 1930 Archer M. Huntington, son of the transportation magnate Collis P. Huntington, and his wife, the renowned sculptress Anna Hyatt Huntington, purchased four adjoining former colonial-era plantations in Georgetown County and built the nation's first public sculpture garden. Named for the main plantation in the tract, Brookgreen Gardens opened in 1932 and was intended to be "a quiet joining of hands between science and art," according to the Huntingtons. Brookgreen Gardens was listed on the National Register of Historic Places in 1978 and named a National Historic Landmark in 1992. The sculpture garden was designed by Frank G. Tarbox Jr., who spent years developing the landscape and collecting and planting native plants and wildlflowers. On the occasion of Brookgreen Gardens' fiftieth anniversary in 1981, trustee president Joseph Veach Nobel described the gardens as a "farsighted concept that embodied aesthetic appreciation and ecological preservation long before sculpture was popular, or ecology became a catchword."[18]

In addition to Brookgreen Gardens, Huntington built a winter home called Atalaya on the property. Archer Huntington passed away in 1955, and Anna never returned to stay in the house again. In 1960 the state of South Carolina leased the twenty-five-hundred-acre property, which is separated from Brookgreen Gardens by U.S. Highway 17, as a state park. The property contains some features rarely found along the Grand Strand today, such as saltwater marshes, three miles of undeveloped beach, rare tracts of maritime forest, and live oaks that are up to 250 years old. Because this acreage contains an almost untouched habitat, birds flock to the park, which some consider the single best birding destination in South Carolina.[19] Several colonies of the endangered red-cockaded woodpecker thrive here.

The lure and majesty of the ocean and the beauty of a sunset over the waves are still magnets for people coming to Myrtle Beach. While the natural environment has changed dramatically with modern development, the city, county, and state continue to work together in a variety of ways to ensure that a measure of the natural resources that drew people to the Grand Strand in the first place will be available for generations to come.

Six

The Ties That Bind Us Together— Religion and Education

*H*orry County geography isolated it from much of the rest of North and South Carolina, leaving those who settled Myrtle Beach to acknowledge not only that their future was in their own hands but also that a prosperous future required neighbors to bond with common purpose. No two institutions cemented that bond better than churches and schools, for they made up the social fiber that drew people closer together in faith and in progress and shaped the character of the burgeoning resort as a family destination. The shared experiences of building these institutions led to lifelong friendships—and marriages—between families that would persist for generations and leave an indelible mark on the city.

Religious Institutions

In the early 1900s religion had a powerful influence on the lives of southerners and was characterized by its generally fundamental and evangelistic nature. In contrast to northern churches of the period, southern Protestants were more concerned with salvation and moral direction. Their northern counterparts tended to focus on social issues resulting from rapid industrialization and urbanization, such as poverty, child labor, and prostitution. Southern churches generally left such issues to the individual and concerned themselves with salvation of sinners. By the early 1920s, however, this regional schism fell away with the establishment of ecumenical efforts to deal with social issues.[1] The history of the development of churches in Myrtle Beach reflects this blending of concerns: salvation of the individual with influence on society and progress. The increased railroad access to the beach, with regular Sunday excursions by 1909 routinely filling up the trains, created a challenge to church ministers, who preached against this violation of the Sabbath. As a result, it can be said that the churches followed the people to the beach. A Baptist church was already well established in the area, and the Methodists began holding Sunday services at the Pavilion and other locations about 1915. Many other denominations would follow in later years.

The people who were instrumental in building the schools, businesses, and hospitality industry in Myrtle Beach were also church leaders, and many of their families are still active in the life of the community. Just a few examples include the following:

> Daniel W. Nance, a prominent building contractor and property owner in Myrtle Beach, was a driving force in building First Baptist Church in the 1930s and 1940s.

> Andrew W. Stackhouse was pastor of Sandy Grove Baptist Church in the 1930s as well as a teacher and principal at Myrtle Beach Colored School.

> Holmes B. Springs Sr., who worked with John T. Woodside and Myrtle Beach Estates in the late 1920s, and his family were early— and lifelong—worshipers at First Methodist Church. His wife Louise was the church's first pianist.

> Annie Burney, who owned one of the earliest guest houses in Myrtle Beach (1923), was on the first building committee for the First Presbyterian Church in 1928.

> George W. Trask, whose family owned G. W. Trask & Sons Farms and Crystal Ice Company, was a leader in the Presbyterian Church in the 1940s. He was also chairman of the Myrtle Beach School Board in the late 1940s.

> One of the first trustees of Church of the Messiah (present-day Trinity Episcopal Church) was Nicholas C. Hughes Jr., who surveyed early plats for Myrtle Beach Farms and others from the 1930s through the 1950s.

In addition, the city's main landowner and developer, along with sister companies, fostered the development of the churches. Myrtle Beach Farms and the Chapin Company, as well as John T. Woodside's Myrtle Beach Estates in the late 1920s, provided land for churches at little or no cost to the congregations. They did this not only for religious growth but also because they knew that the availability of churches would foster residential areas for families. Early survey maps of Myrtle Beach indicate the location of properties to be donated to churches that were on the leading edges of development. "What the [Myrtle Beach] Farms would do," recalled Tempe Oehler, "is . . . give land to a church to build a church [building]. If the church deceased, the land went back to them. That is the way they moved the city limits out. When they gave the land to Trinity [Episcopal] Church, there just was not much at all in here so that helped develop this area [around the church]."[2] Senior partners in Myrtle Beach Farms, Chapin Company, and Woodside's Myrtle Beach Estates were known to make personal donations to newly formed Myrtle Beach churches. Most of these men were active as laypersons in their individual churches and were keenly influential in the character of the community. For example, the *Horry Herald* was thrilled about the beach's new owner in 1926. John Woodside, the editor H. H. Woodward wrote, "is practical enough for the best of us in this county. . . . Moreover he is a God-fearing man, a strict Presbyterian, and he is said to order his life according to the word of the Lord. Under his management we feel certain that the beach will be no resort for gamblers, no center of loose living, but a place where any young man or young woman may safely spend their [*sic*] time surrounded by the best of influences. . . . There will be no wild carousing, no flaunting of sin or iniquity, such as have helped give an evil name to some other places."[3]

Simeon B. Chapin, one of the cofounders of Myrtle Beach Farms Company, went a step further and organized the Chapin Foundation of Myrtle Beach in 1943 to help support the continued growth of religious and benevolent organizations within the city limits of Myrtle Beach. The ability of the foundation to give is directly linked to the success and growth of the city as its endowment is funded by stocks in Myrtle Beach Farms Company, Inc., and Burroughs & Chapin Company, Inc. As of 2005 the foundation had contributed more than $15 million to Myrtle Beach churches, libraries, hospitals, the YMCA, and other civic projects.

By 1980 congregations representing most religious faiths had places of worship in Myrtle Beach. Five of these date back to the early days of the community: First Baptist Church of Myrtle Beach (1870), Sandy Grove Baptist Church (1902), Mt. Olive African Methodist Episcopal (AME) Church (1907), the First United Methodist Church of Myrtle Beach (circa 1915), and First Presbyterian Church (1928). The Baptist, Methodist, and Presbyterian facilities were shared whenever possible with young, growing churches until the latter were able to afford their own church buildings. These churches, and the many others that would follow, served not only as religious institutions but also as social gathering places and forces of change in the community. They faced the same seasonal issues that tourist-related enterprises did: how to support winter congregations of full-time residents while welcoming thousands of summer visitors through their doors.

As Myrtle Beach grew and prospered, so too did the churches. While Myrtle Beach's early population was made up primarily of families who had lived in the area for generations or who had permanent homes in Conway and other nearby towns, those who followed after 1920 came from all over the region—and by the 1940s from around the country. Myrtle Beach churches provided a sense of community that facilitated bonding and life-long personal and business relationships. Indicating the community's level of involvement with its churches, a 1956 newspaper article stated that "the latest census shows that Myrtle Beach has a population of 5,836. There are 4,059 of those on church rolls, which is roughly 70 percent. . . . Splitting it again, there are 74 percent of the white population affiliated with churches in Myrtle Beach and 44 percent of the Negroes."[4]

First Baptist Church of Myrtle Beach, 500 Fourth Avenue North

This church was founded circa 1871, when it was known as Socastee Baptist Church, and had thirty-seven members in 1873. It was renamed Eden Missionary Baptist Church by the late 1880s. The church building was located on Old Conway Highway (State Highway 15) on land that eventually became the main runway of the former Myrtle Beach Army Air Force Base. Fire destroyed the church in 1898. The congregation then moved to land donated by William T. Todd on State Highway 15 near Withers Swash, where it stood for the next thirty years.

In 1933 a new church was built at Fourth Avenue North and Oak Street. It was renamed First Baptist Church of Myrtle Beach in 1937. Construction on the present-day complex began in 1944 on the corner of Kings Highway and Fourth Avenue North, and the sanctuary was completed in 1950.

Sandy Grove Baptist Church, 1008 Carver

The congregation of this church organized in 1902 and met in a bush shelter. The first church building was located near Little River Road (present-day Oak Street). In later years another, larger wooden church was built on Carver Street, south of the current church, on property donated by Myrtle Beach Farms. The existing church was built in 1965 and enlarged in 1970.

Mount Olive African Methodist Episcopal (AME) Church, 1108 Carver

Congregants began meeting in 1879 in homes. The church was officially organized in 1907 or 1910 by a group of black Christian farmers in the area. They built a white, wooden building near modern-day Oak Street and Twelfth Avenue North. The church also served as a schoolhouse for local black children until Myrtle Beach Colored School was opened in 1932. A new church building was completed in 1959.

First Methodist Church, Myrtle Beach, 901 North Kings Highway

The congregation first met as a Methodist Sunday school organized in spring 1915 at the beach with the assistance of Socastee Methodist Church, the South Carolina Conference Board of Missions, friends in Conway, and Simeon B. Chapin. Methodist revivals were held at Myrtle Beach School in 1918, and summer services were held at the Pavilion.

The first church building was constructed near the corner of Ninth Avenue North and Kings Highway and remodeled in 1928. In 1939 the present sanctuary was built. The old, original building was moved next to Carver School in 1960 and was dedicated as a recreation center. It burned down in 1968.

First Presbyterian Church, 1300 North Kings Highway

This congregation was organized in 1928. For the church building, John T. Woodside donated a half-block of land at the corner of Eleventh Avenue North and Kings Highway, the site of the present-day Mammy's Kitchen. After Woodside's operations in Myrtle Beach collapsed during the Great Depression, the church barely survived as many of its members were Presbyterian families who followed Woodside from Greenville to Myrtle Beach; it was down to nine members at one point.

By 1945 the congregation had grown sufficiently to consider building a larger sanctuary, and Myrtle Beach Farms exchanged the half-block for a full block between Thirteenth Avenue and Fourteenth Avenue North and Kings Highway. Ground was broken in 1947 for a new sanctuary, which opened the following year.

St. Andrew Catholic Church, Thirty-seventh Avenue North and North Kings Highway

Catholic services were first held in 1929 when St. Mary's Parish in Georgetown established the St. Andrew mission. In 1938 Myrtle Beach Farms donated land for a building at Twenty-ninth Avenue North and Kings Highway. St. Andrew Catholic Church opened in June 1939. The current sanctuary was built in 1964.

Trinity Episcopal Church, 3000 North Kings Highway

Episcopalians first began meeting at the beach in the mid-1930s, holding services in the Methodist and Presbyterian churches. In 1936 the congregation, which was first called Church of the Messiah, began a building campaign, to which Myrtle Beach Farms donated a lot at Thirtieth Avenue North and Kings Highway. A new church opened in 1939. The first full-time minister arrived in 1949. The church was enlarged in 1950 and one year later officially changed its name to Trinity Episcopal Church.

Meher Spiritual Center

The center is named for Meher Baba, who was born Merwan Sheharian Irani in 1894 in India and died in 1969. He was a spiritual leader who believed that his duty was to awaken the human spirit to the realization of God. Elizabeth Chapin Patterson, daughter of Simeon B. Chapin, met Baba during a visit to New York in 1931 and became interested in his teachings. Baba's popularity during the late 1940s and 1950s may be due to a response to the nation's growing materialism and consumerism of the period. He was reportedly influential with cultural icons of the 1960s counterculture, including Pete Townshend of the rock band the Who.

In 1941 Baba asked Patterson and Princess Norina Matchabelli to find a property in the United States for a center of study and meditation. In 1943 Simeon Chapin gave his daughter five hundred acres that John T. Woodside had originally set aside for a hunting preserve in the late 1920s. She donated it to the Meher Spiritual Center. Baba visited the Myrtle Beach Center in May 1952, July 1956, and May 1959.

By 1980 the center was open year-round as a spiritual retreat. The land has been preserved in its original state and is recognized as a nature and wildlife preserve by the state of South Carolina. It is one of the few sizable tracts of land on the Grand Strand remaining as it was before European settlement.

Education Facilities

Prior to the Civil War, the prevailing doctrine on education among South Carolinians was that a child's learning was the parent's responsibility, not the state's. Even after Reconstruction when the South Carolina State Constitution of 1868 called for a system of universal education, with schools open to all "without regard to race or color," communities were still required to provide much of the financing and maintenance of their local schools. Although the state of education at the turn of the twentieth century in Horry County, as well as in most of South Carolina, was dismal, people were still eager to learn. When a community wanted its own school, it simply built one. In 1899 South Carolina passed laws permitting school districts to levy taxes for their support. Community school districts chose trustees, who hired the teachers, determined the salaries, raised funds, made the rules, and generally oversaw the operations of the schools.[5]

In the early 1900s one of the first schools in the Myrtle Beach area was located on Pine Island Road (near Old Conway Highway, or Highway 15) and was next to George King's dairy, according to the late Mary Todd Nance in an article by Eva Claire Riggs.[6] By 1910, however, the community relocated it near the present-day intersection of Third Avenue North and Broadway.[7]

The building was divided into two large rooms that, with folding doors between them, became four classrooms for grades one through ten. This one-story, white clapboard structure, which was supported by small brick pillars and had narrow brick chimney flues for wood-burning stoves, comprised Myrtle Beach School District, number thirteen of ninety-five districts in Horry County. The district's three trustees in 1910, all farmers in Socastee Township, were Salathiel S. Owens, Joseph C. Dubois, and Daniel J. Cox. In the fall of 1918, the pupils who were to become the first graduates of Myrtle Beach High School in 1930 entered the first grade there. Seventy-one students were enrolled at the Myrtle Beach school as of June 1918.[8]

Although most people in the early 1900s understood the value of an education, the reality was that boys and girls were needed to help support their families. In addition, extra money to pay for teachers and supplies was difficult to come by. In 1920 the school year in Horry County was only 136 days, the shortest in the state. The emphasis on education in coastal South Carolina, however, was soon to improve with the help of the state government. By 1920 the Progressive movement, which on the national level was a crusade for social and political reform, was beginning to affect South Carolina. Because of the limitations of what could be accomplished under the state's one-party politics, Progressives concentrated on public health, morality, child labor laws, and education in South Carolina. As part of these efforts, the General Assembly passed the "6–0–1" Act in 1924, which standardized the length of the school year to at least seven months, with the state paying for the cost of six months ("6") and the local school district required to pay for one month ("1"). The "0" was for county appropriations, which were encouraged but not required. The 1924 act also established minimum standards and salaries for teachers. Before the decade was over, South Carolina schools increased their per-pupil expenditures by 149.6 percent, from $16.02 per white student in 1920 to $39.98 in 1930.[9]

This attention to education was reflected in Myrtle Beach, where a new brick grammar school building opened in 1926 at 505 North Kings Highway (site of the present-day U.S. Post Office), facing Oak Street. The land was donated by Myrtle Beach Investments, John T. Woodside's company. Myrtle Beach's first high school (for whites), the county's eighth one, was built next to it, facing Kings Highway, and was dedicated in February 1928. A new section that connected the two school buildings with a 450-seat auditorium was soon added.

Six students, out of an enrollment total of thirty-three, constituted Myrtle Beach High School's first graduating class in 1930. The members of that class were Arland Cooper, Lonnie Causey, Grace Perdue, Betsy Hollinshead, Annie King, and Jesse Stalvey. Only two students, siblings Ollie and Beulah Owens, graduated the next year. Eight girls graduated in 1933: Ruby Lee Foxworth, Sara Miller Blackwell, Esther Nance, Annie Louise Huggins, Eloise Miller, Dorothy Oliver, Sadie Leona Owens, and Hettie Mae Simmons. Indicative of the continuity and legacy of families in Myrtle Beach is the fact that of these eight women, three married and raised families in Myrtle Beach. All of their children and many of their grandchildren also graduated from Myrtle Beach High School.[10]

No matter what era one occupies, teenagers will find a way to bend and stretch the status quo, whether in a small town or a major city. The senior class of 1939 shared such a story with J. Marcus Smith for his *Myrtle Beach Sun-News* history column on September 7, 1996. They related how the seniors claimed a portion of the second floor of the high school as their domain and prohibited juniors from entering. Or course, the inevitable happened: the juniors invaded and a fight ensued. School Superintendent Lewis N. Clark conferred with the principal Ernie Southern, who knew that Simeon Chapin was promoting a contest among all Horry County high schools for the best essay on Brookgreen Gardens; one winner from each county high school would receive a cash prize, and another student would receive an all-expenses-paid trip to the 1939 World's Fair in New York. Clark and Southern decided that, as an apt punishment for the boisterous young men, all would be required to tour Brookgreen Gardens, write essays on their trip, and within the week submit their entries to the contest. As it happened, the grand-prize winner, Roy Harrelson Jr., came from Myrtle Beach High. Harrelson later became the editor and publisher of the *Myrtle Beach News*. It is uncertain whether he was a member of the group being "punished."

Fire destroyed the grammar and high school complex in the early morning hours in February 1946. The event is etched in the memories of several long-time Myrtle Beach residents. "We lived across the street," recalled Tempe Hughes Oehler, "and the telephone operator called my mother about two or three o'clock in the morning. She said, 'Mrs. Hughes, the school's on fire. Thought you'd like to know.' And she called everybody and a crowd assembled. I remember a classmate, Roddy Rourk, came to help put out the fire. He got hold of the fire hose and directed it at the school but it was so powerful that he couldn't hold it down and that thing was just flipping all around, you know, so it wasn't helping the fire much. A lot of the kids were just rejoicing because the school was burning. But it was a real mess for the next year or more."[11]

Sigmund Abeles was in the fifth grade when the school burned. His mother, Henrietta Abeles, owned Paul's Guest House directly across from the school. Abeles remember, "Firemen were wetting our house down and our roof, because . . . wind was blowing . . . burning shingles. And my mother kept telling me to go back to bed! There'd be no way I could go back to bed! I mean, this whole excitement and everything, the most exciting time. And the school actually smoldered for a very long time. . . . there were school buses that were damaged that were left in the yard that we would all climb in and pretend that we were driving." He also recalled the sound of cans blowing up in the fire. Billy Roberts, who was a high school senior that year, said that those were cans of vegetables that had been prepared in the cannery on the first floor. He said, "We boys taking agriculture and shop built the cannery. I soldered the galvanized tin with which the large hot water vat was constructed."[12]

Roosevelt Bellamy did not know about the fire until the next day because they lived farther away than Oehler or Abeles, but he did recall that it was a Tuesday night. "They had a basketball game there that night and it burnt down that same night," Bellamy remembered.[13] "Jimmie" C. Benton remembered that his school bus driver, not knowing about the fire, picked them up that morning but had to turn around when the bus got to the school. Benton had left photos of his horses in his classroom overnight to show the next day, and they were destroyed.[14]

Students were dispersed to several locations for classes: Lafayette Manor, Sea Side Inn, the former USO facility, and First Presbyterian Church, among others. Oehler said, "I remember when we had our graduation [in 1947]. See, we didn't graduate from the high school; we graduated from the Methodist Church. That's where we had our graduation because we didn't have a school." Billy Roberts, who graduated in 1946, related that their ceremonies were held at the USO building, where his class also completed their last semester of high school. The grade school was rebuilt on its original site and opened in 1946. A new high school was built at 1403 North Kings Highway in 1948 across from First Presbyterian Church. The $150,000 school had a gymnasium with a capacity of twenty-five hundred and ten classrooms.[15]

The education of African American children in the Myrtle Beach area in the first half of the twentieth century did not enjoy the same Progressive influences as did that of white students. Their school facilities were inadequate, teacher salaries were lower than for white teachers, per-pupil expenditures were considerably lower, and few school buses for black children were available, even though many students were scattered in rural areas.[16]

Prior to the 1920s students at Myrtle Beach Colored School met in their churches, primarily Mount Olive African Methodist Episcopal Church. In June 1918 thirty-one students were enrolled.[17] Opening in 1932 at 800 Tenth Avenue North, a new building for Myrtle Beach Colored School was based on designs prepared by the Julius Rosenwald Foundation but was not funded by the foundation. Parents had to build much of the school themselves. Henry Hemingway, one of the original students at Myrtle Beach Colored School, remembered "wood sawing" and selling eggs and oranges to help raise money. Reverend Andrew W. Stackhouse was one of the first principals of Myrtle Beach Colored School. Eleven Horry County black schools built during this period received assistance from the Rosenwald fund.[18]

Myrtle Beach Colored School provided classes for first through eighth grades. Children fortunate enough to go on to high school went to Conway's Whittemore School, although little if any transportation was provided for black youths until the 1950s. They would usually live with other families in Conway while attending. The first three accredited black high schools in South Carolina, of which Whittemore was one, awarded diplomas in 1930. Black high school students from Myrtle Beach attended the Conway school until the spring of 1965, when the first four black students were enrolled at Myrtle Beach High School. Two of these students were Martha Canty and Prince Bowens. Prior to 1929 black schools were not accredited and could not grant high school diplomas.

A decade before integration, South Carolina schools underwent changes that were just as traumatic to individual communities as integration would be. The consolidation of school districts statewide in 1954 was preceded in Horry County by a study requested by Horry County superintendent of schools Thurman W. Anderson, the results of which were published by the George Peabody College for Teachers in Nashville, Tennessee. By 1941 Horry County had eighty-five school districts, an unmanageable and wasteful number, according to the report. Although Anderson wanted to consolidate the schools into one district, which would mean closing smaller schools, he was not able to accomplish this task until 1954, when school buses were available to all areas of the county.[19] That year all the school districts in the county were consolidated into a single school district with about forty schools. Statewide, 1,200 school districts were reduced to 102.[20]

The loss of local control was outweighed by the improvements in education and facilities. Between 1940 and 1962 South Carolina public schools reorganized as the state steadily increased its control over school policy. State spending on education increased from $18 million in 1939–40 to $91 million in 1957–58. This activity was stimulated by the election in 1950 of

Governor James Byrnes. In response to *Briggs v. Elliott* and in anticipation of a decision in *Brown v. Board of Education of Topeka,* Byrnes immediately began a campaign to provide "substantial equality" in school facilities for black and white students. The legislature passed the state's first sales tax to provide increased funding for public education, and by 1956 the state had spent $124 million on new construction and buses, about two-thirds of which went to black schools. While in 1951 only 142,000 pupils were bused to school daily, by 1955 this number increased to 241,000. Governor Byrnes was especially proud of the increase of 50,000 black children receiving school transportation, most for the first time.[21] This significant increase, however, does not reflect the quality of that transportation. "They bussed us from here [Myrtle Beach] to Whittemore [in Conway]," recalled Patricia Burgess. "Bus we rode on was a handicapped bus that they had already wore out. When you got on top of the Conway bridge, most of the time you would not go over, so the guys would have to get out and push it across the bridge."[22]

In 1953 Myrtle Beach enjoyed the fruits of Byrnes's programs with the opening of a new school for blacks, Carver Training School, which replaced Myrtle Beach Colored School. Its opening was just in time as enrollment had almost doubled since 1941, from 164 in 1941 to 361 in 1957.[23] This increase is believed to be due in part to the air force base reactivation in 1954 and reflects overcrowding issues throughout the system in Myrtle Beach. The schools had grown significantly since the opening of the Myrtle Beach Army Air Force Base during World War II, when enrollment at the Myrtle Beach Elementary School increased 39 percent between 1940 and 1945, and from 292 in 1940–41 to 405 in 1944–45.[24]

To ease overcrowding in 1953, the administration moved the seventh grade from the grammar school to the high school. However, because no physical space was available at the high school that first year, the boys attended classes in the City Recreation Room at Chapin Memorial Library and the girls met in the Education Building of First Presbyterian Church.[25] That did not solve all the problems. Within two years the grammar school was again running out of space as the town continued to grow and as the air force base population increased. More than 640 new children were expected to enroll in Myrtle Beach schools in September 1956. Plans had been drawn for a new grammar school with a capacity of 750 students, and trustees sought funds from the federal government to assist in construction.[26] Myrtle Heights Elementary School opened in 1956, and a new junior high was built by 1964, just in time for integration.

The United States Supreme Court unanimously ruled on May 17, 1954, that "separate but equal" was unconstitutional. Eleven years later the Horry

County public schools desegregated with little disturbance. Prior to integrating the students, however, black and white teachers were integrated. Evelyn Brittain, a graduate of Myrtle Beach Colored School and Whittemore High School, was teaching in Myrtle Beach in the 1950s. She remembered, "We were in the building where Swansgate is now [Carver School]. The teachers integrated first and then as years progressed, . . . The children integrated." According to Keith Cribb, who was principal of Myrtle Heights Elementary School from 1957 to 1980, in order to create the right racial balance, "some of our teachers left one school to go to another school. That was a little bit difficult for them but they made the exchange real well. . . . It [integration] was difficult, I won't tell you it wasn't, but I think we made it as smoothly as any school district in the state of South Carolina."[27]

Not only was there a shuffling of teachers, but also the impact within one family might be significant. "Personally," said Cribb, "it was pretty hard because there were five of us in the family . . . all three of my children were in my school. And after it [integration] happened and we were all situated, five of us were in five different schools. My wife was at the high school, I was at the Myrtle Heights Elementary, but each of the children went in different spots. It wasn't real easy, but it was something we knew we had to do and we did it."[28]

Louise Springs Crews, who was a teacher at Myrtle Beach Grade School in 1964, also recalled the difficulty of busing during the integration process: "It was kind of hard at first because we had so many little tiny children in one building. Trying to get them on the right bus, that was hard. We had different colors, tags, on them, everything else. But it worked out all right."[29] An editorial in the *Myrtle Beach Sun-News* on August 26, 1965, entitled "To Credit of Our People" read, "People of this county are to be commended for the manner in which school problems and changes have been handled during the troubled times that now exist in our country. We have gone about our business of educating our children to the best of our ability. The type of education we are offering certainly could stand improvement. So long as we recognize that fact and work toward reaching a higher goal, there is hope. In many counties and cities in our nation there is trouble. Boycotts, sit-ins, demonstration of about every nature plague public education. We have no such experience in our county. For the benefit of all our children, we trust we can write the same 10 years from now."

The Horry County School District activated its formal desegregation plan for the 1965–66 school year. On September 2, 1965, eleven black students, all residents of Myrtle Beach, enrolled at Myrtle Beach High School, and four of those students started classes there in January 1965.[30] More than twenty-eight hundred students started school in Myrtle Beach that year.

During the early 1950s an increased demand for college training was stimulated by the vastly improved high schools, greater economic and career opportunities, and the need to train returning veterans of World War II and the Korean War.[31] The need for a junior college was cited in Horry County as early as 1954 in order to provide continuing education and training for county teachers. Community leaders envisioned a school for students who could not afford to go away to college and workers who wanted to further their education but were bound to the area by jobs and families. Horry County Junior College, the predecessor of Coastal Carolina University (CCU), was born, opening in September 1954 as a branch of the College of Charleston with classrooms at Conway High School. The junior college offered "two years of fully accredited college work for the low sum of $300 per year tuition fee." It became independent in 1958 when the College of Charleston discontinued its extension program. Two years later Coastal Carolina joined the University of South Carolina system as a regional two-year campus. The institution expanded to a four-year college and awarded its first four-year degree in 1975.[32]

The 1960s also brought another higher education option to Grand Strand area high school graduates. In 1958 the South Carolina General Assembly passed a bill to establish twelve technical education schools. Philip Gray of Myrtle Beach was asked to chair a committee to win one of the campuses for Horry County. It was initially conceived as a school to serve not only Horry but also Georgetown and Marion counties and was to be called Horry-Georgetown-Marion Technical School. Gray's committee secured a donation of land from Burroughs Timber Company and funding assistance from Horry County. Marion County eventually dropped out of the project. The school's first building was completed in 1963. Three years later Horry-Georgetown Technical College, a public two-year community college, opened to offer associate degree programs and continuing education programs to meet job training, occupational advancement, and lifelong learning needs of the residents and employers in the area.[33]

Public libraries are another element of education largely taken for granted today, but prior to 1929 no such institution existed in South Carolina. The improvement of the South Carolina public school system in the 1920s and 1930s, however, fostered the need for a statewide public library system. Although the state created an agency in 1929 to aid in its development, the South Carolina General Assembly did not appropriate any funds. The federal government's Works Project Administration (WPA) intervened in 1935, seeking to provide each county with some measure of public library service. Separately but in conjunction with the WPA efforts, the Conway

Library Committee was formed about 1935 to promote a public library, which opened in 1938 in the auditorium of the Conway City Hall. The WPA was working about the same time with the Horry County Board of Education implementing bookmobile services and establishing library services for black citizens through the black schools, largely with discarded and outdated books. This arrangement continued into the 1950s. Etrulia Dozier, who in 1954 was a librarian at Whittemore, Conway's black high school, remembered, "There was a relationship between the school and the public library because at that time, they would bring a box of books over from the public library and I could check them out from the school library and then collect them and have them returned after two weeks." Soon after that, however, the state mandated that all school libraries had to be funded, and Whittemore developed its own collection. When WPA funding ended in 1942 in Horry County, the Horry County Board of Education assumed full responsibility for the bookmobile service.[34]

Myrtle Beach's library had its roots in this WPA program. With five hundred books from the federal government and one donated book, the Myrtle Beach library opened part-time in the fall of 1939. It was housed in what was then the chamber of commerce building in the 800 block of North Kings Highway. Frances Stackhouse, the assistant librarian at Myrtle Beach High School, was its first part-time librarian.

Between 1939 and 1948 the Myrtle Beach library moved several times, and it soon became evident that it needed its own home. In August 1948 the city of Myrtle Beach accepted a grant of forty thousand dollars from the Chapin Foundation of Myrtle Beach to build a library building on the south end of Myrtle Beach Memorial Park, on land that had been donated to the city by Myrtle Beach Farms Company. The grant stipulated that the library, after its completion, should be maintained by the city and named the Chapin Memorial Library after Simeon B. Chapin. The library opened on June 1, 1949, exactly a month before the Horry County Library System celebrated the dedication of the new Horry County Memorial Library in Conway. The opening-day collection, which consisted of eighteen hundred books, two newspapers, and five magazines, also incorporated the WPA collection. Mrs. Frank Norment was the first full-time librarian, and the first library commission included Dr. Cecil Brearley, chairman and pastor of First Presbyterian Church; Claude Epps Sr.; J. Harry Spann; Mrs. James E. Bryan Jr.; and Mrs. Holmes B. Springs. The library occupied the top floor of the two-story brick building, and the first floor housed the city's recreation department. Shirley Walker Boone succeeded Norment as librarian in 1954, arriving two weeks after Hurricane Hazel devastated the area. That did not scare her off, however, because she held that position until she retired in 1990. In the early years Boone was the only full-time employee and would have to lock up the library just to take a lunch break.

The building was renovated and expanded several times, with total space in 2006 measuring twenty-five thousand square feet. The children's section was added in 1959; in 1969 the city's recreation department moved into new quarters and the library expanded to fill the first floor. In 1979 another two thousand square feet were added to the existing building. The Horry County Library System made overtures to bring the Chapin Memorial Library under its authority in the 1970s, but the city of Myrtle Beach determined that its residents were better served in maintaining its own municipal library system. Circulation increased about 24 percent between 1960 and 1970. In the following decade it increased by almost 60 percent, for a total in 1980 of more than eighty-seven thousand books, audiotapes, videos, magazines, and puzzles. Contributing to that increase in the 1980s, in addition to a general growth in population, were the "snowbirds," retirees who traveled to the South from New England and Canada during the winter months. "That was one of the biggest changes in the library," Boone recalled in 1990. "Where before we might have had two visitors register in the winter, now [1980s] there are hundreds. Then our largest circulation was in the summer; but now the winter circulation is much larger."[35] Boone said many times during her retirement celebrations that the best part of her job was serving the community, helping children who eventually brought in their children and sometimes even grandchildren.

Although change has been a constant in Myrtle Beach's history and development, the city's families have provided a base of stability and continuity over the decades. They have been part of the social and political upheavals, built the institutions that nurtured their children, and supported each other in economic downturns and in growing pains resulting from prosperity. They have watched and participated in the transformation of Myrtle Beach from a sleepy summer retreat at the turn of the twentieth century to a nationally recognized and cosmopolitan city. At the same time, these families have been successful in retaining the small-town sense of community, especially through the institutions of education and religion. Time and the emerging new generations of these early families will mold the next century's community of Myrtle Beach, South Carolina.

Seven

The Pavilion: A Monument to Community, Tourism, and Memory

The Myrtle Beach Pavilion not only represented the evolution of the community, visitor demands, and shifting demographics in Myrtle Beach, but it also signified stability, consistency, and history. For many, it meant amusement park rides, the music of the carousel, and the thrill of being at the top of the Ferris wheel and seeing the expanse of ocean. For others, the Pavilion was the dance floor, the jukebox, name entertainers, and the shag. It was also a place to see and be seen, to meet friends, or to catch the eye of someone special. To every person who has spent a summer's evening at the Pavilion, it was a landmark, a place of dreams, excitement, and memory. "Everything that is Myrtle Beach . . . all started on this spot," according to the author Will Moredock.[1]

More than one Pavilion existed in Myrtle Beach over the generations, and all were the products of Burroughs & Collins, whose beach development efforts were rolled into Myrtle Beach Farms Company in 1912. Even during the late 1920s and early 1930s when John T. Woodside and Myrtle Beach Estates owned most Myrtle Beach property, Myrtle Beach Farms retained about thirteen hundred acres, which included the Pavilion, the beach and surrounding property between about Third Avenue North and Ninth Avenue North, and commercial property in the downtown area. In 1980 the Pavilion was still owned and operated by Myrtle Beach Farms.

All the properties known as the Pavilion over the years had different architectural styles and were built of different materials, but they served generally the same purpose—to function as a platform for entertainment and community gathering, a place for people to transform themselves from

Children's rides at the Myrtle Beach Pavilion amusement park in 1965.
Mark Garner Collection, courtesy of Chapin Memorial Library

pedestrian to sunbather. Also for more than a century, each was in generally the same location, physically and psychologically—the heart of Myrtle Beach.

The first Pavilion, built circa 1902, was nothing more than a crudely built beachfront shelter that may have served as a fish camp in the off-season. It was a complement to Burroughs & Collins's new hotel, Sea Side Inn, built in 1901. After a fire destroyed this structure, in 1920 Myrtle Beach Farms built the Annex, a two-story bathhouse, next to which the original Sea Side Inn, or the Strand, was moved in 1926. The Annex had small rooms on the upper floor for lifeguards, performers, musicians, and other staff. A partial open-air first floor provided dressing rooms for bathers, showers, concession stands, and simply a place to get out of the sun. People who rented bathing suits could store their clothes in pigeonhole compartments located behind a counter. Behind, out of view, was a place where employees washed the rented bathing suits. A "[w]ringer" was used to squeeze out the excess water before the suits were hung out to dry. This was operated with a hand crank."[2] Many local and seasonal residents worked at the Pavilion and the bathhouse, just as in more recent times. Captain G. Marshall Nance managed Sea Side Inn in the 1912 and 1913 seasons. A local fisherman, Nance also sold cornbread and fish sandwiches at the Pavilion, in addition to organizing fishing excursions. Vivian F. Platt of Conway, who later became a druggist and major landowner on the Grand Strand, was amusements manager in 1913. Archie, Ernest, and Paul Sasser, sons of railroad conductor Captain Philip Sasser, ran the concessions during more than one season in the 1920s.[3]

In time a venue was needed for more genteel social gatherings. The "dance" Pavilion was built about 1908 and is also referred to as the round Pavilion, although it was actually multisided, with each side containing an open window with no sashes. Adjacent to Sea Side Inn, this Pavilion was connected to the hotel by a boardwalk and complemented its facade with a red shingle roof, gray walls, and white window sills. Its wraparound porch provided a place for vacationers to rock a summer afternoon away or stroll with friends. A Victrola with a small trumpet-shaped speaker and about a dozen records delivered the first music for dancers on a summer night. A string band of black musicians who also doubled as waiters at Sea Side Inn or an orchestra of college boys served as the natural progression from a phonograph, and live music eventually became a required addition to the season. The young people waltzed and fox-trotted. The more daring

The Pavilion was built in late 1923 over the ocean-front boardwalk at the southeast corner of what is now Eighth Avenue N. and Ocean Blvd. In addition to recreational purposes, the upper floor was used as a convention hall until 1930, when Ocean Forest Hotel opened. Courtesy of Sarah Bryan

ones shimmied. The older people watched from and children played on the porch, which was frequently covered with sand from encroaching dunes, according to Annette Epps Reesor.[4] Myrtle Beach Farms added a wing to the Pavilion in about 1923 to accommodate the growing number of people flocking to the beach during the summers.

The Pavilion also served as a community town hall of sorts. Early Methodist congregants met here before World War I. Townspeople and seasonal visitors held an "Allies Festival" in the Pavilion in July 1917 to raise money for World War I relief efforts. In addition to songs, talent acts, games, and food, dancing was enjoyed by everyone. Music played an important role in Pavilion entertainment since its earliest incarnation. Groups entertaining in the 1920s included the Toddling Five Orchestra from Lancaster, South Carolina; Ed Hannant's Night Owl Orchestra from Hendersonville, North Carolina; Connelly's Carolinians; and the six-person Swamp Fox Orchestra.

This excerpt of an anonymous poem, signed only "S," was published on page one of the August 24, 1922, *Horry Herald:*

> *This Is Myrtle Beach*
>
> Tis just a village of a score of houses or more,
> with a hotel, a yacht club,
> and the Blue Moon tea room
> That keeps an open door.
> The stand where the Sasser Brothers,
> Dispense iced drinks, chewing gum and sweets
> To say nothing of the pavilion,
> And its revelry of jazzy feet.
> So friend, if you are tired and listless,
> Or just want a change from home,
> Pack your kit bag and come over
> You can find us by the wail of the saxophone.

Increasing crowds ruled the "dance" Pavilion obsolete, and a large, new oceanfront Pavilion was erected in late 1923. It was built over the boardwalk on the southeast corner of Eighth Avenue North and Ocean Boulevard.[5] A two-story wooden structure, this new Pavilion architecturally resembled the Burroughs & Collins peanut warehouse in Conway. In postcards from the period this building was also labeled "Convention Hall and Pavilion, Myrtle Beach."[6] Conferences for various organizations became an extension of tourism as early as 1920, when Sunday school training classes were held there by the Methodist Training Institute. Perhaps the biggest breakthrough for convention business was when the Conway Chamber of

Commerce invited the South Carolina Press Association to hold its annual conference in Myrtle Beach in June 1922. Not only did this provide business for Sea Side Inn and the new Myrtle Beach Yacht Club, but it also showcased the other facilities, such as the Pavilion and, of course, the wonderful beaches. By the summer of 1924 Myrtle Beach attracted not only a repeat visit of the Press Association and the Methodist Training Institute but also new business from the Baptist Pee Dee Academy, the Presbyterian Sunday School Convention, the South Carolina Conference in Social Work, and Group Six of the South Carolina Bankers Association. After Ocean Forest Hotel opened in 1930, most conferences moved from the Pavilion to this more elegant venue.

In the late 1920s the town saw activity, excitement, and population growth as Woodside's Myrtle Beach Estates built Ocean Forest Country Club and Golf Course and Ocean Forest Hotel, developing the vital infrastructure that would support later growth. In 1927 the Pavilion was repainted and updated, and concession spaces were rearranged. Creative and entertaining diversions for tourists also became prevalent, as visitors from other parts of the country were beginning to discover Myrtle Beach. For example, during the 1927 season Walter Johnson, who was responsible for the exciting menu of crowd-pleasers at the Pavilion, began a series of free

Sea Side Inn, called the Strand at this time, was moved about five hundred feet closer to the beach and turned ninety degrees in 1927. The Pavilion is to the left, and the bathhouse is between the two buildings. Courtesy of Myrtle Beach Postcard Collection, Chapin Memorial Library

Monday night programs. This included a variety of musical numbers and recitations, after which children had thirty minutes for dancing and then adults had the dance floor for the rest of the evening. In July of that year the Henderson Sisters of Charlotte, North Carolina, conducted morning and afternoon dancing classes at the Pavilion. Orchestras, such as the ten-member Carolina Tar Heel Orchestra from the University of North Carolina, which played at the Pavilion in 1930, performed during many summer seasons, usually providing a regular concert on Sundays. The Pavilion also added a roller skating rink and a bowling alley in an attempt to provide a continuing variety of amusements for tourists.

During the off-season, when Myrtle Beach was "returned" to its residents, the Pavilion became the center of community activities that might include tourists but were designed primarily for townspeople. For more than twenty years the Pavilion hosted the annual Halloween carnival, which was sponsored by the local Parent-Teachers Association (PTA) for the benefit of the local school and included a costume parade, games, contests, performances by children, and other activities. By the 1950s the carnival also included teenagers, with a Halloween hop at the Pavilion that included the crowning of a king and queen each year. The PTA discontinued the event at the Pavilion in 1961, and individual schools began hosting their own carnivals. The Jaycees sponsored an annual fund-raiser, a minstrel show usually held in March, at the Pavilion from 1949 until the early 1960s. Entertainment showing white men and women with blackened faces and performing stereotypical and demeaning roles of black people was a popular, though unfortunate, form of theater in many parts of the country from the post–Civil War years into the 1950s. "Blackface" and "minstrel" are not true synonyms; blackface performers were around several decades before the first minstrel shows evolved.[7] Another community activity for which the Pavilion was a focal point was the annual Christmas parade sponsored by the Myrtle Beach Civitan Club and organized in 1939. It usually started at the intersection of Broadway and U.S. Highway 501, proceeded through the business district, and ended at the Pavilion.

Growth in population and tourism was slow but steady during the years of the Great Depression, but the late 1930s brought many changes to Myrtle Beach, including its recategorization as an official municipality. In 1938 the Pavilion was enlarged and renovated with a new facade. The old gabled, sloped roof gave way to a more modernistic flat roof and squared sides. Two years later a concrete walkway from the Pavilion replaced the former wooden boardwalk. Plans were to expand the concrete boardwalk more extensively, but the beginning of World War II dried up available funds. The Pavilion and the bathhouse burned on December 28, 1944, from unknown causes, and rebuilding was delayed because of the war and shortage of materials. A new bathhouse opened in 1947, and a massive poured-in-concrete Pavilion, built to withstand winds of 150 miles per hour, opened in 1949.

A constant presence at the Pavilion was the amusement park rides. By the early 1930s the lot immediately to the north of the 1923 Pavilion, where the 1949 Pavilion would be located, was filled with amusements and rides, including rides for young children, a Ferris wheel, and a carousel, usually set up by traveling carnivals. The first roller coaster, the Comet, was added by 1950. After seeing a small traveling carnival owned by Earl and Sherman Husted at Conway's annual Tobacco Festival in 1948, Edward Burroughs signed them to begin performing at Myrtle Beach across from the new Pavilion. He later hired Earl Husted to manage the Pavilion, with responsibility for food operations, the arcade, the bathhouse, upstairs entertainment, miniature golf, beach concessions, special "free" acts, all ticket sales, company-owned rides, and property management of all leased concessions. Harry Beach owned and operated the portable amusement park rides through the 1950s, paying a commission to Myrtle Beach Farms, which owned the carousel, Ferris wheel, and other rides purchased over time. Husted's responsibilities expanded as Myrtle Beach Farms purchased the rides owned by Beach and continued to revamp the amusement park ride area. This included buying additional properties to enlarge the operation, particularly following the 1967 Montreal World Expo, which inspired visiting Myrtle Beach Farms representatives. New thrill rides and spectacular European-manufactured rides were added each year.[8] When Magic Harbor Amusement Park failed in the mid-1970s, the Pavilion Amusement Park bought its Corkscrew roller coaster and moved it along the Ocean Boulevard corner, extending it along Eighth Avenue North.[9] Husted retired in the late 1980s, at which time the Pavilion Amusement Park was considered the number one tourist attraction in South Carolina and one of the finest amusement parks (as opposed to theme parks such as Disneyworld) in the country, according to the International Association of Amusement Parks and Attractions and *Amusement Business* magazine.

The Pavilion Amusement Park was especially known for its 1912 classic wood carousel, built by Herschill-Spillman of North Tonawanda, New York. It is one of fewer than twenty-five all-wood carousels made by this company at the turn of the last century and still in existence. It contains three rows with a total of fifty-two animals. Husted purchased it from W. E. Morgan of Anniston, Alabama, in 1951 and moved it from Oxford Lake Park in Anniston to Myrtle Beach, where it delighted generations of families.[10] The musical accompaniment for the carousel comes from the 165 rolls of paper music played on a circa-1920 Wurlitzer band organ. The park

The cover of this postcard booklet depicts the Pavilion and the amusement park in the 1950s. Myrtle Beach Postcard Collection, courtesy of Chapin Memorial Library

also held a 1900 German band organ, built by A. Ruth & Sohn from Bayden, Germany. It was originally built for the 1900 World Exposition in Paris, France, and is listed on the National Register of Historic Places. All figures and decorations on the organ are from hand-carved wood. Harry Beach, the amusement park concessionaire, bought it for Myrtle Beach Farms from a wealthy industrialist living in Martha's Vineyard, Massachusetts, and it was shipped to Myrtle Beach in 1954. The organ is eleven feet high and weighs about two tons. Its working parts include four hundred pipes with ninety-eight keys and eighteen lifelike, hand-carved figures—twelve move in rhythm to the music, two play the harp, and four beat drums. Crowning the organ is an angel-like male figure with gold and silver wings. The figure is draped in cloth and holds a harp. The organ plays perforated cardboard sheets of music, most of which were composed more than fifty years ago.[11]

In the 1950s Myrtle Beach was enjoying the benefits of the nation's optimism, affluence, and love of leisure. America was on the road because the highways were improved and connected under the Eisenhower administration. The middle class was expanding with a healthy postwar economy. New motels and motor courts with swimming pools and air-conditioning were cropping up all along the Grand Strand. Nightlife was changing, too, with the emergence of a new counterculture that was expressing its distaste for the established, traditional ways of thinking and behaving. During the 1940s dancing at the Pavilion centered around the jitterbug, a dance that "supported a subculture of fashionable young creative dancers known as jitterbugs."[12] This subculture was not accepted easily by the town. The *Myrtle Beach News* reported on August 5, 1943, that a large group of "jitterbugs and several zoot suiters" were in Myrtle Beach that summer and some of them created a "disturbance." The city recorder was quoted in the same article as saying that "Myrtle Beach was not going to be infested with 'jitterbuggers' and 'zoot suiters' such as had happened on the west coast within recent months. If you have got to fight, concentrate your energies on the Germans and the Japs." The newspaper reported that many of the offending young people ranged in age from fifteen to nineteen.

Up until that time dancing had been dominated by big band swing and jazz, but the war decimated the big bands as many musicians joined the armed forces. The large traveling orchestras of earlier years virtually disappeared in the war years and were replaced by small combos of six to eight musicians. Black musicians were finding an audience with their own brand of gospel blended with rhythm and blues. In Myrtle Beach many of the regular dancers at the Pavilion were adapting the jitterbug with steps picked up from black dancers in clubs such as the Whispering Pines, a nightclub in the black section of Myrtle Beach. The new blend of dance steps came to be known as "the shag."[13] Just as the jitterbuggers were not easily accepted, neither were the shaggers. Conservative townspeople considered it "dirty dancing." According to Helen Milliken, "those caught shagging in public risked being arrested by renowned Police Chief Carlisle Newton. Many old-time Stranders recall passing a cap collecting money to bail friends out of the 'Newton Hotel.'"[14] During this period the Pavilion became a center for rock and roll music and a venue for some of the most well-known pop music groups and soloists in the country.

By 1950 the Pavilion also sought new entertainment venues to please its audience base. Two of the favorite acts of the period were South Carolina native Slim Mims and his Dream Ranch Boys and Girls, and Roy Acuff. In 1950 activities included the always popular fireworks display on the beach in front of the Pavilion at 11:00 P.M.; theater-stage performances of Bingo, a movie and TV chimp actor who had been seen with such celebrities as Marilyn Monroe, Cary Grant, Ginger Rogers, and others; Maxie and Millie, a musical comedy team; Lew Folds, a juggler; and Carol and Reed Simpson, dancers. In early 1951 the Pavilion advertised wrestling matches every Wednesday night beginning in February and a new heating system. Entertainment that summer included the Great Kinzro, a death-defying aerial act performed 165 feet in the air over the Pavilion beach; Rajah Raboid, who predicted the future; Skip and Jerry Yeuman, a music novelty act from Miami; Raveena, a "lovely comedienne"; and John Lucynn, a balancing act, with singing emcee George Akers and the Jerry Mayburn orchestra.

Opening acts at the theater in June 1951 included Hanlon and Clark, a mystifying mental act; Dellen's boxing cats; the Olympics, a "scintillating" skating act; and Les Ross, a juggler and comedian. Every Monday evening was children's night with favors for the kids; Tuesday was variety night; and Wednesday was sports night with professional wrestlers and boxers. On Thursday, Friday and Saturday, after the shows, the floor was open for dancing for no additional admission. Harold Clardy recalled talent shows every Wednesday night and said, "You wouldn't win much, but we'd have fun." He said that these kinds of shows died out later in the 1950s when more theaters and other attractions opened in Myrtle Beach.[15]

One of the biggest developments of the period in which the Pavilion was a major venue was the first annual Sun Fun Festival in 1951. This event, first chaired by Mark Garner, publisher of the *Myrtle Beach Sun* and president of the Myrtle Beach Chamber of Commerce, was initially conceived to attract vacationers during the slow period between the end of the school year and the Fourth of July holiday. Other civic leaders who chaired the event in its early years were Justin Plyler (1952), Ernest Williams (1953), and Oliver Miller (1954–55), supported by various celebrities including the novelist Mickey Spillane, the actress Joan Fontaine, and the golfer Ben Hogan. Every civic organization was involved in one form or another, whether it was to organize and judge the parade entries, the beauty pageant, or the many other logistics of the event, or to manage the Sun Fun Jail (which raised money for the Ocean View Memorial Hospital in the early days).

With an increase in younger audience members, beginning in the 1950s the Pavilion became the "reviewing" stand of all the cars and trucks cruising and crawling down Ocean Boulevard. By the mid-1970s the second story of the Pavilion, which had been the dance hall, was enclosed, air-conditioned, and transformed to an updated dance and concert venue called the Magic Attic, later shortened to the Attic. Before the second floor was a dance hall, the space was used for roller skating, wrestling, and vaudeville acts. The rails around the modern-day Attic were actually for the assistance of skaters of generations past.

Over the years the Pavilion also represented summer jobs for Myrtle Beach's young people. Dr. Charles Joyner, professor of history at Coastal Carolina University, grew up in Myrtle Beach. He worked at several different summer jobs from the time he was thirteen, but he particularly remembered the summer before his senior year at Myrtle Beach High School, when he went to work for James Bryan Jr. at Myrtle Beach Farms. He counted the money made at the Pavilion, a job he held every summer until 1958 when he entered the U.S. Army.[16]

Sigmund Abeles, who graduated from Myrtle Beach High School in the early 1950s, wanted a job so that he could buy his own clothes. He said, "Our whole attitude about Myrtle Beachers was that we were hip, that we wore clothes—I mean, there was all that jitterbugging—that we wore clothes that Conway people didn't know about. And, you know, people were into what you wore. And it was very hard on me, because my mother got a 20 percent discount at Banner Brothers, plus it was her family, so I was supposed to get all my clothes there. And I thought it was very un-hip. So I always wanted stuff at Chapin Company. And I started getting jobs working at the beach, and doing this and doing that, so I could buy clothes I wanted, and buy an easel, which I wasn't allowed to have. . . . I was making good money down at the Pavilion."[17]

Howell "Skeets" Bellamy Jr., a local attorney whose father was president of Chapin Company from 1955 to his death in 1975, also remembers working at the Pavilion:

I was working at the bathhouse at the Pavilion and Poddy Bryan and Lawrence LaBruce and Kenneth and a variety of folks, worked there in the summer. And it was Mr. Bryan [James E. Bryan Jr.] that saved me from working at Chapin Company forever, because my father was going to keep me up there. One day Mr. Bryan came and got me and carried me to the bathhouse, and said, "This is your new job." And my father said, "I don't know about that." And James said, "Oh, Howell, let him go down there. He needs to have some experience with life." Because my father thought I would be tempted down there. And we spent our summers down there, and back in those days, Poddy, everybody was wearing these, what I call zoot suit pants, pants that billowed at your knees, and went about that big. They were called peg pants. And we wore them with loafers, and all that stuff. And we would work at the bathhouse, and we would get all the girls that would come over to the soda fountain . . . to come over and model bathing suits for us at the bathhouse.[18]

While in high school, Myrtle Beach photographer Jack Thompson got his professional start working at Skip's two-minute photo stand at the Pavilion. He remembered, "We had all the props for people to come and put their heads behind the fat and skinny swimmers, stick their heads behind the bars of the old Myrtle Beach jail, and the half moon that had Miss Myrtle Beach on it."[19]

The Pavilion represented one of the few monuments to Myrtle Beach history. It was more than just a building and an amusement park; it evolved with the generations of visitors to Myrtle Beach, providing a visual landmark, a reminder of past summer joys, and a place for creating new memories for the next generation. Just as the visitors who used the first Pavilion in 1902 were amazed, awed, and excited by the spell of the beach and the ocean, so too were the generations that followed. The Pavilion was at the heart of it all.

Eight

Family-Owned and -Operated

A defining characteristic of Myrtle Beach's tourist accommodations from the 1920s through the 1960s was that they were family-owned and family-operated. While the architecture, building materials, and amenities of these accommodations changed over these forty years and guest houses gave way to motor courts, they all shared one common trait—the personal touch, with families inviting other families to stay with them and return season after season.

"Serving the traveler" was an important byword on the Grand Strand as far back as the 1700s. The Grand Strand's earliest innkeeper was perhaps William Gause, who started a tavern for travelers along the old Kings Highway about 1740 at present-day Windy Hill Beach. He hosted the area's first celebrity tourist, U.S. president George Washington, in 1791. In 1893 in Murrells Inlet, William L. Oliver established another such stop for travelers called Oliver's Lodge. However, along the miles and miles of beach known as the Grand Strand, overnight accommodations at the turn of the twentieth century were limited due to poor accessibility for travelers.

Burroughs & Collins changed that in 1901 with the opening of Sea Side Inn and the beginning of rail service from Conway, the county seat, to the beach.[1] Until 1909, when the first summer cottages were built, Sea Side Inn was the only place for visitors to stay overnight at the beach except for campgrounds. Early families who built beach cottages encouraged others to do the same. Even in the face of the turmoil created by World War I, the spread of the boll weevil, and the collapse of farm prices, people still sought escape and respite at the beach. Jobs with Myrtle Beach Farms and concerted promotional efforts by the company and the Conway Chamber of

Commerce combined to attract people who wanted to establish homes and livelihoods along the sands of the Atlantic Ocean.[2]

Early Hotels

Sea Side Inn was the first—and only—hotel in Myrtle Beach for about twenty years, until Myrtle Beach Yacht Club was built in 1922. Located behind the sand hills or high dunes near the railroad depot, Sea Side Inn was built by the contractors Joseph A. Garren of Hendersonville, North Carolina, and Henry P. Little of Conway. It was built in two sections, according to Edward E. Burroughs.[3] Opening day was May 23, 1901. In the June 6, 1901, issue of the *Horry Herald,* the editor, Henry H. Woodward, raved about his tour of Sea Side Inn conducted by Iola Burroughs, wife of the proprietor Franklin A. Burroughs: "We were carried all over the handsome Sea Side Inn. From the front steps to the kitchen, perfect order and beauty reigns. On the broad piazzas are stands of hot house plants, giving the first impression of a refined and homelike welcome. Beautiful palms and ferns grace the spacious hallways, parlors, and dining rooms, and all through the house is seen the magic touch of a refined woman's fingers. In the well furnished bedrooms a delightful sense of coziness and comfort pervades the atmosphere and it is determined that no one who visits there this summer shall contract malaria on the new and improved plans of flies and mosquitoes for there are screens to all the windows and doors, and as extra precaution, canopies over all beds."

Only gas lighting was available when the hotel first opened, but generator electricity was available by 1909.[4] Dining room fare was usually fresh sea bass or other seafood, rice or grits, and vegetables from the Myrtle Beach Farms Company's five-hundred-acre farm. Entertainment included dancing at the adjoining Pavilion, built in 1908, with music provided by a Victrola or an early ensemble of black musicians who also waited tables. Room rates were two dollars per day, six dollars per week, or twenty dollars per month, with a special reduction for families.

The age of the automobile ushered in a new era of growth for Myrtle Beach as road-building efforts progressed, making the beach more accessible.[5] All along the East Coast, automobiles and railroads were bringing tourists to the beaches. In 1915 Seaboard Air Line Railway published a brochure entitled *Winter Golf Courses: Hotels and Boarding Houses* to promote destinations and amenities along its rail line. In Florida, Daytona/Daytona Beach listed forty-seven guest houses and hotels, Miami had twenty, St. Augustine had twenty-seven, and St. Petersburg had thirty. About 28 percent of these properties were owned and/or operated by women, indicative of the key role women were to play in the hospitality industry in Myrtle Beach and elsewhere.

In February 1926 John T. Woodside purchased more than sixty-five thousand acres of Myrtle Beach property from Myrtle Beach Farms Company and set in motion a wave of development not seen in the area prior to this.[6] That summer James W. Ivey, a Florence hotelier, managed the inn and hired college students as waiters in the dining room, which over the July 4 holiday served about 760 people. The new company also started construction on an administration building with guest rooms on the second floor and offices on the first floor. In the early months of 1927 work commenced on the Herculean task of picking up the "old" Sea Side Inn, now called the Strand or the Carolina, turning it ninety degrees, and moving it about five hundred feet to the east with log rollers and mules. The objective was to bring it closer to the beach and the bathhouse. Janis Stewart Smith moved with her parents to Myrtle Beach from Greenville with many of the Woodside employees in October 1927 to run the Strand in the summer and the "new" Sea Side Inn in the winter.[7] "It [the Strand] was a big hotel. It was huge," she recalled. "And the orchestra and the lifeguards and the girls who worked in the dining room lived in the upstairs, kind of like a dormitory. And the men and boys stayed in one end and the girls at the other end. We served three meals and the dinner was really a family affair. It was nice. We were usually full all the time in the summertime."[8]

Woodside also went to work trying to attract postseason visitors and to cement relationships around the region with those who could help him spread the word about Myrtle Beach, and thus increase the demand for guest accommodations. Weekly fox hunts on the beach were organized beginning in October, and on Thanksgiving weekend a ceremony, with full military honors, was held to dedicate the new administration building. This was attended by South Carolina governor Thomas G. McLeod; Brigadier General Albert J. Bowley from Fort Bragg, North Carolina; Percy R. Albright, vice president and general manager of Atlantic Coast Line railroad, from Wilmington, North Carolina; Congressman Allard H. Gasque of Florence; Ben Sawyer, chairman of the South Carolina State Highway Commission; and others. Festivities included a Governor's Ball with music furnished by the Fort Bragg Band.[9]

Demand for guest rooms was so great that by the summer of 1927 the "new" Sea Side Inn was devoted entirely to accommodations for visitors and the company offices were moved out. Lafayette Manor, as it would be called by the early 1930s, served as a hotel until 1960, when it was razed to make way for an expansion of the Pavilion Amusement Park complex.[10]

Another corporate endeavor in the early Myrtle Beach hotel business, Myrtle Beach Yacht Club, was organized in March 1922. The three-story hotel, which was originally planned as a private club, contained thirty-five 12-by-12-foot bedrooms with bathrooms, broad piazzas, and a proposed 370-foot pier. The first floor contained a lobby, a lounge, writing rooms for ladies and men, cigars and a soft-drink stand, a clerk's office, and bathrooms. The 20-by-50-foot lounge was available for meetings and dances. The ground floor or basement contained bathhouses for men and women, with seventeen dressing rooms and three showers for women, fifteen dressing rooms and three showers for men, as well as three servant rooms, a barbershop, a men's assembly or club room, a pressing club, and a sewing room. In the center of the basement was an open space for children to play. The second and third floors contained guest rooms. The hotel was completed just in time for the June 1922 annual conference of the South Carolina Press Association, a first-time Myrtle Beach event that brought newspapermen from across the state to see what Myrtle Beach had to offer. The board of directors of the Yacht Club included James E. Bryan Sr. of Myrtle Beach Farms; Will Freeman, a Conway bank cashier; Horace L. Tilghman, president of a lumber mill in Marion; William J. Wilkins, a Florence architect; John Murchison, a Florence ice cream manufacturer; George Holliday, a Galivants Ferry merchant and farmer; and Charles Muldrow.

By the 1923 season, the Yacht Club ended its private status and was opened to the general public, perhaps indicative of a sluggish state economy and the desire of the middle class to build private summer cottages rather than buying club memberships. According to the *Horry Herald,* "This was done after special consideration of the members who found that it was almost impossible to conduct it as a private venture without great losses every year. . . . At last accounts the club house was full of guests."[11] Records are not available as to how ownership was determined after the club was disbanded, but since Myrtle Beach Farms donated the land for the venture the property may have reverted to the company. In 1937 Sam P. Gardner, who would serve as a city councilman through most of the 1940s and early 1950s, purchased the Yacht Club Hotel and Pier and renamed the complex Ocean Plaza Hotel and Pier. It changed hands one more time in 1955, when Mr. and Mrs. Keith Jones purchased the property. In 1973 the Ocean Plaza was demolished and replaced with the 20-story, 142-suite Yachtsman, the city's first high-rise hotel. The pier still existed in 2005.

Guest Houses—1920s

Combining graceful southern hospitality with a keen business acumen and an eye for opportunity, women of the region positioned themselves as builders of Myrtle Beach's hospitality industry. The introduction of guest houses grew out of a need to provide outlets for visitors who could not afford to rent a summer cottage but wanted a more personal experience than was available at the larger hotels. The degree to which women took advantage of this new opportunity to gain community leadership and economic power was an outgrowth of the times across the United States when women were finding their voices. The transition in South Carolina did not come easily, however. In 1919 Congress passed the Nineteenth Amendment, which authorized woman suffrage, and sent it to the states for ratification. Although the South Carolina General Assembly rejected it, enough states ratified the amendment that it became law in August 1920. South Carolina's General Assembly was forced to pass a law giving women the right to vote, but at the same time they passed another law excluding women from jury duty. In addition, few candidates around the state that fall would endorse the idea of women joining the local Democratic Party. The women of Horry County, however, were not to be deterred. Approximately five hundred women, including two black women, registered to vote there in 1920.[12]

One field where the women of Myrtle Beach defined their individual and communal strength was in the hospitality business. These early guesthouse owners, many of whom bought and sold property on their own in the 1920s, built the foundation for the hotel and motel business in Myrtle Beach. Many were assisted by Myrtle Beach Farms, in the person of James Bryan Sr., who provided reduced land prices and time extensions for buying furnishings, food, and other necessities. Their tenacity and a belief in the future for themselves and their families, however, were testament to their staying power. Some were single, divorced, or widowed. For others who were married to farmers, merchants, or teachers, the guest houses provided second incomes during hard times. Some took up residence and kept their guest houses open year-round, while others were seasonal and returned to homes and jobs in neighboring counties and states during the off-season.

One of the earliest guest houses was owned by sisters Annie and Lela Burney. The May 24, 1923, *Horry Herald* reported that Burney Cottage had twelve rooms and "is located on the Strand on the same side of the beach as the Yacht Club. It is believed that the new place will be a full house for the new season." Annie Burney, age forty-three and single at this time, was familiar with the guest-house business. A North Carolina native, she owned a boardinghouse on Railroad Avenue in Hemingway, South Carolina, prior to coming to Myrtle Beach, and her younger sister, Lela, age thirty-seven (in 1920), assisted her in its management. A third sister, Ina, age twenty-nine and a nurse, also lived with them. The 1920 census showed that they had seven boarders and three servants in Hemingway. All the boarders were professionals, such as teachers, an assistant postmaster, a dentist, a salesman, and a doctor. Once settled in Myrtle Beach, Annie Burney became involved in the life of the community, serving on the first building committee for First Presbyterian Church in 1929. In the July and August 1935 issues of *Myrtle Beach Today and Tomorrow,* a promotional newsletter, a listing for Burney Cottage read that it was open year-round and had steam heat in winter. In the 1930s the Burney sisters also owned Crepe Myrtle Inn, a guest house on Chester Avenue and Seventh Avenue North, although records are not clear as to whether or not Burney Cottage still existed at this time.[13]

Myrtle Beach would have no stand-alone restaurants for several more years. For this reason, in addition to providing rooms, "[m]ost of the guest houses served meals; they had kitchens and dining rooms," according to Harold Clardy, lifelong employee and retired president of the Chapin Company. "We [Chapin Company] would even open on Sundays so that the guest houses could have produce and meats and so forth to cook because they didn't have the advantage of big freezers and things that we have today to keep the food." Into the 1930s the guest houses took advantage of the fresh produce in the area, and a farmers' market existed as early as 1927. "The lady from the Patricia Manor used to drive a Ford truck and come down and select her produce and food, mainly seafood at the time, and then take it back to the Patricia Manor," said Julia Macklen, who with her husband Lloyd operated a grocery store in the late 1930s and early 1940s before they went into the motel and restaurant business. They first bought Travelers Motor Hotel, sold it in 1949, and then opened Lloyd's Motor Court and Restaurant.[14]

Guest Houses and Trailer Courts—1930s

Myrtle Beach guest houses that started in the 1930s were serving more than just tourists. Throughout a dynamic decade that included the Great Depression, New Deal projects, and incorporation of Myrtle Beach as a town, guest houses were filled with workers associated with the main construction projects in the area, as well as those people providing services for this burgeoning, if temporary, workforce. Three dredging companies were working on the Intracoastal Waterway; other firms were working to pave and widen streets, add curbs and sidewalks, build a sewer project, and support the Civilian Conservation Corps in building the Myrtle Beach State Park; and still others were building new homes, churches, and stores. In addition, the truck farms employed hundreds in the gathering, picking, and shipping of produce. Guest houses that were open year-round were interested in boarding these workers as well as summer tourists. In the 1930 census, two sisters from Aynor, both Myrtle Beach schoolteachers in their twenties, had a guest house. Neta Page, age twenty-nine, and her sister Aubrey Page Harpe, a widow at age twenty-seven with two children, had two boarders who were also schoolteachers, Horace Sanders and Harriet Morris. Roberta McMillan owned Blue Sea Inn at 1007 North Ocean Boulevard, and her only boarder at the time of the 1930 census was Henry Trezevant Willcox, thirty-three years old and a stenographer at a real estate office. He moved to Myrtle Beach in the late 1920s to work with Holmes B. Springs Sr. and John T. Woodside and would stay, working in various capacities with the city of Myrtle Beach, the remainder of his life. Philip Gray mentioned staying at the Blue Sea Inn during the winter of 1937 while working on the Intracoastal Waterway but did not stay long "because the heat was not very good." He also briefly stayed at Todlin Inn and eventually ended up at Brunswick Guest House, operated by a Mrs. Swain.[15]

Perhaps one of the best known of the early guest houses was located at 2702 North Ocean Boulevard. Pat Rousseau moved to Myrtle Beach from North Wilkesboro, North Carolina, in 1929 as a single mother with two children, the financial backing of a family friend (her father had been a prominent merchant in North Carolina), and a knowledge of cooking. She purchased a wood frame house and remodeled it into a thirteen-room guest house that she named Patricia Court. In the early 1930s she married Joe C. Ivey and purchased an adjacent lot from Myrtle Beach Farms in 1934, upon which the Iveys built Patricia Manor. They added a three-story building by 1941, Patricia Inn, a square, white, frame structure with green and white awnings. Columns ran along the beachside patio, and the lobby and dining room were decorated in Old South decor and architectural features. A hand-carved banister followed the stairs to the third floor. In 1955, after the structure had been damaged by Hurricane Hazel the previous October, a new, more modern, two-story Patricia Court motel was built with twenty-three rooms facing the ocean. Although the Iveys divorced in the 1950s and both remarried, they remained business partners, selling the complex in the 1970s. It would be razed in the mid-1980s to make way for a high-rise hotel appropriately called the Patricia.[16]

By 1935 the worst of the Depression was waning in Horry County and tourism was improving. Henrietta Abeles, a single Jewish mother with a two-and-one-half-year-old son named Sigmund, arrived in Myrtle Beach in 1936 from New York to be closer to her siblings' families and to make a fresh start. With some savings and a mortgage from Myrtle Beach Farms, Abeles built the eight-bedroom, three-bath Paul's Guest House, located at 506 Kings Highway. "The rooming house was a real struggle at first," recalled Sigmund, who went on to become an internationally renowned artist. "You know, a room for three dollars a night. A very resourceful soul, described by her siblings and their offspring as a 'modern woman,' Mom designed our house and negotiated with . . . Chapin Company and Myrtle Beach Farms for the purchase of the two lots with a wooded back and a mortgage to begin the construction. My mom chose to make her rooming house on the highway [U.S. Highway 17] rather than the ocean front. She could have had her pick at that time of anything she wanted, but because she was hoping to get some of the winter business of people traveling from New York to Florida, which she did, and she was worried about having the house blown away by a hurricane, she chose not to go to the ocean."[17]

Growing up in a guest house gave Sigmund a view of the world he might not have seen otherwise. "From our front steps I viewed the world as a youth; there were indelible occurrences. I witnessed my neighbor Mr. Hollingshead get killed doing a U-turn on his motorcycle; watched the daily shuttle of German prisoners-of-war passing by in army trucks from field labor; saw a huge, stone, winged horse partly covered by tarps enroute to Brookgreen [Gardens] and caught sight of FDR and Churchill in an open touring car with motorcycle escorts heading to [Bernard] Baruch's plantation."[18]

Trying to survive on the income of a seasonal trade, whether one was running a guest house, a restaurant, or a gift shop, was not easy. "Myrtle Beach is now much more of a twelve-month-out-of-the-year place," Abeles continued, "but in those years it was feast and famine. There were at least two days that were sold out—the Fourth of July and Labor Day—and then in the winter I got a choice of any room I wanted. On the other hand it was a fascinating business to see people. And since my work, my art, is focused on faces mostly, people, I know that my interest in being a voyeur came from being in that rooming house, from the good-looking people to the not good-looking people, to the people who were sober to the people who weren't sober, to the good and bad. I mean it was great extremes. People probably are their best and worst on vacation. So it was fascinating."[19]

The next step in the evolution of accommodations across the country and in Myrtle Beach included the cabin camps, or trailer courts. Three varieties existed: an auto camp to which cabins were added; a cabin camp with no accommodations for tents or guest house (an early form of motor court or cottages); and a guest house with cabins added. Several variations of such cabin camps existed in Myrtle Beach in the 1930s. The tendency was to develop away from the beach on the roads leading into town. In 1938 W. L. Bailey obtained a license to operate Bailey's Place, which was also known as Bailey's Tourist Cabins. It had a rough reputation, according to some, with a tavern and dance hall nearby. Trailer City, owned by Horry

Land & Improvement Company, was built in the late 1920s at Third Avenue and Kings Highway near Spivey Beach. Its 1938 license said that approval was granted for the operation of a trailer camp and summer cottages. The Tip Toe Inn tourist camp, located on Old Conway Highway about one and one-half miles from Myrtle Beach, was formerly known as Green Top Inn. In the 1938 license application, camp owner Margie Hettick wrote that during that year she personally operated said camp but during the previous year leased the camp to another party and had no control over or connection with its operation. W. L. Frye in 1939 pledged "to operate a legitimate place" at his tourist court one and one-half miles from Myrtle Beach on Old Conway Highway.[20] By 1940 Myrtle Beach had a rough reputation, particularly along the roads from Myrtle Beach to Conway and Georgetown, where several bars and motels rented cabins by the hour. Sheriff Edward Sessions of Horry County was continually trying to clean up the area; hence the "pledges" on the license applications.

Early Restaurants

Until the 1930s all commercial dining was available through the guest houses, hotels, and the Ocean Forest Country Club. Meals at the guest houses were usually included in the overall cost of the rooms. However, stand-alone eating establishments began to appear in Myrtle Beach by 1935, if not earlier, as a result of the growth of the resident and tourist populations. Many of these eateries were started by Greeks. According to long-time resident and civic leader Henry T. Willcox, Dan Odyssea started the first restaurant on the waterfront, although no documentation found to date indicates what that restaurant was called or where it was located. Early postcards indicate restaurants called Myrtle Beach Grill, Carolina Café, and Kozy Korner in the 1930s on Broadway across from the Chapin Company. On the oceanfront Ye Olde Tavern, located near modern-day Ninth Avenue North and the ocean, opened in the mid-1930s. In 1939 on U.S. Highway 17 and First Avenue, Eli Saleeby opened Saleeby's Grill, which became Fleetwood Restaurant in 1954. The Seven Seas Grill advertised in the 1935 issue of *Myrtle Beach Today and Tomorrow* and was owned at one time by George Anthony, John Cousin, and Charles Cordes.

Guest Houses and Motor Courts—1940s

In the 1940s, especially after World War II, many guest houses were adapted architecturally to a motel style, in which rooms were available at separate entrances from the main lobby or were replaced altogether by a new building. Motor courts were also being built on Kings Highway, where land was cheaper than on the beach for a more spread-out layout, with each usually involving a one-story, U-shaped building of side-by-side units around a grassy court or swimming pool.

In addition, new guest houses were still being built, although many were adapting to motel-style architecture. Chesterfield Inn at 700 North Ocean Boulevard was one memorable guest house that morphed into a motel operation. Steven C. Chapman of Chesterfield, South Carolina, moved to Myrtle Beach in 1936 and purchased a frame house owned by F. C. Todd. Chapman raised the house, built eight rooms downstairs, and named it Chesterfield Inn. After the inn was damaged by fire during World War II, the current structure was built in its place in 1946, with an additional wing built in 1965.[21]

The first motor court in Myrtle Beach, or at least the first one to be named as such, is thought to have been the Ocean Pines Motor Court at 3801 North Kings Highway, which opened in March 1940. Other early properties included Jack Nelson's El Rancho Motel, Palmetto Motor Court, and Travelers Motor Court, all of which were located on North Kings Highway. While guest houses were still viable businesses in the 1940s and most had developed a loyal following with repeat business year after year, few new ones were built after World War II. Many owners of older guest houses redesigned and remodeled them or built annexes to modernize and meet changing market demands.

Motels

While the term "motel" dates commercially as early as 1926 (Arthur Heineman's Milestone Mo-tel in San Luis Obispo, California), motels did not become prevalent across the country until the 1950s and 1960s.[22] The term was a contraction of "motor" and "hotel." The same kind of property might be called motel, motor court, tourist court, auto court, cottages, motel court, hotel court, or cottage court.

The city of Myrtle Beach developed some definitions for these names in its first zoning ordinance in 1947:

> Tourist home or guest house—any dwelling in which rooms are rented for the temporary care or lodging of transients and travelers, for a consideration.
>
> Apartment hotel—an apartment building, under resident supervision, which maintains an inner lobby through which all tenants must pass to gain access to the apartments and which may furnish dining room service for tenants only.
>
> Bungalow courts—a group of two or more single-family dwellings on one or more adjoining lots, having a separate outside entrance on the ground floor level for each single family dwelling.

Motor court—any multiple dwelling or group of dwellings, other than bungalow courts, hotels or apartment houses, which is designed or intended for the temporary residence of motorists or travelers. The term motor court shall include cabin camp, auto camp and tourist camp.

Hotel—a building or other structure kept, used, maintained, advertised as or held out to the public to be a place where sleeping accommodations are supplied for pay to transient or permanent guests or tenants in which twenty or more rooms are furnished for the accommodations of such guests, and having one or more dining rooms or cafes, where meals or lunches are served to such transient or permanent guests, such sleeping accommodations and dining rooms or cafes being conducted in the same building or buildings in connection therewith.[23]

The definition of a motel, however, was not included in the zoning ordinance. New names of properties in Myrtle Beach coincided with the titles in the zoning ordinance, such as Noel Court (312 Sixth Avenue North); T&C Motor Court (212 Kings Highway North); Dunes Village Motel and Apartments (Fifty-second Avenue North at Ocean Boulevard); Haywood Motor Court, which later became Haywood Motel (Twenty-ninth Avenue North and Kings Highway); and Suber Motor Court, which under new owners became Sea Breeze Motel (Sixth Avenue South and Kings Highway). In its simplest form, a motel was usually a one- to two-story structure, often with adjacent small buildings, no formal spaces, and parking spaces for automobiles near the rooms. While guest houses provided comfortable, homelike atmospheres and attracted destination tourists—those who came to Myrtle Beach year after year for several days or weeks—motels represented the freedom of the road for touring Americans beginning in the late 1940s. Motel customers included people who enjoyed traveling to multiple destinations on a vacation and preferred privacy in relative anonymity rather than a group setting. Motel guests wanted a degree of freedom previously unknown in other kinds of accommodations.[24] This new touring vacationer also expected to find air-conditioning, television sets, and telephones in their rooms, and, of course, swimming pools—even if the ocean was right next door. When the price of modernizing began to require greater capital outlays, the small business woman and man had to consider their future carefully.

Several factors in Myrtle Beach affected the proliferation of motels there in the postwar years. First, the city was growing. The year-round population more than doubled between 1940 and 1950, from 1,597 to 3,345. In the next decade it would more than double again to 7,834 residents. This gain in permanent residents followed the growth in tourism, which was supported by the Myrtle Beach Chamber of Commerce and the South Carolina State Chamber of Commerce. In a 1951 manual, the South Carolina State Chamber of Commerce contended that the state was not getting its share of the $9 billion spent annually across the United States by tourists, travelers, and vacationers, and that the roadblocks to success for state tourism were indifference, or a misconception by residents that tourists had no interest in South Carolina, and inadequate accommodations. "South Carolina should get ready to receive tourists in large numbers," the manual said. "Facilities for lodging, meals, and entertainment should be improved and enlarged."[25] The hospitality industry in Myrtle Beach was also banding together and in 1951 formed the Myrtle Beach Accommodations Association, a merger of the Hotel Association and the Motel Association. The organization's objectives were to promote Myrtle Beach, create one voice for the business owners before city council and other bodies, and provide some local industry standards.

Another factor in the transition from guest houses to motels was the building of the federal interstate highway system, the concept for which had begun in the 1930s. The Federal-Aid Highway Act of 1944 was passed by Congress, which expanded the network of roads but provided no specific funds for construction. With a steady increase in automobiles on the road, as well as an increase in automobile deaths, President Dwight Eisenhower was committed to building a safe and effective interstate highway system. Soon after becoming president in 1953, Eisenhower authorized the first funding of the interstate system. While Myrtle Beach was not directly impacted as no interstate system came her way, the hospitality industry nevertheless was affected as it sought the best locations to attract the touring public.

One of the most important factors affecting the industry, however, was perhaps the passage in 1954 of an accelerated income tax depreciation clause to the federal tax code, which "stimulated new construction and tended to limit life expectancy of motel buildings, thus precipitating short-term ownership and cyclical renovation and modernization," according to John Jakle. It remained a built-in mechanism for change until the late 1980s. Equity was sheltered through accelerated depreciation in the early life of a purchase, but in eight to ten years, when amortization payments became greater than depreciation allowances, the property owner had an opportunity to sell and take long-term capital gain. He or she then was ready to reinvest in another motel and repeat the process.[26]

These trends and events joined with a pent-up demand for consumption and travel by the American public in the fifteen years after World War II, and Myrtle Beach benefited. In 1956 American income was 50 percent higher than in 1929, the year of the previous high. Leisure became an industry. Between 1946 and 1953 the number of motels in the United States doubled to about forty-five thousand total.[27] Motel ownership seemed a ready-made investment for families who migrated to resort destinations, and some couples literally did build motels. In 1954 Norma and Blake Whisnant relocated to Myrtle Beach from Hickory, North Carolina, for the sole purpose of building a motel. Along with Blake's brother they built the eighteen-room Hotel Drive-Inn at 501 North Ocean Boulevard and moved in. They sold the property in 1975. Local people, too, got involved in building their own motels from the ground up. Horry and Lucille Benton built South-Bend Apartments and Rooms at Seventh Avenue South and Ocean Boulevard in 1951, when Ocean Boulevard on the south end was not paved and did not have street lights. Horry Benton continued his construction work with Daniel Nance, while Lucille managed the motel.[28]

According to the Greater Myrtle Beach Chamber of Commerce, between 1954 and 1964 a total of $40 million was invested locally in lodging, business, and residential construction, driven by a record growth in tourism. Tourism generated a $48.5 million income for the Myrtle Beach area in 1963, about $37 million of which was spent at local hotels, motels, and other accommodations.[29] The 1960s were a decade of unparalleled expansion, growth, and visibility for the Grand Strand. More than 130 new motels were built during the period. The typical Myrtle Beach motel of the 1960s was two to four stories with flat roofs projecting over exterior hallways. Most common designs were rectangular, L, and U shapes. Rooms were small, and lobbies, each of which was usually carved from a room on the first floor, faced the parking lot, and consisted of a check-in counter and brochure racks, were designed for efficiency. The most distinct features of these motels were concrete block screen walls, which were used as decorative and practical elements, as railing on exterior halls, as fencing along pools, and to hide mechanical elements and stairwells. The walls were cheaper to build than frame construction, could be assembled quickly, were able to withstand hurricanes, and would not succumb to rust and corrosion from the salty sea air.[30]

The trend nationwide in the 1960s, however, showed establishments that were family-owned and -operated giving way to those owned by large investment companies. While in 1948 more than 98 percent of all tourist accommodations were owned by individual families, by 1972 only 59 percent were.[31] Myrtle Beach's first chain was Howard Johnson's Motor Lodge and Restaurant near Twelfth Avenue North and Kings Highway, which opened in October 1954. One of the earliest corporately owned motel chains was Holiday Inn, with its first motel opening in Memphis, Tennessee, in 1952. The chain moved into Myrtle Beach and opened its ninth motel franchise with fifty-two rooms in May 1956 between Forty-seventh Avenue and Forty-eighth Avenue North and Kings Highway.[32] A lawsuit by Bill and Frances Hendrix Smith against the chain ensued, however, because for several years previous to this they had been using the name Holiday Inn on their guest house at 1200 North Ocean Boulevard. As a result, the franchise used the name Holiday Lodge Hotel and was prohibited from using its full name at any hotels within the city limits until the mid-1980s, when the Smiths sold their property and the rights to the name to a company owned in part by Jim Whelan. The original hotel never became part of the Holiday Inn chain. However, Mr. Whelan had an interest in a property that did become a franchise of the chain and began using the full name. In the late 1980s the Smiths regained control of the independent Holiday Inn hotel but took no steps to attempt to revoke the permission that the other hotel had received to use the full name.[33]

While the mom-and-pop motels and guest houses were still present by 1980, they were overshadowed by the high-rise hotels, which were replacing them on the oceanfront beginning in the 1970s. The first guest accommodation to see these changes from family-owned and -operated to corporate-investor ownership was Ocean Plaza Hotel, which was replaced in 1973 by a new $2.5 million, 140-room hotel to be called, appropriately, the Yachtsman.

Hospitality Highlights

What follows is by no means a complete list. Myrtle Beach's guest houses and motels existing from the 1920s through the 1950s are too numerous for a complete account, but those mentioned below are indicative of the whole. Most were family-owned and -operated, but some, such as Sea Side Inn, the Ocean Forest, and Lafayette Hotel, were not.

1900–1920

Sea Side Inn/The Strand. Sea Side Inn opened for business on May 23, 1901. In 1909 it received electricity connection. A garage for automobile storage was added in 1917, and more than 1,700 registered at the hotel that summer. In 1924 the dining room was enlarged and a new, higher boardwalk was built from the hotel to the beach. In 1927 the hotel was renamed the Strand. It was physically moved closer to the beach, adjoining the bathhouse, and was renovated with new lavatories in every room, a new kitchen, and a cafeteria dining room. The lobby was enlarged with entrances on the south and north sides. The hotel regained its original name in the early 1930s. It was razed in 1949.

1920–1930

Myrtle Beach Yacht Club/Yacht Club Hotel/Ocean Plaza Hotel. Myrtle Beach Yacht Club was built in 1922 by a private membership group, which also built the town's first pier from the hotel. In 1924 the facility became public and was renamed Yacht Club Hotel. Circa 1937 Sam Gardner purchased the property, renaming it Ocean Plaza Hotel. In 1950 the hotel was remodeled, the original wraparound porch was downsized, and a grander entrance was added. In 1955 the hotel was sold to Mr. and Mrs. Keith Jones, who redecorated all the rooms by 1960 with wall-to-wall carpeting, added telephones in all the rooms, provided televisions in half the rooms, and added air-conditioning. In 1973 this facility was demolished and replaced with the twenty-story, 142-suite Yachtsman, the city's first high-rise hotel.

Woodside's Administration Building/Sea Side Inn/Lafayette Hotel. In 1926 construction began on what would jointly be offices for Woodside's business interests and a hotel. A radio was installed in the lobby, where guests enjoyed musical concerts and followed the first Gene Tunney–Jack Dempsey boxing match on September 23. In 1927 the administration building became a hotel and was named Sea Side Inn. In the early 1930s it was renamed Lafayette Hotel, and in 1960 the building was torn down.

Myrtle Lodge. Myrtle Beach Postcard Collection, courtesy of Chapin Memorial Library

Kelly Tompkins built Hotel Kelly in 1938. This view is from the mid-1940s. The hotel was located on N. Kings Highway near Chapin Company.

Burney Cottage. In 1923 sisters Annie and Lela Burney opened this guest house. They also owned Crepe Myrtle Inn at Chester Avenue and Seventh Avenue North in the late 1930s.

Hotel Lucky Strike. In 1922 sisters Bessie and Margarete Sessions of Conway bought Myrtle Beach property at 1101 North Ocean Boulevard. Bessie later married Stafford Smith and with him owned and operated Hotel Lucky Strike.

Myrtle Lodge. Built in the early 1920s with ownership unclear but probably Myrtle Beach Farms, this facility was located at Eighth Avenue North near the original Sea Side Inn. Kelly Tompkins bought it in 1935. The hotel was destroyed by fire in November 1938 and was rebuilt with brick. It was torn down in 1969 for expansion of the Myrtle Beach Pavilion Amusement Park.

Parnell Cottage. Located in about the 900 to 1100 blocks of North Ocean Boulevard, Parnell Cottage was owned by Mrs. M. E. Parnell of New Orleans. It existed until the late 1930s.

Hart's Villa. Property at 2106 North Ocean Boulevard was purchased in August 1926 by Mrs. Dot Keefe Monroe, a Florence native and widowed schoolteacher, and Claude J. Gasque, a Florence attorney. It opened in 1927 and was razed in 1998. Monroe also built the Florentine, the Tides, and Court Capri.

Beach City Bungalets. Availability of these guest quarters was advertised in 1926, making them perhaps some of the earliest cottage rentals.

Huckslin Inn. In July 1926 thirty-nine-year-old Rosa Todd Hucks, wife of William F. Hucks, bought a lot at 1903 North Ocean Boulevard in Myrtle Beach for her guest house, which opened in May 1927. She sold meals for seventy-five cents and was one of the first to buy at the Myrtle Beach Farmers Market that year. In 1935 every room had running water.

The Kit Kat. Located at 2401 North Ocean Boulevard, this guest facility was opened in 1927 by Kathleen B. Murphy. It survived until the 1990s.

Pleasant Inn. This inn, listed on the National Register of Historic Places, was built in 1927 by Frank Sessions at 200 Broadway. It was purchased by William Finch Simmons in 1929. His wife, Hettie Lell Owens Simmons, ran it as a boardinghouse. She also owned a grocery store nearby for a time. One block away at 101 Broadway, her daughter, LaZelle Owens Dubois, started LaZelle's Flower Shop in 1946. This shop was still operating as of 2005.

Blue Sea Inn. This inn was owned and operated by Roberta McMillan at 1007 North Ocean Boulevard. Her husband was a furniture merchant in Myrtle Beach. She was listed as a boardinghouse proprietor on the 1930 U.S. Census.

The Patricia. Patricia Rousseau, a single mother of two, bought a house at 2702 North Ocean Boulevard in 1929. She remodeled it into a thirteen-room guest house, naming it Patricia Court. After being expanded several

The lobby of Blue Sea Inn in 1952. Dwight Lambe Collection, courtesy of Myrtle Beach Chamber of Commerce

The Belvedere, 1903 N. Ocean Blvd., in 1951. Courtesy of Dwight Lambe Collection, Myrtle Beach Chamber of Commerce

times, the facility was sold in the 1970s and razed in the mid-1980s to make way for a high-rise hotel, the Patricia.

Kool 'N Easy. This guest accommodation located at Oak Avenue and Eighth Avenue North was owned and operated by Mrs. Daniel Nance.

Ocean Forest Hotel. Popularly referred to as the "Million Dollar Hotel," this facility opened in 1929 and was torn down in 1974.

1930–1940

Crepe Myrtle Inn. Located at Seventh Avenue North and Chester Avenue, this guest house was built in the late 1930s. Although its first ownership is not known, the Burney sisters were the owners in 1939.

The Driftwood. Located at 1600 North Ocean Boulevard, this facility was opened in the early 1930s by L'Nora and Homer Misenheimer.

The Juanita. A boardinghouse located at 2805 North Ocean Boulevard and owned by Neta Page and her widowed sister Aubrey Page Harpe was listed on the 1930 U.S. Census for Myrtle Beach. Neta Page bought the lot for what most likely became the Juanita in 1936. She later married a Mr. Cranston, who worked on the Intracoastal Waterway in the 1930s, and he ran the facility with her.

Villa Ambrose. Built by Howard Ambrose from Conway, this guest accommodation was located at 2600 North Ocean Boulevard.

Dixie Cottage. In 1935 Dixie Cottage was operated by Clara Siewers.

Gregory Manor. The location and ownership of this guest house cannot be verified, but it was advertised in 1935.

Strandola Inn. This facility was advertised in 1935 and was operated by Mrs. Viola C. Overton.

Waterside. Advertised in 1935, Waterside operated at an unknown location.

Paul's Guest House. Located at 506 Kings Highway, this guest house was built in 1936 by Henrietta Abeles, a single Jewish mother of one from New York. She operated it until sometime in the 1980s.

The Pioneer. Located at Fifth Avenue and North Kings Highway, this house was owned and operated by Mrs. George C. Graham.

The Breakers. Property at 2006 North Ocean Boulevard was bought in 1937 by Mattie Mae Avent, who was single and originally from Spartanburg, South Carolina.

Miramar-Reinhart By-The-Sea. May Reinhart purchased 2402 North Ocean Boulevard circa 1936. After consolidation of nearby properties, change of ownership, and new construction, a 328-room resort with five buildings and anchored by Dayton House Resorts existed by the end of the twentieth century.

Gingham Inn. This inn opened in 1930 and was operated by Sam Means of Greenville at an unknown location.

Hobeika Apartments, as shown here in 1955, located at 208 N. Ocean Blvd. Dwight Lambe Collection, courtesy of Myrtle Beach Chamber of Commerce

Erwin House. Operated by Mrs. W. T. Moore of Cheraw, this guest facility opened in 1930 at an unknown location.

Ideal Home. This accommodation opened in 1930 at an unknown location and was operated by Mrs. Light Townsend of Bennettsville.

Welcome Inn. In 1935 Myrtle Gause purchased the lot at 906 North Ocean Boulevard, where this fifteen-room guest house most likely was built.

Todlin Inn. This guest facility opened in the mid-1930s.

Brunswick Guest House. This guest house opened in the mid-1930s.

Kentucky Inn. This inn, located at 1105 North Ocean Boulevard, advertised thirty-five rooms available in 1935.

The Periscope. A building at 2301 North Ocean Boulevard, which was listed on the National Register of Historic Places, was built about 1930 as a summer cottage. Mildred and Able S. Perry, who purchased it in 1937, converted it to a guest house. The facility was purchased by Marjorie and Willie Everhart in late 1950s and was torn down in 2001.

The dining room of the Anchorage in 1951. Dwight Lambe Collection, courtesy of Myrtle Beach Chamber of Commerce

McCormack Guest House in 1954. Dwight Lambe Collection, courtesy of Myrtle Beach Chamber of Commerce

1940–1950

Carolina Inn. Located at 1107 North Ocean Boulevard, this guest house was demolished about 1960.

The Poindexter. The Poindexter, located at 1700 North Ocean Boulevard, was owned by Estelle Poindexter.

Brooker Lodge. This guest lodge was located at 929 North Ocean Boulevard.

The Anchorage. Located at 2104 North Ocean Boulevard, the Anchorage was still serving meals in 1963 long after many guest houses had limited or eliminated the practice, as stand-alone restaurants had become popular.

The Ocean Terrace. Owned by Mr. and Mrs. B. N. Hammond, this inn was located at 1002 North Ocean Boulevard.

Sunset Inn. Located at 1909 North Ocean Boulevard, this inn was opened by Lottie Cline Rogers.

The Ship. This accommodation at 1701 North Ocean Boulevard was owned by Carl and Vivian K. Lineback through the late 1970s.

Harmony House. Located at 302 North Ocean Boulevard, this inn was owned by Mr. and Mrs. Barney L. Harmon.

McCormack Guest House. This facility existed at 1900 North Ocean Boulevard.

Mammy's Kitchen started as a drive-in and counter-service restaurant in 1954 at the corner of Eleventh Avenue N. and N. Kings Highway. Dwight Lambe Collection, courtesy of Myrtle Beach Chamber of Commerce

Tarrymoore Inn in 1950. Chesterfield Inn is to the far right. Dwight Lambe Collection, courtesy of Myrtle Beach Chamber of Commerce

Howard Johnson's, the first chain motel in Myrtle Beach, opened in 1954 at Twelfth Avenue N. and N. Kings Highway. Dwight Lambe Collection, courtesy of Myrtle Beach Chamber of Commerce

Tarrymoore Inn. The address of this inn was 610 North Ocean Boulevard.

Rainbow Court. Located at 405 Flagg Street, this guest facility was listed on the National Register of Historic Places. It was originally built about 1935 but had extensive additions in the 1940s and 1950s.

Chesterfield Inn. The original inn was built in 1936 by Steven C. Chapman of Chesterfield, South Carolina, at 700 North Ocean Boulevard. It was listed on the National Register of Historic Places. After fire damaged that building, the current structure was built in its place in 1946, and an additional wing was built in 1965.

Ocean Pines Motor Court. Located at 3801 North Kings Highway, this inn opened in 1940.

El Rancho Motel. In 1946 this motel opened at 4001 North Kings Highway.

Palmetto Motor Court. The address of this facility was 2202 North Kings Highway.

Travelers Motor Court. This motel existed at 1803 North Kings Highway.

Nine

Tourism

 griculture, timber, and to some extent fishing were the economic mainstays of the Horry County coast until the late nineteenth century. Tourism supplanted them all in the twentieth century. While the business of tourism may have changed and evolved over the period from 1900 to 1980, the ocean and seashore in Horry County continue to draw generation after generation to bask in the warmth, play in the waves, and stand in awe of their beauty and power. Blessings of nature, the social trend of vacationing, improved transportation access, and hard work together created a major national resort area in Myrtle Beach by the last quarter of the twentieth century.

While recent generations tend to take vacations for granted, they are a somewhat modern concept. The term "vacation" did not appear in the mass media until the mid-1800s when railroads began fueling the expansion of resorts in the mountains, by the sea, or at natural springs. The main incentive for travel was to escape disease. Many southern planters traveled to New England, and some moved further inland to such cities as Columbia or Greenville, South Carolina, or as close as Murrells Inlet during the summer months to escape the "fevers" or malaria of the coastal lowcountry. The idea of travel for recreation's sake went against the Puritan work ethic and religious beliefs that idle hands were sure to send one to hell. However, slowly people in search of health or a change of climate traveled to spas and beach resorts to avail themselves of the therapeutic value of sea or mineral water.

By the late 1800s men and women from the emerging middle class began setting aside time for rest and recreation, claiming vacations as a critical marker of their new socioeconomic status. This new middle class, according to the historian Cindy Aron, consisted of self-employed skilled artisans and farmers, professionals and small-business men, male white-collar clerks and midlevel managers, women who married such men, and single women who were schoolteachers or clerical employees. The early 1900s solidified the hold that vacationing had on Americans as the vacation industry became more organized. For instance, American Express introduced the traveler's check in 1891, and by 1906 the *New York Times* and the *New York Herald* were publishing Sunday travel sections. By the 1920s and 1930s the majority of working-class Americans were enjoying annual paid vacations.[1]

A new promotional magazine/newsletter called *Myrtle Beach, Today and Tomorrow* was published in 1935 and stressed the need for a beach vacation in the work-a-day world. The editor described Myrtle Beach as one of those "unique" resorts where there is always something to do; someplace to go; something different to see other than the usual beach activities of swimming, shell collecting, fishing, sunbathing, and surf-bathing; and "as prescribed by your physician as being beneficial to the prevention and cure of certain diseases." There were golf and horseback riding, dancing in the open air, and "automobile trips to famous gardens, old homesteads and places of historical interest." He claimed that even the large truck farms in the area might be of interest.[2]

Railroads played an important role in early beach resort development. Atlantic City, New Jersey, built by the land development company of Camden and Atlantic Railroad, advertised four hundred hotels in 1900. Coney Island became the playground for the New York City masses in the late 1800s beginning with the opening of a rail line in 1875.[3] Myrtle Beach was as dependent on railroads as these other early coastal resorts were to bring the people to them. Access to the Horry County coast was difficult as it was cut off on all sides by the Waccamaw and Pee Dee rivers and their adjacent swamps. Hardy souls traveling to the beach would board Waccamaw River steamboats at Conway and travel south to Wachesaw, formerly located west of Murrells Inlet in Georgetown County. As an alternative, they would move north on the river to Grahamville, which by road is about eight miles northeast between Conway and Nixonville. From there they rode wagons or oxcarts to New Town, as Myrtle Beach was called before 1901, and camped on the beach. Conway-based Burroughs & Collins Company built the Conway & Seashore Railroad in 1900, and people in nearby towns began traveling to the coast in greater numbers. Word-of-mouth advertising spread the word, as did early paid advertising and promotional efforts by Burroughs & Collins. The company built Sea Side Inn and the Pavilion and advertised railroad schedules and hotel rates in the local newspapers. Summer cottages began to appear after 1909. A dirt road for automobile traffic was completed in 1914. All in all, building a tourist destination was a slow process in the early days.

Development of Myrtle Beach was primarily the responsibility of the major landowner Myrtle Beach Farms Company, formed in 1912 as a sister company to Burroughs & Collins. Active promotion of tourism fell to the Conway Chamber of Commerce, which was organized in 1920 to encourage and strengthen economic development of Horry County. The attraction of the South Carolina Press Association was perhaps the chamber's most effective early effort. In the spring of 1922 Marion Wright, a young Conway lawyer who was secretary of the Conway Chamber of Commerce, sent a telegram to Harold C. Booker, secretary of the South Carolina Press Association, inviting the organization to hold its annual meeting in Myrtle Beach. Soon after that invitation was sent, James E. Bryan of Myrtle Beach Farms Company sent a second wire with details about transportation and accommodations. Although about 90 percent of its members had never been to Horry County, the organization accepted the invitation for their June 21–23, 1922, meeting.

Many of the residents in Conway seem to have been involved in some facet of the planning and implementation of this event. They knew that newspaper accounts about the beach and Horry County could have positive results for the area. A group of about eighty reporters and their guests traveled by train to Marion, where after a brief ceremony by the Marion Chamber of Commerce, Conway volunteers drove the reporters to Galivants Ferry. There they were greeted with a large banner proclaiming "Welcome to the Independent Republic of Horry," beside which stood eighteen-year-old Miss Flora Mae Holliday, the state's reigning Queen of Palmafesta. More greetings and refreshments ensued at Aynor and Homewood before the entourage finally arrived in Conway, where informal receptions were held at the Grace and Kingston hotels. Lunch was served at the city hall by the ladies of the Civic League, who proudly proclaimed that all the food was from the soils and farms of Horry County. Then the group proceeded to the beach by car and boat. The meeting was a huge success, and editors extolled the wonders of Horry County in newspapers around the state that summer.[4]

Conventions and meetings have been a significant source of business and exposure for Myrtle Beach ever since that summer. Prior to the building of a convention center in 1967, conventions and conferences were held in a variety of places, such as Ocean Forest Hotel, which opened in 1930; Sea Side Inn; the Myrtle Beach Yacht Club (later named Ocean Plaza Hotel); and the Pavilion, both the one built in 1923 and its replacement in 1949. Attracting convention business was handled largely by the advertising and relationship-building of property owners, Myrtle Beach Farms Company, and visionary individuals. One such individual was James Henry Rice Jr., whose individual efforts attracted a most valuable investor to Myrtle Beach.

Promotion of anything, be it an event, a political cause or candidate, or a region, can have many legitimate objectives. Rice's objective was altruistic to a large extent. He loved the natural bounty of the South Carolina lowcountry, especially the Horry Count coast. A naturalist and conservationist but also a man with a keen sense of the development potential of the coast, Rice used his eloquence in speaking and writing to tell about the wonders and beauties of the coast. He did this mostly on his own but sometimes on behalf of organizations such as the Conway Chamber of Commerce or the Audubon Society of South Carolina. His speech to the 1924 South Carolina Press Association meeting in Myrtle Beach was a pivotal moment for the young resort and for Rice's career. It garnered high praise from newspapers around the state, and the speech was also expanded and published as a book, *Glories of the Carolina Coast*. The book caught the attention of Greenville millionaire industrialist and developer John T. Woodside, who in 1926 purchased about sixty-five thousand acres of coastline from Myrtle Beach Farms Company.

In 1929 Americans spent approximately $2.7 billion on vacation travel, according to a 1937 study by the economist Julius Weinberger.[5] Millions of dollars in investments were being pumped into Florida resorts, such as Miami Beach and Daytona Beach, attracting significant numbers to the state's shores. The increasing ease of travel due to expanded rail lines, the affordability of automobiles, and the construction of better roads around the country rendered vacations cheaper, easier, and often more enjoyable for both the middle and working classes. An astute businessman who had traveled extensively, Woodside understood these trends and was determined to see South Carolina and Myrtle Beach take advantage of them. In the biggest move of his illustrious career, he wanted to create a vacation playground for the middle and upper classes in Myrtle Beach. While his planning and building virtually ceased with the stock market crash of 1929, the millions he had invested between 1926 and 1932 were directly to Myrtle Beach's long-term benefit. This included building the elegant Ocean Forest Hotel and Myrtle Beach's first golf course and country club, surveying new residential neighborhoods, paving Highway 17 from Myrtle Beach's downtown to the Ocean Forest, and adding extensive infrastructure that positioned the town for its next phase of growth. Perhaps more important than the physical structures he left behind, Woodside performed a significant service to the future of the town through his promotions and advertising in cities across the country. He set the stage for achieving what others had been trying to do since the 1920s: expanding the tourist season from the summer months to year-round.

Some off-season activity was evident in the first third of the twentieth century. For example, during the 1930s Ernest Miller, a rancher from Elkhorn Ranch in Bozeman, Montana, would bring his entire crew to Myrtle Beach to spend the winters at Ocean Forest Country Club. According to Jimmy D'Angelo, Miller might fill all the rooms at the golf club and still need two floors at Ocean Forest Hotel. He arranged hunting trips and golfing parties, skeet shooting, tennis, horseback riding, and cookouts on the beach.[6] These kinds of groups were profitable during the off-season, but only to a certain extent because of their inconsistent occurrence. Woodside's Myrtle Beach Estates tried fox hunts in the autumn months, but it appears that this idea did not last long. Washington Park Race Track opened for the first time in May 1938 and that November, with the stated objective of attracting visitors in the off-season, hosted the 1938 South Carolina Coastal Exposition and Races. Ads for the event publicized the Revue Magnificent!, featuring Miss Florence Lalour, whose advertising photograph revealed an artfully draped, scantily dressed showgirl. Other acts included the feminine charms of the Five Avalons, the acrobat artist Marjorie Bailey on the high pole, and other enticing attractions. In addition, of course, there was horse racing.

With the formation of the Myrtle Beach Chamber of Commerce in 1938, a catalyst for promoting tourism during the summer and the off-season took root. The group disbanded in 1941 due to World War II but was restructured and rechartered in 1947.[7] The chamber was strictly a volunteer organization until 1948, when it hired its first executive secretary, Mark Garner.[8] The organization formed its first news bureau in 1955 to change national perceptions that Myrtle Beach had been destroyed by Hurricane Hazel the previous October. The effort was successful and set a precedent for future promotional activities.

Joe Ivey was one of the early and most aggressive promoters of Myrtle Beach in the off-season, according to Harold Clardy, retired president of Chapin Company. In the 1960s Ivey and "Buster" Bryan, who owned motels and had other real estate interests in the area, started advertising "Indian Summers at Myrtle Beach" in New York. By 1973 tourism in the off-season was supplying about 40 percent of the $135 million annual revenue in tourist dollars, with about half of the 350 motels and hotels remaining open from May to November. About 20 percent were open all year by 1973—a great change from the time when Myrtle Beach emptied out after Labor Day.[9] Some of the events and features, organized by both the chamber and private interests, responsible for this change are listed below.

The Annual Sun Fun Festival. Organized in 1951 to attract vacationers during the slow period from the end of the school year to the Fourth of July holiday, this was the chamber's first major attempt at stretching the season.

The Grand Strand Fishing Rodeo. The chamber started this tournament in 1953 to bring attention to the excellent fishing opportunities along the Grand Strand. It was originally held from Labor Day to Thanksgiving but eventually stretched from April through October.

Can-Am Days. A week-long festival that began in April 1961, Can-Am Days celebrations focus on the Canadians who flock to Myrtle Beach during the winter months. The Grand Strand has traditionally attracted about seventy-five thousand or more for this festival.

Myrtle Beach Golf Holiday. The impact of golf on tourism began in the mid-1960s when George "Buster" Bryan introduced Golf-O-Tel, the predecessor program to the Myrtle Beach Golf Holiday. It was a vacation package that combined special rates for hotel, golfing, and

The Sun Fun Festival began in 1951 as a way to attract vacationers in the early part of the summer. This circa 1965 photograph of the parade down Kings Highway was taken looking north from about Ninth Avenue N. Mark Garner Collection, courtesy of Chapin Memorial Library

other amenities. The number of golf courses in the Myrtle Beach area multiplied quickly in the 1960s, starting with six in 1960 and totaling thirty-six by 1980. The major golf season is February through April.[10]

Myrtle Beach Spring Rally. One of the nation's oldest organized events for motorcycle enthusiasts, this rally has been held in Myrtle Beach since 1940. At that time the Carolina Harley Davidson Dealers Association invited customers to join them for the first spring rally, which has been held every year since then on the third Saturday in May. In 1990 about twenty thousand bikers attended the weekend event. In 1980 what would eventually be called Black Bike Week began as the first annual Atlantic Beach Memorial Day BikeFest, sponsored by the Flaming Knight Riders motorcycle club. The organization became the Carolina Knight Riders in 1982.

As a result of the slow expansion of the season and the threat of loss from hurricanes being somewhat minimized with the enactment of the 1968

Fourteenth Avenue Pier, shown here in 1966, was originally built in 1922 as part of Myrtle Beach Yacht Club, which was renamed Ocean Plaza Hotel and Pier in 1937 by its new owner, Sam Gardner. The hotel was demolished in 1973 and replaced with Yachtsman Resort Hotel, the city's first high-rise hotel. Mark Garner Collection, courtesy of Chapin Memorial Library

The concrete boardwalk north of the Pavilion was a gathering place for visitors in the mid-1960s, just as it had been in earlier years. Mark Garner Collection, courtesy of Chapin Memorial Library

National Flood Insurance program, major chain hotels and restaurants began appearing in the 1970s. The first high-rise hotel, the twenty-story Yachtsman Resort Hotel, was built in 1971 at 1400 North Ocean Boulevard on the site of the 1922 Myrtle Beach Yacht Club. The older guest houses were beginning to lose market share to the hotels and motels. In a 1963 survey by the Greater Myrtle Beach Chamber of Commerce, 38.1 percent of respondents were interested in staying in a motel or motor court, 32.6 percent in an apartment, 11.2 percent in a rental house or cottage, 9.2 percent in a hotel, 5.4 percent in a guest house, 2.2 percent at a campsite, and 1.3 percent in a mobile home or trailer park.[11] Henrietta Abeles, who as a single mother started Paul's Guest House on Kings Highway in 1936, noted these changes in a July 14, 1970, letter to her son Sigmund: "Little by little most of the women who ran places like mine have sold out. I met Mrs. Ramsey and she sold; also Mrs. Noel, also Mrs. Copeland in the corner, [we're] getting old."[12] Abeles closed her house to guests in the 1970s but continued to live there until her death in 1983.

For many years the beach was the main attraction for visiting vacationers. Myrtle Beach Farms enhanced this experience with the Pavilion; the boardwalk; amusements such as rides, roller skating, and bowling at the Pavilion; live music and dancing; and organized events. Even in the early

The wooden boardwalk, shown here in the mid-1930s, stretched at one time from the Pavilion to the Ocean Forest Hotel and was believed to be one of the most cohesive bonds for the young resort town. Courtesy of Betty Hartnett Collection, Chapin Memorial Library

years of Myrtle Beach the company was creating summer memories. For example, in June 1917 management organized a big dance and lawn party, stringing lights with one thousand feet of wire around the grounds of Sea Side Inn. Imagine what it must have looked like on the beach while dancing under the stars with no other lights for miles around.

A constant attraction at the Pavilion since the early 1930s was the amusement park rides, which were usually set up by traveling carnivals that included kiddie rides for young children, a Ferris wheel, and a carousel. This kind of arrangement was replaced by a permanent amusement park in 1950 when Myrtle Beach Pavilion Amusement Park was established. Another popular venue near the Myrtle Beach Pavilion in the 1950s and 1960s was Gay Dolphin Amusement Park. Enterprising entrepreneurs also tried theme parks, such as Pirateland Amusement Park, which opened in 1964 on 143 acres south of Myrtle Beach on U.S. Highway 17; Jungle Land, with a tropical setting, petting arenas, and exotic animals; and Fort Caroline, which combined history, entertainment, and nature. During the 1954 season, a group of Seminole Indians set up an Indian village on Highway 501 where fifteen Indians ranging in age from five months to eighty-one years entertained the crowds with their dances, colorful tribal garb, handcrafts, and other attractions.

The Pirateland property has been surrounded with tragedy and controversy since its initial development in 1963. The 143-acre tract with oceanfront was originally part of the property that the U.S. government had taken prior to World War II for the Myrtle Beach Army Air Force base. In 1953 the government deeded the property, known as Seascape prior to World War II, back to the city of Myrtle Beach with the provision that any proceeds from the property were to be used for the operation, maintenance, and capital improvements of the municipal airport. The provision was later lifted. The city signed a thirty-year lease in September 1963 with Golden Cove Inc., which was formed by Mark Garner, Myrtle Beach mayor at the time, and A. P. Gandy, to build Pirateland. The park opened in 1964. Garner sold his interest in 1968 because of concern over conflict of interest, but another controversy erupted shortly after that concerning the fact that Golden Cove signed a sublease with an adjoining campground for more money than the city received from Golden Cove in the original lease. This matter was settled satisfactorily with the city. As a result of never earning the revenues needed to be profitable and the death of a child on a ride in June 1966, the park closed its doors in 1972.

In 1974 a new operator took over the property and renamed it Magic Harbor, opening it to the public in June 1975. By September, however, the North Carolina National Bank took legal possession of the park's assets after the owner failed to make payments on its loan. The bank found another operator, Harry Koch, who reopened the park in June 1976. Months later he and another man were found murdered, supposedly victims of an armed robbery. During the 1970s the Perry family, owners of the adjoining Lakewood Camping Resort, took over the lease, which was due to expire in 1993. However, in 1982 the city signed three new twenty-year leases on the property: one with Blackpool Leisure Park Company of the United Kingdom, which intended to reopen the amusement park on a 42-acre tract; one with Lakewood for 61.9 acres; and a third with Ponderosa Inc., operator of Pirateland Family Campground, for 42.68 acres. The terms of these leases became the center of controversy and civil action in 1983 between the city and Horry County, which manages the city's airport through the Horry County Airport Commission. Although Magic Harbor opened in 1983, it closed its doors for the last time later that year, awaiting a legal decision on the leases and fighting a lawsuit regarding the death of a teenager on one of the rides in April 1983.[13]

Incredible miniature golf courses became one of Myrtle Beach's trademarks. One of the first courses in Myrtle Beach opened at the corner of U.S. Highway 17 and Ninth Avenue North in June 1930, which coincided with the national emergence of the sport in the 1920s. While more of a fad during that era, miniature golf became big business in the 1930s, with three thousand Tom Thumb Golf franchises popping up across the country. The industry waned shortly after that but made a comeback in the 1950s. Rather than the mania of the 1920s, however, it became more of a family-oriented activity, a quiet way to spend a Saturday afternoon with the kids or an evening with a date. Both the Pavilion and the Gay Dolphin amusement parks featured "carpet golf" at one time. By the 1970s Myrtle Beach courses were beginning to develop their own unique style, "characterized by large central rockeries made of sprayed synthetic rock over which water, dyed blue or gold, cascades dramatically into an artificial pond whose color also has been enhanced. Invariably a jungle atmosphere is invoked, replete with palm trees, thatched huts, and fiberglass 'wild' animals," according to John Margolies.[14]

Such entertainment started with a Jungle Golf course built by James E. "Poddy" Bryan III and Al Tirrell in Myrtle Beach in the late 1960s. Soon after that was completed, Edward Burroughs asked the two men to build another course, and they designed the first Around the World in 18 Holes course on property adjacent to the Gay Dolphin on Ocean Boulevard. They

Cruising Ocean Blvd. near the Pavilion was a popular pastime for young people in the mid-1960s. Mark Garner Collection, courtesy of Chapin Memorial Library

designed about every three holes to represent different parts of the world, using, for example, an Eskimo, a polar bear, and an igloo for Alaska and then a jungle-type environment for the next three holes. "But we decided then that we ought to go up in the air, do something different," recalled Tirrell. "Everybody was flat on the ground with miniature golf courses. And we thought why can't we just stick a mountain up in here, like in Tibet, and make it more interesting? And you play up to it, walk up and play down the other side of the mountain, and then put a lake in, and you go around the lake, et cetera. So we did it."[15]

Summer holidays have long been big business in Myrtle Beach, especially the Fourth of July. From the earliest days, all of the tourist accommodations made their biggest money on the Fourth of July, most being booked to capacity year after year. In 1917 Sea Side Inn organized a moonlight bathing party on July 3, a baseball game on the beach on July 4, and a dance that night. More than five hundred attended. In 1926 the crowds had increased to more than five thousand, and within four more years, in 1930, between fifteen thousand and twenty thousand people were expected on the beach for the July 4 festivities. The 1937 Independence Day holiday exemplifies the growth and popularity of the beach resort, with the *Horry Herald* reporting that the beaches had the largest crowds in their history, with a traffic jam at Myrtle Beach that required several hours to untangle. B. F. Vereen, proprietor of a service station and tourist camp about six miles out of Myrtle Beach, told a reporter that cars were parked at intervals all the way from his business to Myrtle Beach. All available rooms and cottages were occupied at the beach, and overflow crowds were looking for places to stay in Conway, Georgetown, and other places. The following year, 1938, more than sixty thousand crowded the beaches, spending up to $750,000 during the three-day holiday weekend. The crowds began pouring in on Friday night, coming in from every direction by car, trailer, bus, and train. By Saturday night, guest houses were forced to turn away many people requesting rooms.

Unfortunately the next season was plagued with a polio panic that kept much of the summer crowds away. Ocean Forest Hotel even had to shut down for a time. The scare was more psychological than real, however. Dr. James A. Hayne, head of the South Carolina Board of Health, published a proclamation that Horry County was free of any danger of infection from infantile paralysis and that no active cases were reported. The local county health office in Conway also issued a statement to the same effect. Fears dissipated with time, and the beach was back in business in 1940, kicking off the season in May with a grand parade, horse racing, a dance, and a beauty contest.[16] The Independence Day holiday continued to grow annually, and

The Bowery, built circa 1944 and shown here in 1965, faces the Pavilion at 110 Ninth Avenue N. It is noted for being the home of the country music band Alabama, which was this bar's house band in the 1970s. Mark Garner Collection, courtesy of Chapin Memorial Library

by 1980 holiday weekend crowds totaled more than three hundred thousand on the Grand Strand.

Between 1935 and 1940 a majority of America's industrial labor force began receiving vacations with pay, "ironically making the decade of the Depression a period when vacationing became more rather than less widespread," according to Aron.[17] Myrtle Beach attractions made attempts to broaden their appeal by targeting diversified population groups. When the Washington Park Race Track opened in 1938, one of its biggest events was Farmers Day, when thousands of farmers and their families gained free admission. The August crowd at the beach was known to contain numerous tobacco farmers and their families who had sold their crops and were ready to relax for a bit. In 1949 Springs Industries built a resort for its mill employees, Springmaid Beach Resort, just north of Myrtle Beach State Park. In 1953 it was opened to the general public. The Grand Strand beaches as a whole, however, were not inclusive of people of color until the 1960s (see the section on Atlantic Beach on page 199).

The growth of tourism on the Grand Strand significantly impacted Horry County and South Carolina, shifting the economic and population center from the county seat to Myrtle Beach and the Grand Strand area. This change occurred mainly between 1910 and 1980. In 1910 the total population of Horry County was almost 27,000, with Conway, the county seat and center of commerce, government, and population, being the largest town with 5,388 people. The smallest township was Dogwood Neck (which included the small summer colony of Myrtle Beach) with 948 people. The county's main industry was agriculture. By 1980 the population shift was dramatic. About 10,240 people lived in the greater Conway area, while the city of Myrtle Beach had a population of almost 19,000.[18] The greatest increase in population, about 550 percent, was between 1940 and 1970, from 1,597 to 9,035, which resulted in the rising price of land and changing land-use patterns. For example, in the 1960s Myrtle Beach Farms began converting its commercial farming land to golf courses, a more profitable use of the land.

A 1966 study indicated that the increase in population and increasing urbanization of the Grand Strand would affect the nature of recreational attractions. According to an article in *Business and Economic Review*, "A great deal of outdoor recreation also takes place in close proximity to these areas [Grand Strand beaches] because many tourists like to walk to the beach from their motel, boarding house or hotel. As the area grows and becomes more urbanized, changes in the landscape either cause individuals to change their recreation requirements in order to continue using the same facilities or change the places where they are able to satisfy their recreation needs."[19] The 1970s saw the beginning of these landscape changes, with hotels getting taller and high-rise condominiums being built. Agricultural land was being lost to development and tourism, a trend occuring nationally. In 1959, 4,988 Horry County farms were listed on the state census of agriculture. Five years later the county had lost more than 1,000 farms (a total of 3,855 farms remained in 1964).[20]

Tourism also affected demographics, notably the influx of people from other states, both as residents and as tourists. The 1900 U.S. Census for Dogwood Neck shows that 95.5 percent of the residents were born in South Carolina, a percentage that did not change much until 1930, when it was 84.5 percent. The majority of the migrating population was from North Carolina. By 1990 only about 60 percent of Horry County residents were born in South Carolina. About 50 percent of the Grand Strand's visitors came from neighboring states North Carolina and Georgia. Significant numbers also traveled from New York, Virginia, Ohio, Tennessee, and the eastern provinces of Canada.

The shift in economic contributions within the county was also occurring by the 1950s. The 1958 Horry County tax valuations of real and personal property indicated that 28 percent of these tax revenues came from Conway and 30 percent came from Myrtle Beach. By 1962 the Greater Myrtle Beach Chamber of Commerce reported that the Grand Strand paid about half of Horry County's real estate taxes while less than one-third of the county's population lived there.[21] In 1959 the Greater Myrtle Beach Chamber of Commerce reported that 29 percent, or $62 million, of the state's total revenue collections came from tourist-related businesses, the majority of which were located on the Grand Strand.[22]

The 1970s saw a continued growth in tourism on the Grand Strand, despite events such as gas rationing in 1973–74 resulting from the oil embargo by the Organization of Petroleum Exporting Countries. The Grand Strand greeted 2.9 million visitors in 1972, and this number increased to 6.5 million by 1978.[23] The historian Roy Talbert attributes this increase to several factors. Interest in golf and an increase in the number of courses accelerated rapidly in the 1970s. Blue laws prohibiting the sale of liquor-by-the-drink ended in 1973. Prior to this, patrons had to bring their own bottles to an establishment. This change created investment interest in the resort by large chain hotels and restaurants. The county's first indoor mall, Myrtle Square Mall, opened, as did the Waccamaw Pottery complex.

Gas rationing in 1974 was actually a boost for the Grand Strand because East Coast travelers chose the shorter driving distances to Myrtle Beach instead of the longer drive to Florida. Despite the rationing, Myrtle Beach experienced a 7 percent increase in business in 1974. Also making travel to the area more attractive, air transportation service to and from Myrtle Beach increased with Myrtle Beach Army Air Force Base allowing joint use of its facilities for commercial carriers in 1975.[24] Airline deregulation in 1978 also resulted over time in expanding flights into and out of Myrtle Beach.

The Grand Strand tourism industry of 1980 far exceeded what the early promoters envisioned as it spread its tentacles northward, southward, and even westward across the Intracoastal Waterway. Managing that growth and adapting to changing entertainment trends and consumer demands created new challenges for the last years of the twentieth century. Through every evolutionary stage of the area's culture and commerce, however, the timeless attraction of the ocean and its sandy shores has drawn new generations.

Ten

Myrtle Beach, the City, 1937-1980

*M*aking a summer getaway or making a home—these two objectives began to meld into one for some people. Myrtle Beach may have started as an adventure, an invigorating splash of sunshine and escape, but it became much more for the families for whom it became a hometown and a livelihood. The town's development, leadership, nurturing, and protection were fostered by Myrtle Beach Farms for decades, but by the mid-1930s residents of Myrtle Beach were forced to face the fact that they had to take responsibility for the future of their community. Myrtle Beach Farms Company could do only so much, and the town was growing too fast for the company's resources.

Between 1930 and 1940 the population more than doubled from about 660 to almost 1,600.[1] Tourism was also expanding, with peak season holidays attracting 15,000 to 20,000 in 1930 and about three times that many in 1938. The infrastructure needed major investment and coordination. Up until this time many of the services normally provided by a municipality had been managed by Myrtle Beach Farms Company, but the needs were becoming too great for one private enterprise to handle. Streets required paving; better drainage was needed; sewage and sanitation facilities were nonexistent; police and fire protection were inadequate for the increasing numbers of people and buildings; and a business licensing program to protect merchants from unscrupulous and itinerant peddlers was essential for retailers and consumers alike. The road to incorporation, however, would not be smooth.[2]

On February 12, 1937, Paul Quattlebaum, S.C. senator, addressed those who had gathered at a town hall meeting in Myrtle Beach to discuss incorporation and form a steering committee. Chaired by Dr. William Rourk, the committee included Simeon Chapin, James Bryan Jr., Dan Nance, Cecil Pridgeon, Bunyon Benfield, Joe Ivey, Jasper Ramsey Sr., Holmes B. Springs Sr., T. P. Pearson, and Clarence Macklen. In April the committee reported to the community that the secretary of state had commissioned a call for an election to decide (1) whether or not to incorporate; if so, (2) the name of the town; and (3) the selection of a city council. What made this election unique was that Myrtle Beach, if voters approved it, would be the first town to incorporate under a new charter for resort communities devised by the South Carolina General Assembly. Passed in April 1937, the act tried to provide an avenue for incorporation for resort communities that had more nonresident freeholders than resident freeholders—in other words, these resort communities had more people who owned real estate there but lived elsewhere than people who had legal residence. The charter provided that five persons would sit on the city council—three residents and two non-residents—and that they would be appointed by the governor of South Carolina. The governor would make these appointments after a primary election in which the electorate would nominate the top three resident candidates. These three names would be considered a recommendation to the governor. The two nonresident council seats would be appointed by the governor without the voice of the electorate. The five council members would then choose a mayor from among themselves. Myrtle Beach's incor-poration committee felt that nonresidents should be included because "a very large portion of the property holders of Myrtle Beach live outside the proposed corporate limit and the progress and development of Myrtle Beach as a resort center up to this time has been made possible largely by the investments and patronage of these non-residents."

On May 25, 1937, the electorate rejected incorporation by a vote of 142 to 124 (from 286 registered voters), largely because of the form of govern-ment proposed. Only seventeen nonresident freeholders voted. Voters also did not like the definition of Myrtle Beach's northern boundary, which stopped south of the valuable Ocean Forest Hotel property; specifically the boundary was the joint corner of the Myrtle Beach Farms Company and the Ocean Forest Company property on the east side of U.S. Highway 17. The seven men running for council in this stillborn election were Jasper N. Ramsey Sr., owner of Nu Way Laundry and Dry Cleaners, with 170 votes; Dr. William A. Rourk, physician, with 150 votes; Bunyon "B. B." Benfield, owner and operator of two Myrtle Beach movie houses and former Dillon, South Carolina, town council member, with 150 votes; Dan Nance, build-ing contractor and real estate investor, with 123 votes; Nicholas Hughes Jr., civil engineer and realtor, with 92 votes; T. P. Pearson, manager of the Stan-dard Dredging Company's operations for the Intracoastal Waterway, with

50 votes; and Earl Jones, a young businessman identified as "interested in the operation of a beach hotel," with 21 votes.[3]

Work got under way immediately to try again, but this time the proposed municipality was structured under the traditional mayor-council form of government. The secretary of state called for another election to be held on August 25, 1937, at the Myrtle Beach school building from 8:00 A.M. to 4:00 P.M.[4] Seven candidates ran this time for the six council seats, and Jasper Ramsey and Dr. Wilford L. Harrelson faced each other in their bids for mayor. Ramsey's son, Jasper Ramsey Jr., recalled that his father had not been interested in being the first mayor but that in "the very first election, he [his father] ran against Mr. Harrelson, who won. But my dad always said it was basically that they had to have somebody to run."[5] The vote, however, was close; Harrelson won by only eleven votes. Incorporation was approved by a landslide—133 to 8. The five candidates receiving the highest votes were elected to Myrtle Beach's first city council. Candidates were Robert Cannon, with 135 votes; Bunyon Benfield, with 132; Dr. William A. Rourk, with 131; Clarence Macklen, with 128; A. P. Shirley, with 111; Robert M. Hussey Jr., with 101; and T. B. Suber, who did not make the cut.[6] Terms of office for mayor and city council were two years and began on March 12, 1938, when Myrtle Beach received its charter of incorporation from the state. The new town limits started on the south at about Midway Swash on the northern boundary of Myrtle Beach State Park. The northern city limit was just beyond Ocean Forest Hotel at Cane Patch Swash, and the east-west depth from the ocean averaged half a mile.[7] Myrtle Beach was officially a city.

The people who would lead Myrtle Beach in the early days of its municipal development consisted of citizens who were not politicians but who cared about their chosen city and had moved to Myrtle Beach to raise their children and earn their living. Until 1956 the mayor and city council changed almost every term. Within the first six administrations of city government, the most regularly elected councilman was Dr. William Rourk, a physician, who served four administrations. He moved to Myrtle Beach in 1929. Several others moved to the town in the 1920s, such as Harrelson (born in Marion County), T. Max Jordan (born in Fairfield County), and Robert Hussey (born in Sumter County). Two were natives of Horry County —Ben Graham and Ernest Williams. Early elected officials with the closest ties to the area were Socastee-born J. Clarence Macklen (councilman from 1938 to 1939) and his brother H. Lloyd Macklen (councilman from 1947 to 1949). The latter would serve four more terms in the 1950s and 1960s.

Most of these men were entrepreneurs committed to growing a city, a home. Myrtle Beach's first mayor, Dr. Wilford LeRoy Harrelson Sr., is a good example. Harrelson was born in Marion, South Carolina, in 1886 and graduated from the Medical College of South Carolina in Charleston with a degree in pharmacy. He operated a drugstore and an automobile agency in Marion before moving to Suffolk, Virginia, to work in the automobile business. In 1927 he relocated to Myrtle Beach to open Delta Drug Store, the town's first pharmacy. He and the former Harriette McKnight had two children, Wilford L. "Roy" Harrelson Jr., who would become editor and publisher of the *Myrtle Beach News* and executive secretary of the Myrtle Beach Chamber of Commerce, and Mary Elizabeth Harrelson.

Creating an environment for raising a family and establishing economic prosperity required some immediate first steps, such as security, for the city leadership. They established a formal police department and appointed J. F. Hamilton as the first police chief in 1938. Up until this time Myrtle Beach Farms, under James Bryan's supervision, paid two policemen, one for daytime work and one for nights, for the community. The company also built the first jailhouse on Tenth Avenue North near Oak Street, which was replaced in 1951. The community organized a volunteer fire department in 1936, the year before incorporation, also with the assistance of James Bryan and Myrtle Beach Farms. It consisted of eighteen volunteers led by Oliver C. Callaway, who would remain as fire chief, a volunteer position, until his death in 1955. At that time a full-time fire chief was hired. The fire department's first station house, located in back of an old sawmill

Downtown Myrtle Beach in the late 1940s was a bustling place with restaurants such as Kozy Korner and Seven Seas Grill. Myrtle Beach Postcard Collection, courtesy of Chapin Memorial Library

Grocery department employees of the Chapin Company in the early 1940s.
The company opened in 1927 in a mission-style, block-long downtown building,
one of Myrtle Beach's first department stores. Courtesy of Harold Clardy

in the area (which was later the location of Cameron Motors), had one used fire engine. It later moved to a station house built in back of the Broadway Restaurant and remained in that location until a new fire station was completed in 1951.[8] In 1959 the police and fire departments shared a new building, but the fire department moved out in 1962 when a separate facility was completed. By 1965 the fire department had five engines, one truck, eight full-time firemen, and fifty volunteers. A rescue squad composed of seven paid members and sixteen volunteers was added to the department.

Early focus was also on infrastructure and modernization. Electricity first came to Myrtle Beach at Sea Side Inn in 1909 via a connection with Paul Quattlebaum's Conway Light & Power Company. The load was powered by small crude oil engines. Horry Benton, who was born in the area in 1912, recalled when Myrtle Beach Farms built a structure across the railroad tracks from the Myrtle Beach depot to house a 25-horsepower diesel engine to power electricity: "A Delco to pull a generator to burn a few street lights from there to the Pavilion. That's about all it could do is burn a few of them lights."[9] In 1926 Woodside's Myrtle Beach Estates began building new waterworks and electric plants, laying drainage pipes, and paving sidewalks as well as Kings Highway north to the Ocean Forest section. In June 1930 New York–based General Waterworks and Electric Corporation, a large utility holding concern operating in more than twenty-five states, purchased Quattlebaum Light & Ice Company in Conway and the electric light and power property of Myrtle Beach Estates.[10] The corporation soon built a 33,000-volt transmission line between Conway and Myrtle Beach. In May 1941 the South Carolina Public Service Authority acquired the system, which by that time was depending on power from a small steam plant in Conway, a small diesel engine generator at Myrtle Beach, and a 5,000-volt line connection with the Carolina Power and Light Company at Aynor. By 1955 the power authority had two 115,500-volt lines to Conway, a 115,000-volt and two 33,000-volt lines to Myrtle Beach, and 33,000-volt lines to Loris, Ocean Drive, Crescent Beach, Garden City, Murrells Inlet, and Pawleys Island.[11]

By the fall of 1949 the city was in a political turmoil, according to Philip Gray, who was a city councilman at that time under Mayor Harry Tallevast.[12] Three men were running for mayor: LeRoy H. Letts, owner of the Pink House restaurant; Jasper Ramsey; and the realtor D. Stowe Crouse. Tallevast, the incumbent, could not run because he campaigned for the Horry County state representative seat that fall, which he lost. Letts was concerned with issues related to the Airport Commission, of which Ramsey was chair, and presented to the mayor written charges of wrongdoing and misuse of funds and privilege on the part of the commission. He was asked to detail his charges to the full city council when airport manager E. A. "Tony" Anthony would also be present, but Letts did not do so. Anthony wanted all issues aired and cleared as soon as possible as the Airport Commission was actively courting Delta Airlines and Piedmont Airlines.[13] Anthony presented a letter, dated September 30, 1949, to the city council from the Civil Aeronautics Administration's district airport engineer stating that the airport's operations deserved special commendation and could be used as an example to other airports.[14] Ramsey also contended that it was a model for other airports that managed revenue-producing facilities transferred to them by the federal government.

On November 4 all candidates for mayor and city council spoke in a public forum at the Pavilion. Several full-page political advertisements were carried in the newspaper, and Letts even used a radio show to make his points. However, Ramsey carried the mayoral vote, and this seventh municipal election was considered to have "the most intense interest ever shown by the electorate," according to the *Myrtle Beach News*. Ramsey received 416 votes, or about 57 percent of the vote. Crouse received 210, and Letts received 95. From a total of 890 registered voters, 727 voted, a record on both counts.[15]

The issue regarding the airport was not a new one, and it would remain an issue for several more years. Myrtle Beach's first organized attempt to tap into the aviation era was during the Woodside days of the late 1920s. Since Woodside sought to attract high-income investors to Myrtle Beach, he knew he had to make the resort accessible by all means of transportation. He built a landing field, which opened August 1928 and was located around present-day Tenth Avenue North and Seaboard Street. Marcus Smith, in one of his newspaper history columns, wrote that in the 1930s football games were played near Tenth Avenue North on the George Trask Farms. The football field was located "at one end of [a] makeshift runway that catered to small local planes."[16] Ben Graham, Myrtle Beach's second mayor, was responsible for building a municipal airport on land purchased during the previous administration on Conway Highway (State Highway 15). In December 1938 Dexter Martin, director of the South Carolina Aeronautics Commission, visited Myrtle Beach and inspected the site for the new airport. He advised that funds were available for use, the Works Progress Administration office in Conway was preparing a project application, and T. Max Jordan of Myrtle Beach was working on the boundary survey, contour maps, and other items. Soon after its completion in 1940, Graham and Holmes Springs offered the airport to the U.S. government as a gunnery and bombing base. It became Myrtle Beach Army Air Base in 1941.

An important result of the decision-making process was that the U.S. Army Air Corps ordered the first aerial photography of the area. These photographs revealed that the area south of Withers Swash, including Spivey Beach, was undeveloped, and most of the avenues north of Ninth Avenue North had not been paved. The first and second rows were most heavily developed from the Pavilion area to approximately Twenty-ninth or Thirtieth Avenue North North of Thirtieth. Little second-row development existed, with the exception of a cluster centered between Thirty-seventh Avenue and Forty-first Avenue North.[17]

The military decided to close the base at the end of World War II. A factor in the decision was that the base's mission in late 1945 had shifted to recruitment and support of special activities. "The speedy demobilization of the Armed Forces caused an almost unbearable personnel shortage. It was difficult for the base to carry out even its severely restricted mission between September 1945 and November 1947," according to the U.S. Air Force Historical Division.[18] In October 1947 the War Assets Administration transferred the property back to Myrtle Beach. Joe Ivey, as chairman of the Airport Commission, hired Tony Anthony to manage the Myrtle Beach Municipal Airport and make it self-supporting—with no funds to do so. Even his salary had to be generated at the airport. Anthony converted former personnel apartments into rental units; started three turkey farms that raised fifty thousand birds per year on the southwest corner of the airfield;

attracted the farm system of the Boston Braves baseball organization to hold spring training at the field for several seasons; and offered some of the buildings at the airport to small industrial companies, such as Electrical Reactance Corporation, which had a plant to make radio condensers and hired approximately 240 women. Part of the property was converted to a modern motor court, and the airport also was winter home to two large carnivals. All revenue generated at the airport was spent to promote civil aviation.[19] Another project approved by the city council to make the airport self-supporting was the sale of some of the timber on the property. Anthony contracted with a forester associated with the State Forestry Commission, who prepared a long-range selective cutting program. Anthony sent bids to all interested lumber companies in October 1948, and five companies submitted bids, with the Canal Wood Corporation offering the best bid of $20,550.

In the meantime, city leaders were working behind the scenes with the United States government to attract the air force back to Myrtle Beach. "My dad began working hard to bring the base back in the early 1950s," according to Jasper Ramsey Jr. "I remember when he was trying to bring it back down here, that they [the air force] said, 'we were there one time and built all these buildings, and you all come to Washington wanting us to leave. You didn't want us there.'" Athalia Ramsey, widow of Jasper Ramsey, said, "A lot of people that built homes up on the Boulevard, they said the noise of the planes, you know, they didn't like all that noise." However, Ramsey, in his campaign to interest the air force in coming back, told the military that the problem was with nonresidents who owned homes there, not the people of Myrtle Beach. In June 1954 the U.S. Air Force accepted the city's offer of the Myrtle Beach Municipal Airport as an air base. However, a delay in transferring troops to the base grew out of discussions between the Civil Aeronautics Administration, the air force, and the city over the use of the field by commercial aircraft. In late 1954 an agreement was reached allowing civilian planes with two-way radios to use the facility. Another delay created difficulties with transferring six plots of land formerly leased by the government to the air force, but an agreement was reached by year-end. In addition, a controversy regarding the air force's desire to purchase twenty-seven acres of beach property from the South Carolina State Park Commission for use as a recreational area for troops caused some friction with the state park system.

To provide adequate facilities for commercial aviation, the city of Myrtle Beach signed a contract on October 9, 1958, with the South Carolina Aeronautics Commission (SCAC) and the U.S. government to relocate the city's civilian aviation operations from the air force base to Crescent Beach

Airport, which was owned by the SCAC. Under the contract, the U.S. government acquired title to properties that the city owned at Myrtle Beach Air Force Base and in return contributed $326,000 toward the development of the Crescent Beach Airport for civilian aviation activities. Work began in early 1959 to resurface the six-thousand-foot runway, buy additional land for an entrance road, expand taxiways and hangar facilities, build a terminal building, and install runway lighting. The terminal was not built until the early 1960s, however. Piedmont, which had been serving Myrtle Beach with seasonal service through the 1950s from the air force base field, was instructed by the FAA to begin year-round service by May 1962. That service would have to be out of Crescent Beach Airport due to base runway limitations. The Crescent Beach airstrip, formerly called the Wampee Strip, was built during World War II by the State Highway Department on 375 acres acquired by the federal government and was used as an emergency landing strip by the U.S. Marine Corps from Congaree Air Base near Columbia.[20] In 1975 Horry County resumed commercial aviation operations from the Myrtle Beach field under a joint-use agreement with the U.S. Air Force. The airport was named Myrtle Beach Jetport until 1995, when it was renamed Myrtle Beach International Airport.

As the young city grew and its needs became more complex, its politics became more contentious, with the voting rights issue changing the dynamics of party politics. The year 1951 was the first time that a Democratic primary was to be held in a municipal election, having been approved in a special referendum the previous summer. Scheduled for October 9, the primary would send the candidate with the majority vote to the general election. Defeated primary candidates or new candidates could run in the general election on an independent ticket. Under protest by former mayor Harry Tallevast, who was running against incumbent mayor Jasper Ramsey, Myrtle Beach City Council agreed on September 22 to cancel this election's primary, on the advice of the county registration board, due to shortness of time allowed for new registrations.

In addition, the 1951 race was among the first in South Carolina in which voters were not required to show their poll tax receipts in order to vote. Strom Thurmond, who was South Carolina's governor from 1947 to 1951, was instrumental in gaining voter approval for a constitutional amendment repealing the poll tax as a qualification for voting.[21] Requirements to vote included the following: voters must prove the ability to read or write any section of the state constitution; if unable to read or write, the voter must own property assessed at three hundred dollars or more and have paid all taxes collectible on the property in the previous year; and the voter must have resided in the state for two years, the county for one year, and Myrtle Beach for at least four months. The whites-only primary had been abolished in July 1948 by a federal judge who ruled that excluding African Americans from the Democratic Party primary was unconstitutional. About thirty-five thousand black voters in South Carolina voted in the Democratic primaries in August 1948. In Myrtle Beach only two black people registered, Charlie Fitzgerald and his wife, Sarah. However, according to the *State* newspaper, they "voluntarily" asked Mayor Tallevast, manager of the Horry County executive committee (for the Democratic Party), to strike their names from the rolls. "Fitzgerald told the mayor, 'I don't think this is the right time to put our names on the book.' He said their names were the only Negroes on the books and he wanted their white friends to know that he asked that his name and that of his wife be taken off the roll."[22]

Tempe Oehler's parents, Nicholas and Jessie Hughes, often worked as poll managers during Myrtle Beach elections. In the 1930s and early 1940s they would take Tempe and her sister to the Myrtle Beach school where voting was held. She did not remember when the first African Americans voted in Myrtle Beach but did "remember that one of the poll managers would ask the blacks how to spell 'aurora borealis.' Now, how many white people then knew how to spell that?" She also remembered the first person who wanted to register as a Republican: "This lady and her brother came here from New Jersey. Mrs. Farrington was her name. She wanted to register Republican and nobody knew how to register a Republican. She had voted Republican back in her home area. Oh man, that was big news."[23]

The 1951 election would prove to be just as rousing as that of 1949 but with different issues. About five hundred people attended a candidates' rally on November 1, 1951, which was organized by the Jaycees and held at the Pavilion. It was "liberally sprinkled with women."[24] The two main issues were the franchise granted to Seacoast Telephone Company and the city's proposed purchase of the electrical distribution system from the Public Service Authority. Other local issues included cleaner beaches and streets, adequate sewage facilities, and the paving of streets and the building of sidewalks, especially in the area south of the Pavilion, which some contended was not receiving the kind of street maintenance and improvements that areas north of the Pavilion received.

The issue surrounding whether or not the city should purchase the electrical distribution system could not occur without voter approval, Ramsey contended. It appears that no serious consideration was being given to the purchase, but rather that it was being studied and used as a negotiating tactic by his administration to gain a lower rate on street lights. Ramsey contended that he was only examining all the facts before presenting the issue to the voters. The main issue regarding Seacoast Telephone Company's so-called franchise was whether or not the company should get such a commitment from the city. Ramsey countered to Tallevast that funding for further improvements to the system could not be gained without the strength of a conditional franchise. Tallevast implied that the city had not made a sound business decision by entering into an agreement with the telephone company.

Extended telephone service began in Myrtle Beach during the Woodside era about 1927, when Myrtle Beach Sales Company installed a triple trunk line from Myrtle Beach to Conway. This included phone service at the "new" Sea Side Inn with phone lines to several rooms and connections with other buildings. In 1936 Seacoast Telephone Company began service in Myrtle Beach with twenty-five telephones and a switchboard located in Lafayette Manor Hotel. By 1941 the town had ninety subscribers to phone service. Ten years later about five hundred phones were in Myrtle Beach homes and businesses, and Seacoast Telephone Company had significantly improved long distance service and established dial service. Still, many said that phone service simply was not adequate to the needs of the rapidly expanding community. By applying some pressure in the right places and entering into a franchise agreement, Ramsey claimed that his administration was able to make some constructive improvements to the town's phone service.

The full-page newspaper advertisements presented a roaring battle between Tallevast and Ramsey about these issues, as well as different philosophies concerning management and budgeting and how best to make the city grow. Both clearly wanted to see the air force base return to Myrtle Beach, with an underlying note of concern about the threat of attack fueled by cold-war fears. However, the voters sided with Ramsey and returned him to office. Councilmen who were also reelected were Philip Gray, James Porter, and Sam Gardner. Newly elected councilmen were Edward Broedel, Ernest Williams, and H. Lloyd Macklen, who had previously served under the Tallevast administration.

Another major issue during the 1950s was the need for a community hospital, funds for which were raised entirely by the community with no federal or state assistance. Holmes Springs Sr. is credited with the original idea, and he worked closely in the early planning with Sherwood Forrest and Mr. and Mrs. Walter Hosier, as well as with the Myrtle Beach Chamber of Commerce. The plan to build the twenty-five-bed Ocean View Memorial Hospital required $350,000. Eight acres of land were donated by Myrtle Beach Farms Company at Seventy-seventh Avenue North and North Ocean Boulevard. Initially the community expected to raise $150,000 from the public, which would be matched under the Hill-Burton Federal Hospital Act and a contribution from the state of $50,000. By December 1950 more than $100,000 had been raised through every kind of fund-raiser imaginable—dances, pencil sales, fish fries, horse races, car raffles, golf tournaments, and much more. However, because Horry County already had two hospitals and ten or more counties in South Carolina had none, Ocean View Memorial Hospital did not qualify for federal funds. Therefore, the board of directors, discouraged but not defeated, voted to go it alone, even though the news put a major damper on the funds drive. All the money raised was invested in federal bonds. In December 1953 the board voted to use the monies that were invested in bonds and break ground for the hospital, a visual reminder to the public that the project was still alive. By August 1955 volunteers began a new drive to raise $50,000, a goal reached by year-end in large part due to the efforts of the hospital's Ladies' Auxiliary, but $200,000 was still needed to open the hospital doors. By early 1956, when it appeared that no state or federal assistance would be forthcoming, the board hired a fund-raising company, Charles A. Haney and Associates. Community members had done all they could up to that point.

By November they reached their goal in cash and pledges—with no help from the state or federal government and not one cent of taxpayer money. It was a night of great celebration for an uphill battle that had lasted six years. When the total was announced, the excitement and happiness in the crowd of more than one hundred was palpable. Everyone got in their cars and mounted a caravan, which traveled from the Holiday Lodge motel, where the meeting was held, down Kings Highway to Ninth Avenue North. "There, as music pealed from the steeple of the Methodist Church across the street, and to the din of automobile horns, chairman [Robert H.] Jones mounted a fire department ladder and painted the campaign thermometer out to the top, and on skyward to indicate the subscriptions yet to come to the cause, which is to give Myrtle Beach its first hospital and to provide the area for the first time with nearby hospital protection," according to newspaper reports.[25] Leadership of the campaign in its later years was credited to Mrs. S. C. Lind, president of the women's organizations that, after the Special Gifts Committee, raised the most money. George W. "Buster" Bryan, chairman of the Special Gifts Committee; campaign director William R. MacMillan; Bill Gasque, chairman of the men's organizations in Myrtle Beach; and C. A. Burgdorf, chairman of the campaign organizations in the area outside Myrtle Beach, also received high praise, as did Springs and many others.

On July 2, 1958, Ocean View Memorial Hospital opened with 50 beds, twenty-nine employees, and fifteen physicians on staff. By 1970 the hospital had 96 beds and a new emergency room wing, but community needs and growth were rapidly outpacing the hospital's capabilities. In 1973 community leaders came to the conclusion that a bigger facility was needed and announced plans for a new hospital, which included selling Ocean View's building and land. On September 14, 1977, ground was broken for a new $9 million facility at Eighty-second Avenue North. It would contain 124 beds and be a three-story, full service hospital. It opened in April 1978 as a Hospital Corporation of America facility and was later renamed Grand Strand Regional Medical Center.

Myrtle Beach experienced explosive growth in the second half of the 1950s, and civic leadership considered the need for professional city management. In a special election in December 1960, voters decided to move to a city manager, or commission, form of government. Several municipalities in South Carolina had adopted this form of government, the changes for which included increasing the mayor's term of office to four years and dropping two council seats. The remaining four seats would be divided equally between two-year terms and four-year terms the first year, and after that all terms would be for four years. Existing city department heads would come under the supervision of the city manager. Under the mayor/council style of governance, city council members were assigned certain departments to oversee. The public approved the referendum by a significant majority but on a low voter turnout; only 32 percent of eligible voters participated. A total of 357 voted for the change and 227 opposed it. The next step was to elect the new government, and a primary election was scheduled for March 21, 1961. Incumbent mayor William Cameron was renominated to serve the city's first four-year term as mayor. From a field of nine candidates for council, Dr. Holmes B. Springs Jr. and Dwight Lambe won nomination, but the other two council seats went to an April runoff, at which time Lloyd Macklen and James Tyson were elected. In order to facilitate a smooth transition to the city manager form of government, the previously elected city administration would remain in office until January 1962, at which time the newly elected mayor and four councilmen would begin their new terms. In October 1962 the city hired its first city manager, Edward Leroy Blackwell, whose job also began in January 1962.

The year 1962 also marked the reemergence of the Republican Party in Horry County. Its first county convention was held in March, with all officers being Myrtle Beach residents. The state convention followed later that month and was attended by about thirty people from Horry County. Horry County Republicans entered two candidates in the 1963 race for two council seats, but they were defeated by Democratic candidates Robert Grissom and Cliff Hammond. This was the party's first bid for local office in Horry County since Reconstruction in the late 1800s. The party did not

In 1962 the Republican Party ran candidates for Myrtle Beach City Council, its first bid for local office in Horry County since the Reconstruction era. The party lost that race but was organized enough in 1964 to have a Barry Goldwater campaign head-quarters at Thomas Cafeteria on Kings Highway. Mark Garner Collection, courtesy of Chapin Memorial Library

enter any candidates in municipal elections again until 1971. They would have their biggest wins in 1973, when Robert Hirsch was elected mayor and two Republican candidates for council went to a runoff with two Demo-cratic candidates but emerged victorious. The main issue? Growth and its effects on the city.

The 1960s and 1970s saw rapid growth and expansion of the economy, the built environment, and the population along with saturation of tourist accommodations and the resulting growing pains. On the political front, Mark Garner, publisher of the *Myrtle Beach Sun-News,* was elected mayor in 1965 and served two terms, through 1973. From 1940 to 1970 Myrtle Beach's population grew by more than 550 percent, from 1,597 to 9,035. As an indication of just how quickly the market became overbuilt, retail sales of building materials in Myrtle Beach between 1963 and 1979 increased 2,850 percent! No other category of retail sales came close to this percentage increase.[26] In addition, expansion did not slow down until the late 1970s, when an overbuilt real estate market and a depressed economy forced the city to examine the effects of this rapid growth on the quality of life and on the environment.

The municipal elections of November 1973 were a platform for this concern about the effects of growth and drew a record turnout. Republican candidate Robert Hirsch challenged incumbent Mark Garner on issues revolving around environmental protection, planning and orderly growth, and the effect of expansion on city services. During the campaign these issues also spurred the formation of a nonpartisan group called Citizens for Progress with Protection, which sought to gather information that would provide specific and rational guidelines for city growth.

In addition to candidates for mayor and councilmen, the ballot included a referendum on changing the present commission form of city government to a council-manager form. The day-to-day operations would change little under the proposed system. The main changes would include increasing the number of city councilmen from the present four to six and making the office of city manager mandatory. Prior to this, the position was created by virtue of a city ordinance that the council could repeal. It could not abolish the position under the council-manager form. Changes also involved giving the city manager responsibility for hiring and firing all department heads, which previously was city council's responsibility.

The city's 1979 comprehensive plan noted some of these concerns about growth, which included the dangers of storm damage on an overbuilt and dense oceanfront.[27] Until the mid-1950s, Ocean Boulevard had been dominated by residential development. That changed significantly after the 1963 National Flood Insurance program was implemented, resulting in the replacement of homes by motels and high-rise hotels. The prospect of flooding was greatly increased by the large number of asphalt and concrete parking lots and other manmade development for which little or no drainage considerations were planned. Beach erosion was related to the drainage problem. Most storm water runoff east of Highway 17 was channeled by storm drainage pipes into the ocean, resulting in sand being washed out to sea in areas around the drainage pipes. Associated with this were the high level of pollutants being carried out with the storm water and the runoff of chemicals and pesticides associated with golf course development.

Perhaps the greatest problem associated with water resources and development, the report said, was the gradual decline in the Black Bear aquifer system, the city's main water supply, as a result of the rapid increase of population in the Grand Strand area since the 1950s. Trees also were major environmental victims from the rapid development of Myrtle Beach. In response the city of Myrtle Beach adopted a landscaping ordinance that contained requirements to landscape areas of new development with natural vegetation and incorporate existing trees into the design. In terms of other natural resources, the study noted the deterioration of dunes and natural vegetation along the beaches. Secondary sand dunes had been destroyed by houses and motels, and many of the primary dunes had been bulldozed for parking lots, swimming pools, and outdoor modern recreation areas. Visual pollution was also a problem, with signs, billboards, overhead utility wires, drabness of unbroken concrete development, and haphazard and poorly planned parking areas and other structures.

By 1979 new development, with accompanying demand for public service and facilities, had achieved a momentum that threatened to outdistance the community's ability to guide and control it. "The benefits of growth are numerous," the 1979 Comprehensive Plan noted, "but so are the telltale signs of the consequences that have invariably followed such growth. The standards of living in Myrtle Beach are rising. However, the long-term quality of life is being endangered by mounting tax burdens, costly and unimaginative urban sprawl, an inadequate thoroughfare system, and an unbalanced seasonal economy." The challenge for the remaining two decades of the century would be how to manage growth, plan for future development, and find solutions for the growing pains of the previous decades.

From 1938 through December 1961 the mayor and all six city council members were elected at the same time.

Myrtle Beach City Government, 1938–1980

Mayor
Dr. Wilford L. Harrelson, March 1938–December 1939

City Council
Bunyon B. Benfield (Mayor Pro-Tem)
A. P. Shirley
Robert H. Cannon
J. Clarence Macklen
Robert M. Hussey Jr.
Dr. William A. Rourk

During this period the local government began paving streets and adding curbs and sidewalks. It also issued bonds to install a sewage display plant and sewer system that was tied to a 3 percent tax on the assessed property value within city limits. City government was organized, various municipal ordinances and regulations were passed, and land was purchased for a municipal airport. The first police department was organized, with J. F. Hamilton as the first police chief.

Mayor
Ben M. Graham, January 1940–December 1941

City Council
Albert A. Springs (Mayor Pro-Tem)
Dr. William A. Rourk
A. P. Shirley
T. Max Jordan
T. B. Suber
R. E. L. Brown

This government replaced the wooden boardwalk with a concrete one from the Pavilion to Ocean Plaza Hotel. It was financed by property owners and was to extend further north, but the project was interrupted by World War II. Much of this boardwalk was destroyed in 1954 by Hurricane Hazel. The government also secured property rights on either side of Ocean Boulevard from Sixteenth Street North to First Avenue in order to widen it to sixty feet. The thoroughfare was called Ocean Drive until 1940 and had no sidewalks, curbs, or gutters. In addition, a municipal airport was built, and the city council and mayor worked to convince the U.S. government to convert it into a gunnery and bombing base.

Mayor
Dr. Wilford L. Harrelson, January 1942–December 1943

City Council
Bunyon B. Benfield (Mayor Pro-Tem)
Dr. William A. Rourk
F. C. Cummins
Robert H. Cannon
Oliver C. Callaway
Sam P. Gardner

During this time the city government signed a deal with the U.S. War Department to take over the airport. The city's financial structure was improved.

Mayor
Oliver C. Callaway, January 1944–December 1945

City Council
John A. McLeod (Mayor Pro-Tem)
P. G. Winstead
George W. Trask
Dr. N. C. Ridgell
R. G. Green
Sam P. Gardner

The two administrations of Mayor Oliver C. Callaway (fourth from right), 1944–47, included (from left) P. G. Winstead, Dr. N. C. Ridgell, Jasper Ramsey (not an elected official), Sam Gardner, John A. McLeod, George W. Trask, and R. G. Green. Ruth Gore Collection, courtesy of Chapin Memorial Library

During Callaway's two administrations, the city government installed sixty-four street lights and three hundred parking meters and added ordinances such as a requirement to use garbage cans instead of cardboard boxes. Street delivery of mail began in 1947. Residents were required to mark their homes with house numbers, and the city began erecting street signs.

Mayor
Oliver C. Callaway, January 1946–December 1947

City Council
John A. McLeod (Mayor Pro-Tem)
P. G. Winstead
George W. Trask
Dr. N. C. Ridgell
R. G. Green
Sam P. Gardner

The U.S. government transferred the U.S. Air Force Base land back to the city of Myrtle Beach in October 1947, and the city implemented several ideas for making the airport and surrounding land self-supporting.

Mayor
Harry W. Tallevast, January 1948–December 1949

City Council
Ernest W. Williams (Mayor Pro-Tem)

Rae H. Farrington
Philip Gray
G. Wallace Harrelson
Dr. William A. Rourk/Dr. Waldo H. Jones (Rourk died while in office and
    was succeeded by Jones.)
H. Lloyd Macklen

Rae Farrington was the first woman elected to the Myrtle Beach City Council. The government ended its policy of political appointments for city
department managers and hired managers in police, water, sewer, and street
departments who remained in their jobs over several administrations, lending continuity to important municipal services. The two-lane Highway 501
opened.

Mayor
Jasper N. Ramsey, January 1950–December 1951

City Council
M. A. Bennett (Mayor Pro-Tem)
Furman W. Hardee
T. Max Jordan
Philip Gray
Sam P. Gardner
J. A. Porter

At this time the local government worked to attract the U.S. Air Force back
to Myrtle Beach and worked with the community to raise money for a local
hospital.

Mayor
Jasper N. Ramsey, January 1952–December 1953

City Council
Edward P. Broedel (Mayor Pro-Tem)
Sam P. Gardner
Philip Gray
Ernest W. Williams
H. Lloyd Macklen
James A. Porter

The election that put this administration in office was the first to divide the
city into two voting precincts, divided north and south by Ninth Avenue
North. It was also the first for which voters were not required to show poll
tax receipts in order to vote.

Mayor
Ernest W. Williams, January 1954–December 1955 (Williams died while in office and was succeeded by Cameron.)

City Council
William E. Cameron (Mayor Pro-Tem)
Mark C. Garner
James E. Allen
Gordon S. Beard Jr.
John S. Divine
L'Nora Misenheimer

This government oversaw the final negotiations with the U.S. Air Force regarding base reactivation and an agreement regarding municipal airport facilities. Evacuation, shelter, and rebuilding from Hurricane Hazel in October 1954 required strong teamwork between local, area, and state authorities, led by Mayor Williams. He died of a heart attack in August 1955.

Mayor
William E. Cameron, January 1956–December 1957

City Council
Mark C. Garner (Mayor Pro-Tem)
E. A. Anthony
Gordon S. Beard Jr.
Edward P. Broedel
F. Cliff Hammond
H. Lloyd Macklen

Mayor
William E. Cameron, January 1958–December 1959

City Council
Gordon S. Beard Jr. (Mayor Pro-Tem)
Mark C. Garner
E. A. Anthony
Arthur Vereen
Edward P. Broedel
Dan Winstead

This administration signed a contract with the South Carolina Aeronautics Commission and the U.S. government to relocate the city's civilian aviation operations from the air force base to Crescent Beach Airport. Kings Highway was widened from Eighth Avenue North to the base. Sidewalks were added on Ocean Boulevard to about Thirty-first Avenue North. Highway

501 was widened to four lanes. Ocean View Memorial Hospital opened in July 1958. A third voting precinct was added in 1958.

Mayor
William E. Cameron, January 1960–December 1961
City Council
Dwight Lambe (Mayor Pro-Tem)
Arthur Vereen
Robert M. Grissom
James Tyson
George Inabinet
H. Lloyd Macklen

In December 1960 voters approved a referendum to move to a commission-mayor form of government, which meant increasing the mayor's term of office to four years; eliminating two council seats, for a total of four; and hiring a city manager. For the first term the four seats would be divided into two two-year terms and two four-year terms; thereafter four-year terms would be served. A primary was held in March 1961, at which time Cameron was renominated for mayor, and Dr. Holmes Springs Jr., Dwight Lambe, Lloyd Macklen, and James Tyson won nomination for the four council seats. They would not take office until January 1962, and the previous administration (see above) would continue to serve until that time. Ed Blackwell was hired as the first city manager.

Mayor
William E. Cameron, January 1962–December 1965
City Council
Dr. Holmes Springs Jr. (Mayor Pro-Tem, 1962–63), January 1962–
    December 1965
James Tyson, January 1962–December 1965
Dwight Lambe, January 1962–December 1963
H. Lloyd Macklen, January 1962–December 1963
(A midterm election was held in November 1963 for two council seats held by Lambe and Macklen.)
Robert M. Grissom (Mayor Pro-Tem, 1964–65), January 1964–
    December 1967
F. Cliff Hammond, January 1964–December 1967 (Hammond resigned
    in December 1965 due to a criminal conviction.)

Two Republicans participated in the election for this council but were defeated. It was the Republican Party's first bid for local office in Horry County since Reconstruction in the late 1800s.

Mayor
Mark C. Garner, January 1966–December 1969

City Council
John Singleton, January 1966–December 1969
William J. Southerland Jr., January 1966–December 1969 (Southerland resigned midterm due to relocation of his job.)
Warren S. Cromley, January 1966–December 1967 (Cromley was elected to fill the remainder of Hammond's term.)
(A midterm election was held in November 1967 for two council seats held by Grissom and Cromley and the unexpired seat of Southerland.)
E. Allison Farlow (Southerland's unexpired seat), January 1968–December 1969
Warren S. Cromley, January 1968–December 1971
Robert M. Grissom, January 1968–December 1971

Under this administration the Myrtle Beach Convention Center and U.S. Highway17-Bypass were built.

Mayor
Mark C. Garner, January 1970–December 1973

City Council
John Singleton, January 1970–December 1973
Ned Donkle, January 1970–December 1973
(A midterm election was held in November 1971 for two council seats held by Grissom and Cromley.)
Robert M. Grissom, January 1972–June 1975 (Grissom resigned in 1973 to become Horry County treasurer and was succeeded by Charlie Cook.)
E. Allison Farlow, January 1972–June 1975

The November 1973 election for mayor and two council seats also included a referendum on moving to a council–city manager type of government. The principal changes from the previous commission-mayor government are that (1) the position of city manager could be eliminated only by a referendum of voters, not by the council and mayor; (2) city department heads would report to the city manager, not to individual councilpersons; and (3) two additional council seats would be added, for a total of six. This would also change expiration of terms.

The first African American to run for city council, Reverend Leroy Weathers, pastor of Mount Zion AME Church, was on this ballot. He lost. James Futrell would be the first elected African American city councilman, serving from 1982 to 1991.

Mayor
Robert Hirsch, January 1974–December 1977

City Council
Fred Holland, January 1974–June 1977
Arthur Vereen, January 1974–June 1977
(A special election was held in March 1975 to elect two new councilpersons;
*   this had been delayed one year by lawsuits.)*
George J. Bishop, March 1975–June 1977
Dr. Holmes B. Springs Jr., March 1975–June 1975
(A midterm election was held in May 1975 for three council seats held
*   by Springs, Cook, and Farlow.)*
E. Allison Farlow, May 1975–December 1979
Dr. Holmes Springs Jr., May 1975–December 1979
Erick Ficken, May 1975–December 1979

During this administration the Republican Party won the mayoral seat and
two council seats.

Mayor
Erick B. Ficken, January 1978–December 1981

City Council
Peter Pearce, January 1978–December 1981
Marjorie Stonebrook, January 1978–December 1981
Ted Collins, January 1978–December 1981
(A special election was held in April 1978 to fill vacancies created by
*   the death of Councilman Farlow and a successful bid for mayor*
*   by Councilman Ficken.)*
Wilson Cain, April 1978–December 1979
Gordon Beard Jr., April 1978–December 1979
(A midterm election was held in November 1979 for council seats held by
Beard, Cain, and Springs.)
Gordon Beard Jr., January 1980–December 1983 *(Beard died December 14,*
*   1981, and a special election was held March 9, 1982, to fill the remainder*
*   of his term.)*
Wilson Cain, January 1980–December 1983
E. A. Thomas, January 1980–December 1983

A new Myrtle Beach hospital, owned by Hospital Corporation of America,
opened in April 1978, replacing Ocean View Memorial Hospital. Four new
voting precincts were added in 1979.

Eleven

Grand Strand Leisure

*F*eeling the sand between your toes, the warm sun on your skin, and the spray from the crashing waves on your face are some of the simplest forms of pleasure at the beach. However, the Grand Strand has offered many other simple—and not so simple—pleasures to those who have lingered on her shore over the past generations. Before Myrtle Beach was a travel destination and the beach attracted sunbathers and surfers, it was a hunting and fishing paradise. Fishing is still prevalent, but wild game and fowl hunting has moved much further inland due to land development.

Duck hunting was a grand passion of the people who hunted for sport and those who hunted to put food on the table. The freshwater lakes in the area just north of Myrtle Beach are engulfed in private developments now, but in the 1920s they were known as the "duck ponds," according to Franklin G. Burroughs. They included

Long Pond, located on the Meher Spiritual Center property and known
    for the cattails along its banks
Mud Hole Pond, where there were not many ducks but an alligator
    lived
Round Pond, the main lake for hunting ducks in the past
Little Round Pond, later renamed Arcadian Lake and along which
    a house was built during World War II for the U.S. Coast Guard
    unit that patrolled the coast
Forked Pond, later renamed Lake Arrowhead
Sand Hill Pond, which had a resident alligator.[1]

Burroughs recalled three possible routes to the lakes area, the most popular being Little River Road, which was little more than a sandy trail at the time. It left Myrtle Beach near the commissary, running somewhat parallel to what is now U.S. Highway 17, and led to the settlement of Little River. Today a portion of this road remains and is called Old Little River Road. Hunters would turn off Little River Road near the Chestnut family farm (in the vicinity of present-day Restaurant Row) to Myrtle Beach Farms property and then follow a road to a small clearing near Round Pond. This was where most of the hunting parties that came down to the ponds would stay. Myrtle Beach native Horry Benton, who worked for the Ocean Forest Country Club and Golf Course in the late 1920s as a bellhop and porter, remembered driving club guests to the lakes. He said, "Most of the people I hauled were guests going up to the lakes duck hunting before daylight. And carrying them home of the evening."[2] Another approach to the ponds was by the beach, but only at low tide. It was also possible to reach the ponds by going out by the Conway Road to Wampee and then cutting through the sandy woods to the pond area. Today that route would require crossing the Intracoastal Waterway, but it was not in place at that time.

Hunters were limited to a catch of twenty-five ducks, and no regulations regarding baiting existed, according to Burroughs. The kinds of ducks they saw included scaup (better known as bullneck, black head, or blue bill). Black heads were numerous, as were ruddy ducks, or butterballs, and Blue Petes, or coots.

Briarcliffe Acres, a six-hundred-acre stretch of land a few miles north of Myrtle Beach, is in the vicinity of the lakes. Before it was developed in the late 1940s, Briarcliffe Acres was a habitat for numerous forms of wildlife, such as birds, bears, deer, foxes, possums, rabbits, squirrels, and snakes, including black snakes, copperheads, and rattlesnakes. Alligators, ducks, fish, herons, and water moccasins lived in the lakes and marsh area. The Meher Spiritual Center, which borders Briarcliffe Acres on the south, is a state wildlife preserve. Recounting the bounty of nature on the center property when he first saw it about 1944, Darwin Shaw wrote, "In these early days . . . The lake was teeming with rather large fish. Seabirds would come to the lake to catch their meals. . . . Large alligators also lived in the lake. . . . There was a large flock of wild turkeys that inhabited the property south of the main road through the Center. Wild pigs could be seen in the area now known as Briarcliffe."[3]

Annie Chestnut Squires recalled growing up in the Surfside Beach area south of Myrtle Beach in the 1920s and 1930s:

> This place was an unspoiled wilderness. Deer were plentiful. My dad could go out with one of his hound dogs and in a short time return with a deer, or he and my brothers could go out in the afternoon

and bag a couple dozen quail or doves. Whatever our appetite called for. In the fall I've followed my dad up or down to the lakes nestled behind the sand dunes, and lying flat on my belly, look over the top and see hundreds of wild ducks swimming around unaware of danger. We could carry as many as we needed home.

Uncle Sabe Rutledge, who lived in what was called Freewoods, ran the fishery, which was located where the pier now stands. I would ride in the boat sometimes when the crew went out to make a haul. The crew used large oars to paddle the boat in a semi-circle and the net was laid out as they made the run. People on the beach would get both ends of the net and drag it in on to the beach. It was so exciting to me to explore the oddities and strange things that came in with the fish.

People came with wagons, boxes and barrels to buy fish to salt down, and many campfires were built to fry fresh fish and roast sweet potatoes in hot sand close to the fire. The aroma would tantalize you real fast. Down at what is now Garden City beach, we would gather oysters and clams (that never heard of pollution) and head home with anticipation at the thought of either delicious golden fried oysters, bubbly hot oyster stew, or clam chowder.

In those days we didn't see rods and reels like you do now, so the cane pole was the thing to use. One day in particular, some ladies and children, including myself, had cane poles with long lines. We waded out as far as we could go and cast our lines out. We must have been casting out into a school of fish because immediately we would have a fish on our line. We filled our buckets, but were exhausted walking in and out of the water.

Uncle Benny Vereen from Murrells Inlet used to come with his fox hounds on beautiful moonlit nights and we would stand outside in the cool night air and listen to the chorus of hounds, hot on the chase after a fox. Foxes were plentiful, bobcats, otters, skunks, fox squirrels, opossums, coons and something we had to be on the look-out for, rattlesnakes.[4]

Anyone living in Myrtle Beach in the 1920s and 1930s knew Joe Sarkis's fishery near Withers Swash. "When the mullet were running, he and a bevy of hired help seined the bounty from the sea," remembered Annette E. Reesor. Mary Canty, one of the first students in Myrtle Beach Colored School, which opened about 1932, remembered when the older students took a field trip to the fishery: "Professor Stackhouse would take us from here [the school] all the way down to the beach and we would walk to 29th

Avenue South to a fishery for our field day. They would cook fish and we would fish and we would walk back." Mary Sarkis Hobeika, Joe Sarkis's daughter, said that her father "came to Myrtle Beach and went in the fishing business. We would come every summer and stay until November. He had about fifty Negroes working with him to haul in the nets. We lived in a small beach shack at the fishery. Daddy used to catch fish by the hundreds of barrels. They don't catch fish like that anymore. When he caught those big hauls of fish, people would come from all over to buy salt fish for the winter."[5]

C. Burgin Berry remembered the seine fishing north of Myrtle Beach in the Crescent Beach area: "When Labor Day came, the beach, I always said it dropped dead on Labor Day, there was no one here. But then the fishermen came in. They would set up a net, or they would set up a fishery, and there were probably a dozen on the Grand Strand here. Up and down the Grand Strand. They had nets that were probably about 1,400 feet long. And they'd put them on a boat, you know the fish migrate south in the fall, and they would catch a school of fish going south and they'd put that net out in front of them and swing it in and pull them ashore. Of course, a good haul would bring in twenty thousand pounds or more sometimes. I've seen them so loaded they couldn't get the net to the hill [the sand dune]. You'd have to take a smaller net and go inside and scoop out some of them until they could get to the hill." The fisheries were prevalent in the 1950s and 1960s, Berry added. "There were some up until about ten or twelve years ago, but I think they're all gone now."[6] Part of the reason for the decline in seine fishing was the increase in recreational fishing as promoted by the Myrtle Beach Chamber of Commerce through the annual Fishing Rodeo, which started in 1953. By 1961 an effort to curb "netting" by commercial fishermen was under way because it depleted the supply of fish for tourists or diverted remaining fish into deep water. Approximately twelve commercial fisheries operated on the Grand Strand in 1961.[7]

In 1939 pier fishing became so popular that workers were busy extending the reach of two existing piers at Myrtle Beach. The 530-foot-long Second Avenue pier, built in 1936, was owned by the Coastal Corporation and managed by St. Julien Springs. Its length was nearly doubled to 1,034 feet in 1939. The Ocean Plaza Pier was built in 1922 and owned by Sam Gardner, who also owned Ocean Plaza Hotel, Myrtle Beach Inn, and Ocean Beach Hotel. He almost tripled its length to 650 feet. By 1958 pier fishing was a million-dollar industry on the Grand Strand with eleven piers that stayed busy from May to late November. Even in 1954 after Hurricane Hazel knocked out all of the piers, most were rebuilt quickly. In addition to pier fishing, many people remember crabbing and catching shrimp in the

The first recreational fishing in South Carolina is believed to have started in the Little River area north of Myrtle Beach in the 1920s. This photograph was taken at Little River in the mid-1960s. Mark Garner Collection, courtesy of Chapin Memorial Library

swashes. During the summers deep-sea fishing was popular from charter boats, many of which were based in Little River.

The first offshore recreational fishing in South Carolina is believed to have started in the Little River area in the 1920s when local men began taking people fishing for a fee, first in row boats and then in power boats. One of the earliest was Bob High, who began taking people in the *Eugenia* to the blackfish banks in 1923.[8] As more people came to the area and demand increased, better boats were added to the fleets. Besides taking fishing parties out, boat owners found a market for renting rowboats to fishermen, vacationers, and even the U.S. Army Corps of Engineers when they were surveying the proposed Intracoastal Waterway in the late 1920s. World War II impeded the business as no boats were at that time allowed to take parties offshore.

By the mid-1950s the recreational fishing industry was back in force, and it was to experience its peak between 1955 and 1975. Changes that affected the industry included the passage of the Merchant Marine Act of

1956, which created safety requirements on vessels carrying more than six people. Many companies began taking smaller parties to troll for game fish in the open sea. While many of the boats used up until this time were war surplus or otherwise recycled vessels, boats that were designed and built especially for charter and party work were coming on the market. In the late 1960s Frank Juel introduced half-day fishing trips to inshore blackfish banks. Because of the speed of his boat, it could leave the dock and put in at a fishing spot within an hour, allowing satisfactory time for fishing for most people. Gradually half-day trips came to dominate the blackfish party business. Prior to World War II all the ocean fishing took place on the blackfish banks five to twenty-five miles offshore. This expanded in the early 1950s to overnight trips to the snapper/grouper banks fifty or more miles offshore. Today trolling for pelagic fish can occur from the breaking waves for Spanish mackerel to the outer shelf for marlin, sailfish, and yellow fin tuna. In between the breakers and the shelf, the catch may include king mackerel, dolphinfish, bonitos, or bluefish. River fishing in the fall nets spot, whitefish, and croakers. Weakfish, red drums, and flounder are prevalent all year but especially in the summer and fall.[9]

Racing, whether by horses and harnesses, stock cars, or motorcycles, has been an almost continuous part of the Myrtle Beach sport scene since

Washington Park Race Track, located at Twenty-first Avenue N. and Oak Street, was open from 1938 to 1947. In 1939 fifty horses from five states were stabled at the track. Myrtle Beach Postcard Collection, courtesy of Chapin Memorial Library

1938. The brothers Paul and Parrot Hardy from Mullins, South Carolina, began the tradition when they leased acreage at Twenty-first Avenue North and Oak Street from Myrtle Beach Farms in 1938 and built Washington Park Race Track. Previewing it in May to sportsmen and aficionados of harness racing from six states, the Hardy brothers and the Myrtle Beach Racing Association met with an excellent reception. The forty-thousand-dollar race track contained a steel grandstand that held fifty-two hundred people and was designed to allow unobstructed views of the race, from the start line to the home stretch, as well as of the ocean. A white, vertical board fence surrounded the park, and a white wooden rail outlined the one-half-mile oval track.

On opening day, June 3, 1938, about five thousand tourists, residents, and guests, including South Carolina governor Olin Johnston, Charleston mayor Burnet Maybank, and Myrtle Beach mayor Dr. Wilford Harrelson, cheered on the three races of three heats each. Races were held on Wednesday and Saturday afternoons throughout the summer season. Although harness racing had been in decline since 1900, it enjoyed a comeback in the late 1930s and early 1940s after Roosevelt Raceway in New York introduced harness racing under the lights with pari-mutuel betting. The Hardys also opened the tracks in November 1938 with a fair and races in an attempt to attract tourists in the off-season. The South Carolina Coastal Exposition and Races, held November 1–5, 1938, advertised show girls, bands, special acts, and harness racing. By May 11, 1939, fifty horses from five states were stabled at the track. The state's aversion to gambling, however, spelled the end for harness racing even though track owners, supported by the city of Myrtle Beach, tried what they hoped would be more acceptable forms of betting. The track lasted until 1947, when South Carolina associate supreme court justice G. Dewey Oxner ruled against the form of betting generally referred to as "equal mutual guessing."[10]

Washington Park Race Track was reincarnated in March 1951 as Myrtle Beach Raceway with three harness races, the first since 1947. The following February, Edward Canne, who leased the site from Myrtle Beach Farms, announced that he intended to turn Myrtle Beach into a key harness-horse training center. He held an exhibition and races on February 20, 1952. Plans called for weekly programs of three events with five horses each. No betting was allowed, but the rebirth did not last long.

By the following year, some of the property from the race track was being used as a golf driving range, lit for nighttime play and operated by Lloyd Chinnes. From May 1955 through 1957 National Association of Stock Car Auto Racing (NASCAR)–sanctioned stock car races were held at the site, which was renamed Coastal Speedway. James Earl Hardie was the promoter and planned races for each Saturday night during the season. However, in May 1956 motor court and property owners went before the Myrtle Beach City Council to protest the loud noises caused by auto races. Hardie admitted that the previous Saturday night's races had started rather late and lasted until after 11:15 P.M., leading council members to rule unanimously that races or trial runs could not start before 6:00 P.M. or run after 11:00 P.M.[11]

By 1958 racing moved away from Kings Highway to a new track five miles west of Myrtle Beach on U.S. Highway 501. The track opened on May 24, 1958, with a one-half-mile, high-speed clay track designed to meet NASCAR standards. The Racing Association of Myrtle Beach, Inc., or RAMBI, was led by Howard Holmes, Dwight Lambe, Don Easterling, Robert L. Bellamy, James Tyson, V. A. Taunt, J. E. Cooney, M. H. Smith, and Bill Hedgepath. The organization offered stock certificates to the public, and within a week more than 230 people joined RAMBI. In a gesture to the past history of horse racing, RAMBI opened the 1959 Sun Fun Festival with six turf events featuring thoroughbred horses and opened the 1960 season with motorcycle races. In 1968 the track was sold to Nick Lucas, who renamed it Myrtle Beach Speedway. In 1978 he replaced the dirt track with asphalt, and in 1987 Billy Hardee became a co-owner. Over the years fans of stock car racing have witnessed legendary racers Richard Petty, David Pearson, Donny and Bobby Allison, Ned Jarrett, Ralph Earnhardt, and Dale Earnhardt Sr. and Jr. at the Myrtle Beach Speedway track.

While amateur athletics for children, teens, and adults were prevalent in Myrtle Beach, as in most other communities, National League baseball was not. However, from 1949 to 1953 the farm club of the Boston Braves organization held its spring training in Myrtle Beach on the former air force base, which the United States government had returned to the city of Myrtle Beach in 1948.[12] In 1950 nine to ten ball clubs came to Myrtle Beach in their off-season to train, along with four hundred players, scouts, instructors, and officials, paying the Airport Commission thirty-five hundred dollars for the use of the premises and facilities. The Braves built four baseball fields in the shape of a cross at the end of a runway, the old base hospital housed the athletes, and the former lecture and movie hall was converted to a cafeteria. Not only was their presence a source of income for the city, but it also brought considerable publicity for Myrtle Beach. The *Myrtle Beach News* appropriately asserted that "with sports writers here during the training period and a special publicity program arranged, some ten or more states were covered in news releases and radio broadcasts and there is no way to estimate at this time the value received from the Boston Braves' minor league teams training and playing exhibition games here."[13] Contracts were not pursued after 1953 as the United States Air Force had already announced that it would be returning to open a base in Myrtle Beach.

The game of golf was alive and well in the Southeast by 1926 when John T. Woodside built the Ocean Forest Country Club and Golf Course in Myrtle Beach. One of South Carolina's oldest golf clubs is the Camden Country Club, started in 1903. Pinehurst in North Carolina was built even earlier, in 1898. By 1915 more than forty-five courses were being advertised by Seaboard Air Line Railway as "Winter Golf in Dixie." The courses were located along its railroad route through Virginia, North Carolina, South Carolina, Georgia, Alabama, and Florida.[14] Woodside wanted his Myrtle Beach golf club to stand out and hired Robert White, the first president (1916–19) of the Professional Golfers' Association, to come to Myrtle Beach in 1926 to design the twenty-seven-hole course and serve as its first manager. Casper Benton of Myrtle Beach managed the construction of the course, after spending three months training on golf courses in Long Island, New York. By December 1927 construction of the one-hundred-thousand-dollar clubhouse, designed by R. O. Brannon of Lynchburg, Virginia, and built by Morris McKoy Building Company of Greenville, South Carolina, was under way. In the early 1940s when golf was at a low ebb, a portion of the original golf course was sold for land development, but by 1961 the course had eighteen holes.[15]

Myrtle Beach's second golf course opened in October 1949. Designed by Robert Trent Jones on 270 acres of land donated by Myrtle Beach Farms (in exchange for five thousand dollars in club stock), the Dunes Golf Club was the brainchild of George W. "Buster" Bryan, his brother James Bryan Jr., the newspaper publisher William A. Kimbel, and the hotelier Joe Ivey. Jimmy D'Angelo, who would become the head golf pro of the Dunes, came to Myrtle Beach first as a winter golf professional at the Ocean Forest Country Club in November 1937 and again in January 1939. He returned in May 1948 to sell stock in the Dunes and never left. In 1954, seeking a way to get publicity for the club, D'Angelo organized a testimonial dinner for Robert Trent Jones and invited golf writers who were on their way to the Masters Tournament in Augusta, Georgia. The Golf Writers Annual Myrtle Beach Tournament became an annual event, attracting up to one hundred journalists.

The year 1954 was a landmark one for Myrtle Beach golf in another way. Henry Luce, publisher of *Time* magazine, sent a group of sixty-seven executives to Pine Lakes by train that year to plan a new sports weekly, which became *Sports Illustrated.*[16] The Dunes also hosted the U.S. Golf Association Women's Open Championship in 1962. By 1980 the Grand Strand had thirty-six golf courses, the majority of which were built in the previous decade.[17] What caused the explosion of golf courses? The attention received from the golf writers and the *Sports Illustrated* birth in 1954 helped. Another key event, however, was the development of the golf package in 1966, which linked golfing and motels, with the objective of attracting golfers to Myrtle Beach during the winter months. Buster Bryan, the king-pin behind the Dunes Country Club, also owned Caravelle Motel on North Ocean Boulevard, and he introduced the first golf package, which included a week at a motel, breakfast, and golf for one price. He brought seven motels into the early promotion and called it Golf-O-Tel. Myrtle Beach Golf Holiday, a similar package involving eight golf courses and ten hotels, was formed in 1967 by Cecil Brandon, an advertising executive. The two organizations merged in 1969 after Bryan's death. Another key associate in the development of this promotion was Clay Brittain. By the late 1970s golf contributed more than $340 million a year to the Grand Strand economy and received the principal credit for extending Myrtle Beach's season into the winter months on a regular basis.[18]

In the name of tourism, sport evolved from individual pastime and, in the case of fishing and hunting, economic necessity to big business on the Grand Strand as local business owners sought ways to diversify, add new attractions, and extend the tourist season. Some ideas had to morph to a variation, adjusting to consumer demands and limitations imposed by development. Seine fishing gave way to deep-sea and pier fishing, harness racing was replaced by stock car racing, and hunting simply had to move to other areas as the town grew and coastal development became denser. Besides the beach and the ocean, golfing has had the greatest impact on the tourist economy in the Myrtle Beach area. Farmland and undeveloped property were transformed into beautifully landscaped magnets for golfers around the country and the world who have made the winter months in Myrtle Beach part of "the season."

Twelve

Hurricane Hazel and Its Transformation of the Grand Strand

*H*urricane Hazel slammed into the upper South Carolina coast on the morning of October 15, 1954, a landmark event in the development of Myrtle Beach and the Grand Strand. The destructive storm virtually erased the oceanfront of this quiet summer colony, as well as adjacent beach communities to the north and south of Myrtle Beach. Some contend that Hazel's devastation cleared the way for building the national resort destination that exists today, but Myrtle Beach's transformation was well under way before Hazel. The hurricane only accelerated the process, just as she accelerated up from the Caribbean, along the Atlantic seaboard, and into Horry County history.

Prior to Hazel, the building blocks of a dynamic tourism industry were already in place. Horry County business leaders had worked to bring visitors to the beach since the turn of the century, but this effort was implemented in a more strategic manner with the reorganization and rechartering of the chamber of commerce in 1947.[1] At about the same time, the state of South Carolina was actively working to attract more out-of-state visitors. In a 1951 manual the South Carolina State Chamber of Commerce contended that South Carolina was not getting its share of the $9 billion spent annually across the United States by tourists, travelers, and vacationers. The state earned an estimated $50 million in tourist trade in 1951. Only two states, North Dakota and Rhode Island, realized less from the tourism industry than did South Carolina that year.[2]

On the local level, citizens also were engaged in a drive for increased tourism, as noted in an editorial in the October 13, 1954, *Myrtle Beach News:*

"In the July 29 edition of the *News*, we suggested adoption of 'Miracle Miles' as a descriptive term for the grand sweep of modern hotels, businesses and residential development along Highway 17 through the heart of Myrtle Beach. When people around the nation say, 'What are these Miracle Miles?' we may proudly tell the story of the organization and development which has transformed pine forests and oak ridges into a nationally known resort city in the few short years of its young life." Ironically the editorial appeared two days before Hurricane Hazel blew in.

The Storm Approached

As the residents of Myrtle Beach and adjacent beach towns went to bed Thursday evening, October 14, 1954, few suspected that their world was about to change dramatically overnight. The Horry County coast of South Carolina was about to be broadsided by the year's eighth hurricane, Hazel, a Category 4 storm packing winds of up to 130 miles per hour. None forgot the next eighteen hours or the visual and economic long-term impact.[3]

On October 5 Hazel was identified as a hurricane just east of Grenada in the Caribbean Sea with winds clocked at 95 miles per hour. The small island of Curaçao was the first to feel Hazel's punch. By October 8 at 5:00 P.M. a weather advisory from the San Juan, Puerto Rico, weather bureau reported that Hurricane Hazel was pushing winds up to 125 miles per hour ranging over a 100-mile radius around the center. Then about 345 miles due south of Port au Prince, Haiti, and 1,000 miles southeast of Florida, Hazel faced no immediate land areas. She appeared to be moving westward. Unexpectedly swinging north on October 12, Hazel slammed the island of Haiti in the early morning hours, leveling whole towns and leaving up to one thousand persons dead. The next day the hurricane continued northward through the Windward Passage between Haiti and Cuba into the Atlantic and on her way to the Carolina coastline.

Hurricane Hazel came as a surprise to residents of South Carolina, not because they did not know that the storm was in the Atlantic but because meteorologists predicted that it would pass land and stay out at sea. Hazel was also moving very fast. The National Hurricane Center, based in Miami, Florida, issued storm warnings about the storm at 11:00 A.M. on October 14 for the area between Charleston and the Virginia capes, noting that the storm was expected to stay offshore while moving northward. Ashby Ward, who worked as an announcer at Myrtle Beach's WMYB Radio, wrote that he broadcast hurricane advisories as they cleared the teletype and that they consistently indicated that Myrtle Beach would be touched by winds of only thirty or forty miles per hour.[4] In addition, Horry County coastal residents thought that hurricanes rarely struck the area because of the curved nature of the coastline, which is a fallacy, according to Horry County emergency management director Randall Webster. At that time the last major (Category 3 or higher) hurricane to hit the Grand Strand had done so in 1906, almost fifty years previous. It was about to be the Grand Strand's turn again.

Thursday, October 14, was a lovely fall day even though the weather had been abysmally hot and dry. In fact, since South Carolina had been in a drought situation for months, the thought of an offshore hurricane kicking up some rain was welcome news. The tourist season had ended, and the community of about four thousand persons was busy with civic, school, and neighborhood activities, unaware of what was lurking not far from their shore. Ocean Drive police chief Merlin Bellamy and his wife, Joyce, were grilling steaks for Polly Lowman and her husband that evening when he got a call from Jack Cummings, chief meteorologist in Charleston, alerting Bellamy to the possibility that Hazel might hit north of Charleston. "I said I wasn't even aware there was a hurricane anywhere near. I knew there was one down in the Caribbean. I couldn't envision how this thing had fast-forwarded, we'll say, and moved so fast," Bellamy recalled.[5]

Hazel had sped up. It may have taken her nine days to get to the Carolina coast, but she was moving twenty-five to thirty miles per hour by early October 14 and fifty miles per hour when she first struck land. The average hurricane travels ten to fifteen miles per hour. Confusion over the path of the storm, which was erratic to begin with, and the chain of communication regarding weather advisories delayed some of the crisis planning in Myrtle Beach.

Around 7:30 P.M. on October 14 the heavy rain started. Most people went to bed that evening not worried about a possible hurricane. "It was raining and we knew there was a storm brewing out there, but nobody seemed to call it a hurricane. Or maybe they did. We didn't have a phone," recalled Dagmar "Wickie" Moore, who with her husband, Donald, and their two children were living in Windy Hill. They owned a large house on the beachfront that was divided into rental apartments, and they were living in the garage apartment behind the house.[6]

The 8:00 P.M. advisory from Miami indicated that the storm had veered slightly to a north-northwesterly course, meaning that Myrtle Beach could expect higher winds of up to fifty miles per hour. WMYB Radio decided to stay on the air until 11:15 P.M. in order to report the advisory before sign-off. Then Hazel made another unexpected maneuver. Pulled by a low pressure area over the mountains of Tennessee, she turned west ninety degrees and headed directly for the upper South Carolina coast. Ward wrote that around 10:00 P.M., while he was waiting for the 11:00 P.M. bulletin to be sent, Walt Tabler, the station's chief engineer, burst into the control room and told him, "Harry, that thing's turned this way. The weather bureau called the mayor and told him to alert the rescue groups. He's on the phone and wants to talk to you now." After leaving to take the call, Harry came back into the room and reported, "The bureau says Hazel will hit land just north of us. Mayor Williams wants us to remain on the air until 1 A.M. in order to warn people."[7] The station would end up staying on the air through the night, until mechanical difficulties abruptly ended transmission around 9:00 A.M. Chief Merlin Bellamy got a similar call from the Charleston Weather Bureau office about 10:00 P.M. He was told that if Hazel continued her current course, the storm would produce tides in the Ocean Drive area higher than twelve feet. Immediate evacuation was advised.

Jane E. Perry, Red Cross assistant field director from Shaw Air Force Base, arrived in Myrtle Beach about 1:00 A.M. Red Cross representatives from Atlanta soon followed. Perry worked closely with the Horry County Red Cross chapter setting up shelters at the grammar school and the high school, the city hall, First Baptist Church, Ocean Forest Hotel, and the American Legion Hut. Members of the Myrtle Beach Pilot Club assisted them, making hundreds of sandwiches and gallons of coffee for the sheltered families and the police and military on duty. A first aid station was established at the high school. After the storm passed, the Red Cross would set up a headquarters for disaster relief and for a communications base at Wilma's Cafeteria.

Hoyt Bellamy, who was a lieutenant with the Myrtle Beach Police Department, was one of the police officers patrolling Ocean Boulevard with his sirens blasting and lights flashing, waking up everybody he could find on the first and second rows to get them away from the ocean. If Bellamy and his partner saw a parked car at a property, they banged on the house door to see if anyone was on the premises.[8]

By 2:00 A.M. on October 15 the winds were getting stronger and Mayor Williams received a call from the weather station confirming that the storm was headed directly toward Myrtle Beach. Even if Myrtle Beach leaders had erred on the side of caution, they jumped into action when the storm's course appeared inevitable. By 3:00 A.M. the mayor had established disaster headquarters at the city hall and gathered his team, which included representatives of the police department, the Horry County sheriff's department, the Myrtle Beach Civil Defense Council, the Civil Air Patrol, the Red Cross, and Myrtle Beach Air Force Base. The African American community was sheltered at the new Carver Elementary School. Water storage tanks were filled, and city maintenance workers and utility crews were standing by, as was the fire department. Other beach communities were alerted as well.

One of the places where people gathered was Kozy Korner on East Broadway. Tony and Angie Thompson leased the restaurant for many years. Their son Dino, who was eight years old at the time, recalled, "They didn't start evacuating . . . until about 2 in the morning. That's when I remember the bullhorns, cop cars, sirens. Then it got spooky." About thirty-five people joined Dino, his parents, and his grandmother at the Kozy Korner, most of them downtown merchants and their families. They taped up the windows of the restaurant. Dino and several others watched the storm and played cards from the street level until the wind threw a galvanized garbage can through their front window. Then everybody went downstairs.[9]

The men of the 727th Air Craft and Warning Squadron of the 507th Tactical Control Group had just recently been transferred from Shaw Air Force Base to Myrtle Beach Air Force Base. At 3:00 A.M. they closed operations at the base to help the civilian population of the area. They supplied a portable power unit to hook up to the Myrtle Beach radio system. They also repaired the police radio antenna and furnished power to the police radio system and the local telephone exchange system.[10]

Billy Roberts, a lifelong Myrtle Beach resident, was awakened in the early morning hours of October 15 by the sound of generators on trucks parked next to the radio station across from his home at the corner of Twenty-eighth Avenue North and Oak Street. "We turned the radio on and found out that a hurricane was imminent. And my mother and I rode around in our 1952 Chevrolet all during the hurricane taking photographs. I couldn't get directly on the Boulevard because it was too dangerous in the first place, and of course, if the police found anybody on the Boulevard, they chased them off of there," Roberts recalled.[11]

Meanwhile in Ocean Drive and on the northern beaches Chief Bellamy pulled together a task force with the fire chief, the volunteer fire department, and other citizen volunteers. He marked off a grid on a map of the Ocean Drive area and assigned two people to each zone to knock on every door to warn people. They also canvassed the communities around them. Donald and Wickie Moore in Windy Hill remember the sound of a car horn waking them up about 3:00 A.M., and it was Chief Bellamy. "He leaned out of the car and yelled 'Get out! The storm's comin' in!' So we went out without anything," the Moores recalled. The family headed for Briarcliffe Acres, where Donald's mother lived. Then Donald, a seventh-grade teacher in Myrtle Beach, went back to the Windy Hill house, thinking that he would have to get ready for work later that morning.[12]

At 4:00 A.M. on October 15, Radio Station WMYB reported that the Weather Bureau at Charleston said the hurricane had made a ninety-degree turn, its winds were up to 135 miles per hour, and it would hit the Myrtle

Beach area within the next five to six hours. Marcus Smith and his wife, who was expecting their first child in a matter of weeks, were awakened by the continuous ringing of their door bell. Their friend Allen Ericson told them that the hurricane had turned toward the coast. They loaded the car and headed for Smith's parents' home in Conway. "The two-lane road [Highway 501] with water-filled gorges on each side was frightening. Gale force winds rocked the car and sheets of heavy rain blasted the windshield," he remembered.[13]

The Hurricane Hit

Chief Bellamy recalled that by about 4:00 A.M. Hurricane Hazel was "on" in his area. He recalled, "The wind was so strong coming out of the east and the rain was just pouring. It was just about at an angle like this [holding hand out flat]. . . . The water came up to about 18.5 feet deep on Ocean Boulevard. Water was over the traffic light [main intersection in Ocean Drive at Ocean Boulevard]. We saw waves offshore that looked like they might have been fifty to sixty feet high and in those waves you could see portions of buildings."[14]

Also in Ocean Drive, Eatofel Vereen Thompson Arehart went to bed Thursday night thinking she was going to need to get up early to get to her teaching job in Wampee the next day, regardless of whether or not there was a storm. When she started getting ready to go Friday morning, her husband, Alton Thompson, said that he did not think she would need to go. She replied, "Well, I must go. It is a bad storm but children away from the beach will go to school and we will be needed even if we can't teach." She did agree to let him go onto Ocean Drive to find out about the storm, however. When he came back he said, "The waves are breaking over the street light at Ocean Drive. No school." They eventually left home to go to the shelter at the Baptist church. Eatofel Arehart reported that "that was an awful trip. I don't see how we got there. If we had been going in another direction, I am sure the car would have flipped over."[15]

When Donald Moore rose from bed sometime before 7:00 A.M. at his Windy Hill garage apartment, the waves were breaking over the front of their big house, so he went to pick up Wickie in Briarcliffe and brought her back so that they could pack up a few things. Wickie remembered the trip: "We came down what is now Windy Hill Road [on the way back to Briarcliffe]. There's a stoplight there now and a CVS [drugstore] on the corner. We went down that road. And on the Boulevard was a big restaurant called Eyerley's. We started down the Boulevard to go to our apartment and the water was coming. It looked like a ten-story building, the waves were coming up so we couldn't get through. So he [Donald] backed up and went through the third row. By that time the water had taken most of the big house. The sounds of the wind and the rain were very loud, a howling. We just wanted to get out of there."[16]

Areas to the west of the coastline were also feeling the strength of Hazel. Frank Davis, who was eight years old in 1954, said that he lived in Jordanville, west of Conway, and because they did not know about the hurricane, his parents took him to school as usual in Aynor. Davis remembered, "We came back, I guess, within the hour. The wind started picking up and raining extremely hard. There were two large oak trees on either side of our house, very old trees. Well, we got in the middle of the house. There was a hallway in the middle and that is where we got. Anyway, we finally opened the doors to the hallway and I could see into [the window in] Mother and Daddy's bedroom, which was off the hall, and I watched one of those big oaks fall on the house. The sound of the wind, I remember that more than anything else."[17] At 8:00 A.M. the storm reached the stage where everyone in Myrtle Beach was forced to take cover and ride it out. Telephone lines were soon down, and electrical current was cut off.

The power failed at the radio station at 9:12 A.M. on October 15. Ward wrote that through the windows they could see trees being uprooted and boards flying through the air as if on wings. He remembered, "We were afraid to venture outside because of the terrific wind and flying debris, and afraid to stay indoors because the massive tower directly behind the station was swaying ominously and looked as though it might fall on us at any second. We could scarcely hear our own prayers above the screaming of the wind as it ripped past the building. From our position, we could see the roofs being lifted off of houses. The gray green waves ate away the foundations and in minutes the houses leaned drunkenly and disappeared into the swirling sea. At the height of the blow, the monstrous waves were cresting at forty feet; then they would crash thunderously on the strand and race upward across two hundred feet of sand to chew huge bites out of Ocean Boulevard. As they went, they toppled houses into twisted heaps of wood and brick."[18]

Dino Thompson remembered his father going for a ride in his Jeep during the hurricane:

Even though I thought it was a great adventure, I was looking outside and I remember thinking "not really, we're not really going for a ride" because big things are blowing, big signs, big trees that were uprooted and our windows blown open, and the wind's howling through there.
. . . I distinctly remember him opening the door and the door just slamming open. He lost the door once. The wind caught it and he

had to do everything he could to fight to get it back and lock the door. There's an alley right here and the Jeep was sitting right there so it was a little bit out of the wind when we went out there [right outside the kitchen]. And I remember he was tying me to the Jeep. He just got some clothesline and he was lashing me to the Jeep and . . . we drove from what was a foot of water to what became two and three feet of water. . . . Of course the wind was blistering your face. I could hardly open my eyes and we drove to what is now the Yachtsman area. The fishing pier was called the Seaside Pier and on top of it was the Seaside Restaurant. We parked on the lee side, the windless side of Nu Way Laundry, just right against the building and we sat and watched the hurricane and just a little bit of the pier had broken off and Dad had to back the Jeep up twice because every now and then a wave would crash completely over the Boulevard and hit us. We kept backing up as needed and stayed there until the pier just blew to smithereens. But they [the waves] were crossing the boulevard. When those waves would get real big, that was frightening because they were black. They looked like a mountain. I don't know how big they were but to me they were thirty-five, forty-five feet [high].[19]

Then the eye of the hurricane was over Myrtle Beach. While most people knew when this happened and stories abound about where it actually hit, the National Hurricane Center reported that the eye officially hit land just north of Ocean Drive, close to the North Carolina–South Carolina border. Dino Thompson remembered clearly how beautiful the sky looked at that point. Eatofel Arehart said the same thing: "The wind stopped blowing, the rain stopped and the sky did not clear but it was much brighter than it had been. Not a breath of breeze of any sort. Everything was so calm and still."[20]

Many people did not know there was an eye or what it meant. When the wind stopped blowing, they thought the storm was over and ventured out. Donald and Wickie Moore were at Briarcliffe when the eye passed over. "It got so quiet. We all rushed out to the car because we were listening to the car radio. We were going to come back [to Windy Hill] and all of a sudden, the wind started and we ran back into the house," Wickie said.[21]

Burgin Berry remembered going out about 9:00 A.M. and walking down to Baldwin's Construction Company office in Crescent Beach. He said, "And Jimmy Baldwin was there, he had been down on the front, had on his boots. And I said, 'Jimmy, is there any damage down on the ocean front?' He said, 'Well, you couldn't believe it.' I said, 'Don't kid me now. Is any house really off its foundation?' And he just looked at me and shook his head."[22]

"One thing I remember very clearly," said Hoyt Bellamy, "is that morning when it settled down . . . The eye came right over and I was on the south end. All of a sudden it was clear like the sun. I opened the car door at 29th Avenue South. It was coquina then, I believe, right there close to the Boulevard. And I saw the sun and it was calm. All of a sudden the wind came back from that direction and it almost blew me down. And I got in the car right quick. And there was the ocean. There weren't any buildings like there are now, nothing hardly. And I saw the ocean going out and it was weird looking, because it was something like two hundred yards of beach and sand. I can see it almost moving. That scared the dickens out of me because I didn't know what was going on. Watching the sea move out. Then it stopped but the wind was blowing then of course."[23]

Merlin Bellamy noted the eeriness of the tide being pulled out when the winds shifted. He recalled, "I saw two things I hope I never see again: the water so high and by the same token whenever that eye switched and that northwest wind came, it made the lowest tide I've ever seen. If Tilghman Beach Pier had still been there, I feel like I could have driven around it very easily."[24]

David Michaux, who was in Murrells Inlet, also remembered that tide receding. He had driven to Murrells Inlet from Chapel Hill, North Carolina, where he was attending the University of North Carolina, in order to secure his parents' home. "The amazing part was the fact that when the water went out, it went out so fast, you could almost walk as it went down. Not running, I mean walking slow. It came in real quick and went out real quick," Michaux reported.[25]

The Aftermath

By 10:00 A.M. Friday morning Hurricane Hazel had moved north into North Carolina and the South Carolina coast was finally quiet. Within hours the sun broke through the clouds to reveal devastation and destruction all along the strand, from Pawleys Island to Little River. In addition to the destruction of property, the sand dunes had been obliterated and flattened, and sand seemed to cover everything. In some places in the Ocean Drive area five feet of sand covered the roads. Few power poles were left standing. Roads that were not covered by sand were washed away. "And in the East Cherry Grove section," Chief Bellamy said, "there wasn't a single house left on their foundations. Most of the houses were reduced to just timbers, refrigerators, washing machines, and such. Two hotels that were on the waterfront were affected. The MacArthur was three stories and when the hurricane was over, it had been reduced to two stories. The Ocean Drive Hotel was three stories. We could find no trace of it."[26]

Of four thousand telephones served by Seacoast Telephone Company, about eighteen hundred were out of service. In Myrtle Beach two major breaks in the water system had almost depleted the town's water supply, but these were soon dealt with and water service was restored quickly. Several sewer pumping stations were flooded and required immediate attention. The most important one was restored to service within a few hours.

Clarence Gramling, an engineer for the Santee Cooper power company who was based in Moncks Corner, headed directly for Myrtle Beach with T. M. Watson, manager of transmission and distribution, as soon as the hurricane passed. Gramling remembered,

> We crossed the Winyah Bay Bridge and Mr. Watson took a notepad and started writing down everywhere he saw trees on the line and after about a mile or two, he threw the pad in the back and said, "Phooey on this. I mean, it's just all torn down." We turned into Pawleys Island and it was a wreck. We couldn't even get to the Boulevard because it was so messed up. Went on up to Garden City and the hurricane had just ruined it. At Garden City it pushed the houses off of the waterfront back into the creek behind the ocean, and as I recall there were only two houses left on the oceanfront at Garden City. Went on into Myrtle Beach and the power was off everywhere. Mr. Callaway [the Santee Cooper manager at Myrtle Beach as well as the fire chief] had had a heart attack prior to this and he was not in shape to handle this thing. So Mr. Watson left me at Myrtle Beach to handle restoration of service.[27]

Electrical power in Myrtle Beach was off only for a few hours. In the business section service was restored by 3:00 P.M. Friday. Service to the northern beach communities took longer, however. The problem, according to Gramling, was that everything on the waterfront north of Myrtle Beach was wiped out. He said, "The main feed line was on the waterfront and it was gone. So you had houses that were back from the waterfront and in good shape but no way to feed them [electricity]." In its annual report for 1954, the South Carolina Public Service Authority reported that all distribution lines to Garden City were lost and all facilities along the first three streets in Windy Hill, Crescent Beach, Ocean Drive, and Cherry Grove were almost entirely lost. These facilities were to be rebuilt at a cost of approximately $250,000.

Cleanup after Hazel

Each community had its own share of problems. One common loss was the nine fishing piers on the Grand Strand: Pawleys Beach Pier, Garden City

Pier, Surfside Pier, Myrtle Beach State Park Pier, Second Avenue Pier, Ocean Plaza Pier, Windy Hill Pier, Tilghman Pier, and Cherry Grove Pier. Most were rebuilt by the 1955 summer season. All communities had houses—or parts of houses—and trees and other debris blocking public roads, all of which had to be cleared as quickly as possible. The towns north and south of Myrtle Beach were the worst hit, losing most of their first and second rows of beachfront properties. Because Myrtle Beach was the most heavily populated community with a more involved infrastructure to be affected, its challenges were a bit different.

Requiring immediate attention was the safeguarding of the approximately sixty miles of beachfront from looters. By the evening of October 15, National Guard units were mobilized and sent to the Grand Strand to guard the beach. The units were from Marion, Hemingway, Mullins (two units), Charleston Heights, Conway, Georgetown (two units), Andrews, Charleston, Florence, and Lake City. All but two units were demobilized by October 24. In addition, all available personnel from Myrtle Beach Air Force Base were assigned guard duty in a five-mile stretch along Myrtle Beach's oceanfront on a twenty-four-hour basis for seven days following Hurricane Hazel's passage. Only property owners with passes were allowed on the oceanfront.

Another major issue that was addressed quickly was rebuilding the sand dunes along the entire Grand Strand beachfront. Hazel had completely flattened them. A twenty-four-mile-long artificial sand dune barrier was completed on October 30 by the U.S. Army's 981st Engineer Construction Battalion from Fort Bragg, and this was believed to result in a more rapid, natural buildup of larger dunes.

People all over the country heard about the Myrtle Beach area, perhaps for the first time, because of the news coverage on Hazel's destruction. Photos and articles were carried not only by major newspapers in the region but also by wire services and major news magazines; *Time, Newsweek,* and *Life* picked up the story. Because of this coverage and the fear that people would erroneously think that Myrtle Beach had been destroyed, the Myrtle Beach Chamber of Commerce began a massive letter-writing and promotional campaign to newspapers, magazines, travel agencies, and other outlets to say that Myrtle Beach would be ready for the next summer season.

Construction in 1955 was not limited to properties affected by Hurricane Hazel. More than $2 million was spent in the coming year on new construction, which included 485 new rooms in motor court and hotel additions, apartments and apartment hotels, as well as the modernization and expansion of guest houses and motor courts. Most of this construction would have been done even if Hurricane Hazel had not blown through Horry County. However, the types of buildings that replaced those destroyed on the beach emphasized to people the differences in Myrtle Beach before and after Hurricane Hazel—the transition from a quaint summer colony to a high-rise resort city. That transition was gradual, not sudden. While an individual, historic event may influence and affect the future, rarely does such an event create change by itself. Change is the product of various forces. In the case of Myrtle Beach development, Hurricane Hazel was only one of those forces, albeit a powerful one. She simply hurried along one significant phase of the Grand Strand's evolution, setting the stage for modernization and expansion along the oceanfront.

Hurricane Hazel's Impact on Individual Communities
Myrtle Beach

In Myrtle Beach about 80 percent of the homes on the first row were damaged and Gay Dolphin Park, within two blocks of the Pavilion, suffered severe destruction. The Pavilion and its amusement park, however, were largely spared; most of the rides had been taken down after Labor Day and stored for the postseason. Only light damage occurred along the second row and in the business district.

Some of the biggest problems were with infrastructure. The bridge over Spivey Swash had to be rebuilt. Two major breaks in the water system almost depleted the town's water supply. Four sewage pumping plants required emergency repairs as sand and mud clogged the pumps and motors. The concrete boardwalk, which went from Twentieth Avenue North to Third Avenue South, and the embankment on which it rested were destroyed. Some credited that embankment with reducing property damage in Myrtle Beach by retarding the destructive wave action caused by Hazel. A temporary replacement for the boardwalk provided access to about forty-four hundred square feet of beachfront property. By nightfall of October 15 most electricity and local telephone service had been restored in Myrtle Beach.

Jack Thompson, who was eighteen and working for Skip's Photography in October 1954, recalled, "I ran to the oceanfront [after Hazel had passed] and by the time I got to the oceanfront, there wasn't a cloud in the sky. I never saw the blue, absolutely deep deep blue sky like it was that day. No clouds. The beach was actually down to the gumbo; it was black. And the ocean was black. You could almost walk to the end of where the pier [Second Avenue Pier] had been . . . because the ocean had receded so far back that it was just unbelievable. And instead of the surf, there was only a little ripple. And when I mean a little ripple, the water, the surf, was flat. And you could see palmetto trees, cars, refrigerators, all kinds of appliances, mattresses, toilet fixtures, things you would not imagine out in the ocean."[28]

Ashby Ward, radio announcer for WMYB in October 1954, said, "As far as the eye could see, there was nothing but ruin. On every side of Ocean Boulevard loomed tottering walls and piles of twisted lumber and brick. Like gaping wounds, walls had collapsed, revealing immodestly the scattered and broken furniture and soaking rugs. Strewn over the sand were ranges, refrigerators and other expensive appliances. On lawns that were once well tended, now lay a thick scum of mud and sand. Every so often, the sheer naked force of Hurricane Hazel was impressed on us by huge, concrete slabs that were once foundations for homes, slabs weighing tons that had been picked up and tossed, as though they were just cardboard boxes, over piles of rubble."[29]

Hoyt Bellamy, member of the Myrtle Beach Police Department in October 1954, remembered, "That morning I thought we were ruined, our town is ruined. But that afternoon or sometime right about noon, it was like a hive of bees. People who owned property were coming in down there and cleaning up. More the next day. Just really cleaning up and trying to salvage what they could."[30]

Dino Thompson, whose parents ran the Kozy Korner restaurant in downtown Myrtle Beach, was eight years old in October 1954. He remembered, "When we saw how bad things were, Dad cranked up the Jeep and started riding around checking on people, people he knew. I remember seeing this lady sitting on what looked like a 200-year-old oak tree and you know the roots are fifteen feet up. She was just sitting on one of the big branches crying and I thought somebody had died and Dad said, 'Are you alright? Can I get you anything?' The roof on her house was gone, but it was the tree she was crying about. 'This tree's been in my family all my life.' She was about 75 years old and I remember thinking her children had probably swung on it."[31]

Billy V. Roberts, who lived at the corner of Twenty-eighth Avenue North and Oak Street in 1954, remembered Hazel like this:

> We turned the radio on, and that's when we learned that the hurricane
> was coming, and it was going to be bad. So, my mother and I, we got
> in the car to ride around a little bit, just to see how things were. As we
> were riding down the highway and the other roads, there was always
> some kind of debris coming at us in the wind, or even passing us
> going in the same direction we were going. Maybe tree limbs and
> garbage cans and all kinds of things, maybe signs, and fortunately

nothing hit us, but if it had hit us, it would have been bad. We were just excited. The full impact of that hurricane did not hit us until it was over.

After the hurricane, everybody was in a real cooperative way with each other. People helped each other, sawing trees that were fallen in yards, lending all kinds of help that you would never have dreamed about if something like that hadn't happened. Very often it takes a catastrophe to bring people together.

The forest and trees were really devastated in our area. Between Oak Street and where Broadway at the Beach is now was a great big wooded area with huge trees and some of those trees as much as three feet in diameter were uprooted and blown over. Some of them were broken off halfway up and those with shallow root systems were blown over.[32]

Ocean Drive, Tilghman Beach

Ocean Drive and Tilghman Beach suffered heavy losses. Not only was everything on the first and second rows destroyed, but many businesses further back were also heavily damaged or destroyed. The Roberts Pavilion was reduced to a pile of broken timber. In its request for federal assistance, Ocean Drive reported that fifty-three houses needed to be moved from public rights-of-way. Public roads that had been washed out had to be repaired, and emergency labor and materials were needed to restore temporary water service. Of the 380 homes in Ocean Drive and newly incorporated Tilghman Beach, 200 were completely destroyed.

Merlin Bellamy, Ocean Drive chief of police in October 1954, stated, "I felt possibly like a father that had a number of children and he lost all of them at one time. . . . When we started going out making a survey, looking north from Main Street, there wasn't anything right on that corner. Every bit of it was gone. The pavilion was gone. Looking north, there was a three-story hotel, the Ocean Drive Hotel. We could find no part of it. We don't know what happened to it. Just a short distance from that was the Douglas MacArthur Hotel. And it stood proudly, three stories. But after the storm it wasn't but two stories. It was just like if you had taken a saw and cut the bottom floor completely off of it."[33]

Eatofel Vereen Thompson Arehart was a Wampee schoolteacher living in Ocean Drive in October 1954. She said,

> "I remember standing at the back [of the Baptist Church, where people sought shelter during the hurricane] and looking out a back window and those great big pine trees that were standing around,

just snapped off like matches. Like you take a match in your finger and break it. . . . The next day was the most beautifully bright day you have ever seen. But what devastation!"

"I remember reading *Pilgrim's Progress* and my vision of the River of Styx and that is the only thing I could think of every time I had to go toward the beach. There were many houses that were still standing, in the places that they stood in the beginning. And others—every board was ripped apart, broken into, some of them standing up, some of them piled up on top of each other. There was one house that I had to pass every day and there were no curtains in the window and inside that house stood a table that had been set. The plates and cups and saucers and things were still sitting on the table."[34]

Crescent Beach

At Crescent Beach nineteen houses had to be moved off public rights-of-way. The Ocean Strand Hotel was completely destroyed. A letter from Annie Kemp Alexander to her family on October 17, 1954, tells what she saw at Crescent Beach:

> You just can't imagine what the destruction on the ocean front is. Most of the damage is on the front line houses. The little La Tina apartment next door to our place was the only thing I recognized. There was a pile of kindling wood even with the back of the apartment that was the back end of the house, lying almost flat, and hanging there was our sign, Moring Cottage. I brought that home, also an iron frying pan, all that we could salvage from the wreckage. We didn't see signs of the furniture. I guess it was somewhere all in splinters. . . . I don't know what time will do for our lovely, lovely beach, but yesterday it was a waste, strewn with brick pillars, concrete blocks, old pipe, pans, chairs and all sorts of odds and ends. The road was blocked with parts of houses and all sorts of trash. . . . The top of the Blaylock place was far across the road in a swamp—all that is left. And on and on the same until it seems that you can't bear to see any more.

Cherry Grove

Cherry Grove and East Cherry Grove suffered great destruction. Thirty houses had to be moved from public rights-of-way, and a county road was washed out and had to be rebuilt. In East Cherry Grove there were no houses left standing. "It's [East Cherry Grove's] not there," according to one person. The sandbar that had been built to connect Cherry Grove and East Cherry Grove had been washed out, leaving the latter virtually an island.

Clarence Gramling, who coordinated repair efforts for Santee Cooper in October 1954, recalled, "As you moved on further north to Windy Hill and Atlantic Beach and Ingram Beach and Crescent Beach and Ocean Drive and Tilghman Beach and Cherry Grove and East Cherry Grove, the first couple of roads were just totally demolished and sand washed up on Ocean Boulevard was two, three feet deep of sand. And I mean it was just massive piles of debris, which was much worse than it was at Myrtle Beach. Between Cherry Grove and East Cherry Grove, it actually washed out the causeway. Didn't even have a roadway over to East Cherry Grove."[35]

Atlantic Beach

About thirty-five homes in Atlantic Beach were destroyed. Willie L. Isom, resident of Atlantic Beach in October 1954, recalled, "When Hazel came down, our building, the Bluebird Inn, was the only block building at the time. Everyone came there for protection. All the other buildings were wooden. When Hazel came in the ocean came all the way up to First Avenue. There was a hotel down there called the Lodge Hotel. They had to get the Coast Guard to blow it up because all that was left was debris. The drugstore had no medicine because the drugs were washed away in the ocean."[36]

Windy Hill

Of eighty-nine homes in Windy Hill, about fifty, mostly from the first row, were completely gone. Nine houses had been moved by Hazel into the streets and had to be removed. Part of the Windy Hill Pier ended up in the front yard of a house in Briarcliffe Acres.

Donald and Wickie Moore, who were residents of Windy Hill in October 1954, remembered, "We were making our way back to Windy Hill from Briarcliffe as soon as the storm passed. We came down the Boulevard and saw that Charlie Byars' lot was cleaned. He had two duplexes and they were completely gone. I saw our garage apartment and said, 'Well, I've got part of it.' It was pretty devastating. All I could think about was all the damn mortgages I've got to pay with nothing there to rent."[37]

Surfside, Garden City, Murrells Inlet, and Pawleys Island

Hurricane Hazel made almost a clean sweep of the oceanfront on the south end of the Grand Strand. On Pawleys Island 2 homes were left standing. In Garden City, of 275 homes, 3 were in a livable condition. At Surfside, of about 70 homes, only 3 or 4 were left. Thirteen houses had to be moved from public rights-of-way.

Nelson and Mary Emily Jackson, who owned a summer house in Garden City in October 1954, reported,

We started down Surfside Drive and on down the front to Garden City. And sand, a foot or more deep, and we got down there and saw one house standing, and we had a hard time recognizing it, because none of the landmarks were around it, and it was our house. We were left standing, one of three houses left of over three hundred. And the houses were floating out on the horizon and they were floating in the inlet, Murrells Inlet.[38]

On the beach were parts of airplanes that had crashed, because all along the sand dunes here had been target practice [during World War II] and the pilots had not pulled their planes up properly. We found fishing gear, parts of airplanes, uniforms, and all.

David Michaux, who was a student at the University of North Carolina–Chapel Hill in October 1954, recalled, "Many of the homes from the Garden City beachfront were deposited in Murrells Inlet when the tide went out, many of them largely intact. The rest of them, they were all out here at what we call the Point, like matchsticks. Everything in a million pieces.[39]

Tuck 'Em Inn was the family summer cottage of Pratt Gasque in Murrells Inlet. The following is from *Rum Gully Tales* by Gasque: "We drove in to the back of the house, and I gave Pratt Jr. The key to the front door. He came running back to tell me that we didn't need a key because there was no door. It had been smashed in by winter and water. There was trash all over the yard, mud and trash in the house; all the front doors were gone and the windows above the floor. All beds, chairs and other furniture looked as if someone had put it all in a giant washing machine and turned on the switch. Looking towards Garden City we could see no houses standing, and we counted forty-two houses strewn in the marsh between the inlet and the beach. We had four small boats in the open garage behind the house and they were all gone. Later we found two of them on the beach about a mile north of the cottage and the other two in the marsh two miles south."[40]

The African American Community

*M*yrtle Beach would not have been able to grow and prosper without the hard work and dedication of its black men and women. The African American community in Myrtle Beach has a heritage as rich and deep as that of the white population, but the lives and history of these people have been largely unsung and unappreciated outside of their own neighborhoods.

The experiences of the twentieth-century African American in Horry County, while similar to racial experiences throughout the South, bore certain differences. The population ratio of blacks to whites in Horry County was considerably less in the nineteenth and twentieth centuries than in other South Carolina counties. For example, in 1960 blacks comprised 34.8 percent of South Carolina's total population, while in Horry County the ratio was 26.7 percent in 1964.[1] This relatively low percentage was due to the fact that Horry County historically did not have a large black population. The county's agricultural lands could not support vast antebellum plantations, and therefore the slave labor that came along with them was not required. The freedmen who lived in or moved to Horry County after the Civil War and emancipation were interested in acquiring land and an education after gaining their freedom in 1863.

Many of these former slaves settled in or near Freewoods, which is today part of the Burgess community located on State Highway 707 between Socastee and U.S. Highway 17. Evidence suggests that the settlers in the Freewoods area purchased tracts from former planters because the area borders the old Oregon and Longwood plantations, which were owned by John D. Magill and Joshua Ward, respectively. Much of the area is wetlands and consequently was not valued highly by other landowners for farming.

According to deed records in Horry County, land was purchased by the Freewoods settlers as early as 1873, although the majority did not purchase land until ten to twenty years later. These farmers generally purchased homesteads with capital raised as sharecroppers on the former Waccamaw River rice plantations in Georgetown County. Sharecropping was the most prevalent form of labor in the late 1800s because planters could not afford to hire wage laborers and were forced to make some kind of tenancy agreement. For most freedmen and many white farmers, sharecropping meant a hand-to-mouth existence with little chance of improvement in their quality of life. In the months preceding harvest, a family was advanced food and supplies by the landowner or local merchant. By the time the extended credit was subtracted from the family's share of the crop, the sharecropper usually broke even or went further into debt.

Because landownership was important to them, however, many black farmers managed to save and buy farms, which gave them a measure of self-respect, self-reliance, and independence. The main crops on Socastee Township farms, which included the Freewoods community, were Indian corn, with farms of 2–10 acres yielding on average twenty to twenty-two bushels, and sweet potatoes, with 1–1.5 acres yielding fifty to two hundred bushels. Many black farmers also sold timber to the lumber mills and produced naval stores. Sugar cane was converted to molasses, and bees were kept for honey and wax. Most African American farmers kept hogs, chickens, and other stock.[2]

At the turn of the twentieth century, many of these sharecroppers migrated toward what would become the Myrtle Beach area to work for Burroughs & Collins (later Myrtle Beach Farms) in naval stores, timber, and farming businesses. Some settled in the Wampee area northwest of Myrtle Beach, and others had farms around Murrells Inlet in Georgetown County, just south of Myrtle Beach. Horry County had the highest percent increase in black population in South Carolina between 1920 and 1930, which may be attributed to a higher recorded birth rate and new population migrating to the area for jobs.[3] John T. Woodside's development of almost sixty-six thousand acres along the Grand Strand, the Intracoastal Waterway, and major road- and bridge-building projects supplied many jobs for workers during this period.

Walter Geathers remembered that the people in Myrtle Beach were looked after during the Depression: "There wasn't no city then. The train came on the farm and we loaded [it] up with sweet potatoes and such. Peas, corn, sweet potatoes grew up aplenty. We stayed in Myrtle Beach Farms houses with no rent, in some houses where Oak Street is now. There was plenty to eat. Myrtle Beach Farms, they fed you and if you had nothing, you told them and they credited you food. If you got sick and couldn't pay, they looked after you. Everybody who wanted to work, worked." Even the children worked on the farms. "We worked around there [Myrtle Beach Farms and Trask Farms] as little kids. We'd pick up around the packing houses, push baskets, and load them up," said Leroy Brunson.[4]

The work was hard, physical labor. Rubin Wineglass's father, Samuel Wineglass, was one of the brickmasons who built Brookgreen Gardens and also worked on U.S. Highway 17. Wineglass recalled, "They didn't have the machine [for the road work]. Most of them were doing it with their hands, with shovels." Although most of Wineglass's career was in restaurants and country clubs in Myrtle Beach and the Pinehurst area, he also worked for Moore Construction in the late 1940s, with one of his projects being the 1949 Pavilion. He said, "I was up there, me and another guy from New York I think it was, and we had to stand on the scaffold and sand all that building down."[5]

Jake Abraham, a native of Bishopville, South Carolina, started working about 1938 for ninety cents a day at Myrtle Beach Farms, "like plowing and planting white potatoes, corn and stuff like that. Myrtle Beach Farms had a corn mill. They would grind their own meal on Friday to take to the store. And George Trask had a farm that [raised] all kinds of things, like kale, radish, cabbage, onion, all that kind of stuff. It used to be that farm down there would raise all of that, down in there where you see Sam's [Club] and all that [Tenth Avenue North near Seaboard Street], all of that was farming." Abraham recalled that people on the farms would saw wood and then deliver it, and digging ditches meant shoveling them out. Garbage pickup was literally that, with workers picking up the large galvanized drums and then lifting and emptying them into a truck by hand. After serving thirty-two months in the army overseas during World War II, Abraham returned to South Carolina and went to work for the city of Myrtle Beach for sixty-five cents an hour. He retired in the 1990s after almost forty years of service.[6]

As Myrtle Beach's tourism industry grew, more jobs became available in the guest houses and other tourism-related businesses. The 1930 census provides a glimpse of the jobs that black men and women were performing: auto mechanic; general laborer; servant with a private family; porter, cook, dishwasher, or maid at a guest house or hotel; light plant operator; railroad porter; public-school teacher; and truck driver.[7] Many white families, especially the children, remembered their black servants with great fondness. "Our Negro servants came with us year in and year out," recalled Annette Epps Reesor in her memoirs about her childhood at the beach in the 1920s. "They shared our sorrows, anxieties and joys. It was pleasant to hear them humming during meal preparation, or singing spirituals somewhere around the place after the supper dishes were done. At first they had as complete freedom of the beach as did their employers, but when 'foreigners' came from such sophisticated places as Sumter, Florence, and Columbia, the Jim Crow laws limited their activities. Now I realize the loneliness these good people must have experienced with their leisure time activities so limited."[8]

Wineglass is one of those who left construction work and worked his way up to waiter at various establishments, going to work for LeRoy Letts at the Pink House for many years. His professional life involved several noted establishments, including working at the Southern Pines Country Club in Pinehurst, North Carolina, for more than thirteen years and the Caravelle for twenty years. He was also a member of the Cooks and Waiters Club, which had a clubhouse in Atlantic Beach and members who were all involved in the hospitality industry. More a social organization than a trade association, it nevertheless provided an outlet for people in the same trade to meet together.

While many believe that the Myrtle Beach area was perhaps more tolerant than other places that were still bound by a tradition of racial prejudice, the white community generally had limited understanding of blacks' living conditions and lack of opportunities for improving their lot in life. Wallace Evans remembered what it was like before integration of the schools in 1965: "I went to all-black schools. We walked to school. We got buses finally, we got the used buses. We got used textbooks. All the new books went to Wampee. In 1963, I was playing basketball at Chestnut [High School]. I was a junior in high school and the guys from Wampee got off practice, so they came by the gym. And we were just talking. Finally we decided we'd play a game. We played a scrimmage that night just with each other. The next morning they [the principals] almost fired the coaches. We didn't have an incident, we just played a game. . . . They almost fired the coaches because we got blacks and whites on the same court playing ball." Also during this same general time period Evans was working in Ocean Drive at a diner. He remembered, "We made doughnuts, and we served eggs over easy, and scrambled eggs. You know breakfast and all that stuff. Now we put our hands in the doughnuts and mixed the dough. We made the orange juice, we flipped the eggs, did all that, made the toast, put our hands on it, but we couldn't sit on the counter side and eat it. We put our hands in it, and made it for them. My boss told me, he said, 'When you go around in front of the counter, always have a broom in your hand. Never go round there empty-handed because I don't want people to think that you are not an employee.'" While such unjust attitudes may have made him angry, Evans said that his parents taught him not to fight back: "My parents told me never to retaliate, because that lowers you to the people's level. Never fight back, just go on. That's how you survived."[9]

In the rural areas, however, blacks and whites worked more closely together and with more tolerance. Genevieve "Sister" Chandler Peterkin remembered a relative who claimed that in all the time she was growing up in Myrtle Beach she knew only two black persons, a woman who would come and help her mother sometimes and Joe White.[10] Peterkin said, "My experience was absolutely different because we were in the country instead of a little town. We did things together that people in towns wouldn't have thought of. Blacks and whites would pull shrimp nets together for instance. . . . The creek made a tremendous difference in our relationships. The blacks didn't own creek-front property, but the white people who did would never have said a black person couldn't cross their place to get to the creek. They might even leave their boat on our land, if they had one, so that they could come and go. I know the creek made a difference in the fact that we were in the country. In Myrtle Beach there were definite sections for blacks and whites."[11]

Medical care could be an issue in a small southern town. Not only were lack of transportation and money chief deterrents to getting quality medical care, but finding a doctor who would treat black families was also a factor. For the farmers in the Freewoods community, the nearest physician could be many miles away, although some doctors, such as Dr. Dick Chandler, would visit black families in the area. In Myrtle Beach, Dr. Trask and Dr. William Rourk were among the few white doctors who would see black families. Even in the 1970s some doctors in small Horry County towns still had separate waiting rooms for blacks and whites. A sick black patient had to wait until all the white patients had been treated before he or she could see the doctor.

Consequently many blacks learned to use natural remedies, such as herbs, roots, and other natural sources, for healing. Wallace Evans's father told a reporter that he could not afford to go to a doctor much and was forced to find his own remedies, which might be made from a variety of retail products, for example a brew made of cod liver oil, castor oil, quinine, honey, whiskey, and black draught, which was "supposed to give the body a good tonic if taken at night. A lot of his old-fashioned cures come from the woods. Snakeroot or dollar-leaf to treat a fever, calamus root for stomach problems, a mixture of pine-leaf tops, sassafras, holly-bush leaves and sweet-bay leaves to combat colds."[12]

In the late 1960s Jane Barry Haynes and Elizabeth Chapin Patterson, through their work at the Meher Spiritual Center, reached out to Myrtle

Beach's black community to meet needs they saw firsthand. It started by accident, remembered Wendy Haynes Conner, who was thirteen years old at the time: "Elizabeth had a wonderful housekeeper, maid, cook named Bessie [Graham] and she lived in the Booker T. Washington community, which is the black community right off 10th Avenue North. One Saturday I went with Elizabeth to pick her up. Bessie raised her grandchildren and they were out in the yard playing in the mud. It had been raining. I was so upset by it," Conner said.

The following week the three children came to the Meher Center to play, and the following Saturday they asked to bring other children. Within a few months more than one hundred children were part of what they called "Happy Club." Conner said, "From getting to know the families of these children, we came to know the conditions in that neighborhood. There was no running water at that time. This was in 1966! It is like right there next to the main drag in Myrtle Beach and there was all this incredible poverty. And there were no paved roads. So Mother [Jane Haynes] started the first free clinic there. Actually what she did was we would go around and knock on doors and say 'do you need medicine?' We knew they couldn't afford it. So Mother got one doctor, then got four doctors to volunteer one Wednesday a month. So that's how that got started and that became known as Community Volunteer Services."[13]

In some ways the black community insulated the harshness of life in Jim Crow South Carolina through the warm mantle of tightly knit communities. The Myrtle Beach neighborhood was always close, according to Mary Canty,

Black children in the area attended Myrtle Beach Colored School from 1932 to 1954, when the children and teachers moved to the new brick Carver School at the corner of Dunbar St. and Mr. Joe White Ave. This photograph was taken by the S.C. State Insurance Board in the 1940s. Courtesy of Horry County Museum

who started her education at Myrtle Beach Colored School in the late 1920s. She said that parents, teachers, and community all had worked together to raise their young people. "If I got in a fight or if I was ugly, Miss Jane or Miss Sues or Aunt Mamie was sitting on her porch as I was just passing by. There was no phone then but by the time I got home, they [her parents] would know about it. They didn't have to wait until Sunday to get the report from the teacher [while at church together]. The proverb now that everybody is real caught up with, 'it takes a village to raise a child,' that's the way we came through. It took a village to raise us and believe me, they reared us."[14]

Getting an education was a priority, but it did not come easy for the black students and teachers. *Plessy v. Ferguson* (1896) may have ruled that facilities would be separate but equal, but black schools were far from equal until the early 1950s, when the state government in South Carolina realized that the only hope of avoiding integration was to begin an immediate and far-reaching program to provide equal facilities for each race. Governor Jim Byrnes's 1951 program also provided a basis for the state's defense of the racial status quo and the doctrine of separate but equal.[15] Prior to this, black schools had fewer materials and books, which were usually secondhand; facilities that were crowded and worn; buses, if they got them at all, that were no longer wanted by the white schools; and teachers who were paid far less than their white counterparts. A study of Horry County schools that revealed the harsh realities of a decidedly unequal education for black and white students was published in 1946. For example, the per capita spending on each student at Myrtle Beach Elementary School was $93.21; at Myrtle Beach Colored School it was $36.03. In 1946 Horry County white elementary-school teachers were paid $1,030.00 each and black elementary-school teachers were each paid $640.00. The salary difference was only a bit less for high-school teachers: $1,405.00 for whites versus $1,113.00 for black teachers.[16]

However, even then the black educators persevered in teaching and fighting for their pupils' right to an education. As one white student recalled, at a bonfire to celebrate the end of a school year white students were throwing their used workbooks into the fire. An African American teacher asked them not to burn the materials as he could reuse them with his students. Today's generation may find it difficult to understand and appreciate the kind of sacrifices and efforts that their parents, grandparents, and great-grandparents made. "It's a lot of hard work that they'll never know about that has made it easier for black children to get an education today," according to Etrulia Dozier, retired librarian from Whittemore Middle School in Conway.[17]

Henry Hemingway remembered that he was among the first blacks born and raised in Myrtle Beach who went to college [Voorhees College in Denmark and Benedict College in Columbia]. He said, "I don't believe I could have gone to college then because money was tight. My mama had a job making three bucks a week. My dad worked at the sawmill making nine dollars a week and they called us big shots [laughing]. It was a time. Ol' Mister George Cook used to go down to the fish house and get fish heads and put them in a barrel and bring them back and feed the area. Give everybody a mess of fish heads. I had cornbread with no grease and fish heads for the whole season. But I made it." Things changed greatly between 1930 and 1970 in terms of educational opportunities and civil rights. Leroy Brunson, a former student at Myrtle Beach Colored School, said that while he did not go to college, all of his children graduated from college, including one who earned a graduate degree. There are many other families like his, whose children born in the second half of the twentieth century are enjoying greater opportunities than their parents and grandparents did.[18]

Many of those opportunities are a direct result of desegregation in the 1950s and 1960s. The civil rights movement swirled violently in some parts of South Carolina and the rest of the South during this period. However, major events did not fracture the general racial stability of the Myrtle Beach area, although the black community was not silent. According to Annie Bellamy Futrell, a teacher in Myrtle Beach schools since 1959, the church played a vital role in the movement: "The church is about the only thing that we can say belonged to us in our communities. So the church has always been an anchor to us. That's where the civil rights started, right within a church, because that was about the only place you could stand up and feel free to express yourself."[19] In Myrtle Beach the local chapter of the National Association for the Advancement of Colored Persons (NAACP) took the lead in many of the civil rights activities of that era, backed by the local churches.[20] This partnership also spurred other activities, such as the formation of the Horry County Progressive League, an organization formed in 1963 to register African American voters. Its five hundred to six hundred members registered nearly two thousand voters in the county within a six-month period.

One of the more dramatic incidents of racial tension in Myrtle Beach occurred in the summer of 1950 when the Ku Klux Klan (KKK or Klan) began a period of terror and intimidation in Horry County and neighboring Columbus County, North Carolina. Their supposed objective was a North Carolina recruitment drive by a strong South Carolina base, which involved activity not seen since the 1920s. While the organization had a significant membership in Horry County (the Federal Bureau of Investigation [FBI] estimated that about thirty-five hundred KKK members were from Horry County), most white South Carolinians rejected the KKK in the 1950s and 1960s just as they had in the 1920s. Activities first began swirling in late July when the KKK paraded through the black neighborhoods of Conway, which many blacks thought was meant to scare them away from the polls the following week. Then on Saturday, August 26, the Klan, led by South Carolina grand dragon Thomas Hamilton, turned its attention to Myrtle Beach.[21]

That summer many young people, black and white, enjoyed the music and dancing at Whispering Pines, a club owned by Charlie Fitzgerald. It was located about one mile west of the Pavilion on Carver Street in the black neighborhood called the Hill. Long before black groups were allowed in the local white clubs, all the great rhythm and blues groups played the Hill: these included, among others, Billie Holliday, Little Richard, Fats Domino, and B. B. King, according to Dino Thompson.[22] The Klan did not like the fact that Fitzgerald allowed the white men and women into the black establishment to listen to the music and dance and decided to show its displeasure. A caravan of more than twenty-five cars, the majority of which had South Carolina license plates, assembled near the Pine Island bridge and proceeded into Myrtle Beach. Myrtle Beach police chief W. Carlisle Newton knew the afternoon before the parade that it would occur, as organizers had requested help with traffic control. "It is their duty to render traffic assistance in a parade of any kind that is lawful in the state," according to a statement by Mayor Jasper Ramsey (*Myrtle Beach Sun,* September 1, 1950). A cross of red electric light bulbs was attached to the front left bumper of the lead car.

"The night the Klu men came through," recalled Mary Canty," they [the Royal Courts of King Solomon] were having a party at my grandparents' house. We were on the porch, you know. And all of the cars were coming through Harlem [a neighborhood along Canal Street] with the lights on. And everybody was wondering, 'What's the matter? What's the matter?' So one of the men, I don't know who it was, got off the porch, and went to the road, and attempted to cross the road. And somebody told him 'don't you cross that road.' And he had to stay there. He stood there and watched them go through. And then they went on the Hill. And then later on, they came back. And . . . they just rode through the first time, and that's when the shooting occurred, the second time they came."[23] After the parade had gone down Carver Street, someone, probably Charlie Fitzgerald, called the police to complain and to let them know that there might be trouble if the Klan returned. Instead of sending police to the area to protect a frightened constituency, someone got the message to the Klan that Fitzgerald was daring

Beach Scene at Atlantic Beach, S.C.

Atlantic Beach was settled in the early 1930s as a recreational area for the black community. Before integration few beaches in South Carolina were open for black families to enjoy. Myrtle Beach Postcard Collection, courtesy of Chapin Memorial Library

them to return. In the meantime, the caravan proceeded to Atlantic Beach, parading through the crowded streets of vacationing black families.

It is unclear why, but Horry County sheriff C. E. Sasser sent sixteen law enforcement officers to Atlantic Beach the next day, and they were met by a contingent of merchants. According to Sasser, as reported in the September 1, 1950, *Myrtle Beach Sun,* these men told him that "it is our desire and wish to give you our full cooperation in preserving law and order at this beach. There are about 10,000 colored people here now and you don't see not even one [person] drunk or disorderly. We feel like we have better order than the white beaches. We don't feel like the Klan has any right to move in on us by parading. . . . We are 100 percent southern Negroes and we have our beach and in Conway, Myrtle Beach and other places, we try to live separately, not having any desire to mix churches, schools or anything else. We only have ninety days to make and pay our rent here [in other words, earn a living during the tourist season] but with the Klan coming [we might] just as well fold up. When you visit the white beaches, you don't see any colored unless they are employed." Sasser promised that he would ensure their security. Around 11:15 P.M. Sasser reported that Hamilton had heard about the complaint/warning about the return of the Klan to the Hill.

He accepted what he considered a challenge from a black man, and the Klan caravan made its way back to Myrtle Beach.[24]

Upon arriving at Whispering Pines, the white-robed men jumped out of their cars, relieved Fitzgerald of his gun, and threw him in the trunk of one of the cars. They then proceeded to shoot up the place, break windows, overturn and smash tables and chairs, and shatter the jukebox. One Klansman was shot and killed; one black man, Gene Nichols, a waiter at the Pink House, was shot in the foot; and Cynthia Harrel was beaten on the back. The Myrtle Beach police force did not respond to the trouble because "[t]hey were out on call to stop two free-for-all fights at various places on the beach at the time of the gunfight." The Klansman who was shot died at the hospital. The emergency room staff found a policeman's uniform on him when the white robe was removed. The dead man was James Daniel Johnson, a forty-two-year-old Conway policeman. He was killed by a .38 caliber pistol, with the bullet entering his back. Klansmen drove Fitzgerald to a remote swamp, beat him severely, and cut off part of his ear. When the doctor who treated him reported this, the sheriff and a deputy came and arrested the victim. He was transported to Columbia, supposedly for his own safety. Although there was no evidence to tie him to the death of

In the 1940s Atlantic Beach was in its heyday, with nightclubs, shops, motels, restaurants, amusement park rides, summer cottages, and year-round homes. Myrtle Beach Postcard Collection, courtesy of Chapin Memorial Library

the Klansman, he served a term in prison for the distribution of lewd literature.[25]

As to why the Klan focused on Fitzgerald's place, Sasser publicly commented that a rumor had been circulating that Fitzgerald was keeping white women for immoral purposes. He also said, "To my knowledge some white women and men do go to this place on special occasions to hear the orchestra and see the colored people dance. I have on many occasions told them it was not a good policy." It was a well-known fact that Fitzgerald was a successful businessman, which might have fueled the animosity of the Klan. In addition to the club, Fitzgerald operated a motor court, a barbershop, a beauty shop, and a taxicab company at one time. Another factor might have been that he and his wife, Sarah, had taken a stand in 1948, after the whites-only primary was outlawed in South Carolina, to register to vote, the only two to do so at that time in Myrtle Beach.[26]

Sasser told the community through a formal statement on radio and in the newspapers that Dan Johnson, the officer who was shot, was "a victim of circumstances" and would not have been there if he had known that Hamilton had "murder in his heart." Sasser also admitted that he knew a few men who were members of the Klan but stated that they were "led into this unfortunate thing with no intentions of committing a crime" (*Myrtle Beach Sun*, September 1, 1950). Immediately prior to Sasser's public address on the radio, his department began arresting a handful of Klan members for the attack on Fitzgerald's nightclub. Hamilton was the first, and he was quickly released on bond. By the following day ten Klansmen had been arrested, all charged with conspiracy to incite mob violence. In October the Horry County grand jury cleared them of all charges. Even with substantial proof of their involvement, five Klan members, including Hamilton, were cleared. All other Klansmen charged in the case were released after an earlier preliminary hearing found no probable cause for their arrest warrants. A coroner's jury ruled that unknown persons caused Officer Johnson's death. His murder was never solved.

Mayor Ramsey and Chief Newton, however, had no sympathy for the Klan. "I do consider that the visit of the Ku Klux Klan was uncalled for, as well as undemocratic and absolutely not welcome in this city, and their visit has been very detrimental to the progress of our beach" (*Myrtle Beach Sun*, September 1, 1950). The aftermath of the Klan raid was a short-term economic loss to the guest houses and motels as many black employees left town Sunday and Monday out of fear, and some establishments reported that they were without domestic help of any kind. The following weekend was Labor Day weekend, one of the biggest tourist events of the season behind the Fourth of July.

A decade later the fight for civil rights once again came to Myrtle Beach. Up until the 1960s, all twenty-six of the South Carolina state parks were segregated. Only seven admitted black persons, and only one of those, Hunting Island State Park, was on the ocean. The issue of blacks and whites sharing the waters of the Atlantic Ocean from taxpayer-supported facilities was first raised as early as 1951. Robert Morrison, a black man in Charleston, suggested the possibility of a lawsuit to open white state-owned beaches to Negroes: "Unless there can be some beach found for Negroes to go to, the courts may be called on to open the state park beaches for whites at Edisto Island and Myrtle Beach to all people of the state." Edisto Beach State Park closed for a period due to an outcry by the white citizenry opposing this possibility.[27]

On Tuesday, August 30, 1960, seeking to fight the state's segregation of public parks, a group of fourteen black people and one white man arrived at the gate to Myrtle Beach State Park and attempted to enter. They were advised that the park was closed and were denied admission. However, white people were using the park and had not been asked to leave. According to the *Myrtle Beach Sun and Ocean Beach News*, the white man was Gerald Friedberg and the black man in the lead car was Isaiah DeQuincey Newman, a Columbia preacher and executive secretary of the state chapter of the NAACP. Earlier that day Friedberg and his wife had tried to lead two carloads of blacks into the state park. According to the local newspaper, the group was greeted by South Carolina State Law Enforcement Division officers and a closed gate to the state park. Friedberg and his wife pulled their car to the closed gate and were questioned by Chief Pete Strom of SLED and a plainclothes police officer from Myrtle Beach. The two cars of Negroes were detained briefly and an order was issued to move the vehicles. When the group told the officers that they wanted to go into the park, they were told that the park was closed because it had a capacity crowd and the superintendent had advised that no additional persons be admitted.

This incident was then used in a class action lawsuit, *J. Arthur Brown et al. v. South Carolina State Forestry Commission,* Civil Action No. AC774, filed on July 8, 1961, and alleging that the use of public park facilities in the state of South Carolina was denied to the blacks solely because they were Negroes. The lawsuit asked that laws allegedly requiring racial discrimination in the state park system be declared unconstitutional and that the defendants be enjoined not to prohibit them and other Negroes from making use of the public parks and beaches owned and operated by the state of South Carolina. In 1962 state authorities tried to appease the black audience somewhat by stating that Huntington Beach State Park would be divided in half, with one side for blacks and the other for whites. On July

10, 1963, U.S. district judge J. Robert Martin Jr. in Greenville issued an order that the South Carolina Forestry Commission desegregate the state parks system under the authority of the Civil Rights Act of 1954. To avoid desegregating the parks, the South Carolina Forestry Commission decided to close all of them on September 8, 1963, the day the court order went into effect.

The law to which the plaintiffs referred was a 1956 bill known as Section 14 of the Permanent Provisions of the General Appropriations Bill, which the head of the South Carolina Forestry Commission stated was their basis for operating a racially segregated park system. A confidential memorandum from Charles H. Flory, state forester, to all park superintendents on March 25, 1960, stated, "It seems reasonable that we should continue to have Negro laborers who will perform certain duties within the confines of a white park and that some of our white personnel will continue to officially visit Negro areas. Likewise there will be occasions when white leadership will take a Negro group into a Negro park, and when a white family will have a Negro maid or servant with them on their visit to the white parks. It seems we should continue to permit this practice in a very limited manner and with as little attention directed toward it as possible." After extensive public hearings in the effected communities, state park director E. R. Vreeland reopened all parks effective June 1, 1964. The swimming pool and cabins remained closed at Myrtle Beach State Park, however, until June 30, 1966. This park was allowed to do this due to a stipulation in the act as passed stating that a seacoast park on the request of the majority of the county delegation could open other facilities for Negroes or close camping.[28]

The issue of sharing the beach and the ocean was also considered in the early 1950s when negotiations were under way to reactivate Myrtle Beach Air Force Base. The United States Air Force wanted to purchase about twenty-seven acres of beach property from the South Carolina Forestry Commission for use as a recreational area for the servicemen, blacks and whites. Although the base began reactivation by September 1954, beach property was not included.[28] About 10 percent of the approximately four thousand servicemen stationed at Myrtle Beach were black in 1956.

While integration came slowly, by the mid-1960s most tourist accommodations and venues as well as schools were open to all races. Integration in politics would take a bit longer. Horry County elected its first black councilman in 1980. James Futrell was elected to Myrtle Beach City Council in 1982 and served until 1991. Myrtle Beach's black community experienced many changes between 1900 and 1980 in terms of personal and economic opportunity, all of which were the result of hard-working, determined men and women who wanted better jobs, better schools, and better neighborhoods for their children and grandchildren.

A Beach of Their Own

Before 1930 African Americans had few choices for enjoying leisure time at the ocean. Jim Crow laws of the time would not allow them to have fun alongside whites on Grand Strand beaches, including that of Myrtle Beach State Park, which opened in 1937. Leroy Brunson remembered that when children got out of school in the 1930s and 1940s they could go anywhere but toward the beach. He said, "That was the white area. We couldn't go there. If they caught you walking up there, it could be trouble."[29]

In 1933 George Tyson took an option to purchase two tracts of land north of Myrtle Beach from Ernest V. and Robert V. Ward, white residents of Little River Township, and named the parcel Tyson's Beach. Later one section became Atlantic Beach and the other became the Black Pearl. When Tyson ran into financial troubles in the early 1940s, he was forced to sell the land to about ten black professionals, who banded together to buy Tyson's mortgage and ensure that the property stayed in black hands. Dr. Peter Kelly, who lived in Conway, led the effort to find the doctors, college presidents, and other professionals who jointly put together the money to form Atlantic Beach Company. Dr. Leroy Upperman, a retired physician and surgeon from Wilmington, North Carolina, was one of the investors. He recalled, "Before getting into the real estate thing, I would drive down there with my wife or just take the afternoon off and go to Atlantic Beach. It was the only beach, except for the small beach of Sea Breeze, which is about fifteen miles from Wilmington, that blacks had available to them."[31] Atlantic Beach Company had ten stockholders led by Dr. J. Ward Seabrook, president of Fayetteville State College in Fayetteville, North Carolina. The first vacation home was built circa 1934 by Dr. A. J. Henderson, one of the founding members.[32] The corporation owned more than one hundred lots, of which less than 10 percent was in private hands. Dr. Robert Gordon from Dillon, who built the two-story Gordon Hotel on the corner of Atlantic Street at the oceanfront, and Dr. Peter Kelly of Conway owned at least 40 percent of the lots. Atlantic Street was the most developed street.

Atlantic Beach quickly began filling a pent-up demand in the Southeast for a spot where black men, women, and children could congregate freely, dance, eat, play in the ocean, and just generally have a good time vacationing without fear of reprisal or discrimination. In the 1940s the town grew with nightclubs, shops, motels, summer cottages, and year-round dwellings for black professionals and working-class people alike. Early accommodations included Marshall Hotel, Bluebird Inn, the Patio, and Rainbow Inn. In addition to the many motels, several clubs and restaurants, a movie theater, two grocery stores, two liquor stores, two service stations, a beauty shop, and a barbershop could be found in Atlantic Beach during its heyday. Amusement park rides, such as bumper cars, a Ferris wheel, and a merry-go-round, pleased the younger set. There was also a sidewalk photo studio, and the community had its own weekly newspaper.[33]

Just as at the pavilions in Myrtle Beach, Ocean Drive, Spivey Beach and other places, the Cotton Club, Atlantic Beach's first open-air pavilion, hosted top-name entertainers who would jam into the night. These were groups that entertained at the other beaches but because of their race were not allowed to sleep or eat there. So they gravitated to Atlantic Beach after hours, to the delight of its patrons. The town became a home away from home for famous black entertainers, such as James Brown, the Tams, the Drifters, Ray Charles, Martha and the Vandellas, and many more. "It was busy, really busy through the winter and the summer months. My wife and I had a novelty stand, toys and the like, and if we opened on Saturday, we would have sold out on Sunday. That's how money was turning," according to Willie L. Isom. "We had all the places wide open. Quite naturally our people couldn't go anywhere but right here, so you can imagine how clustered Atlantic Beach was at the time. People would dance in the street and you can see the dust flying."[34] Annie Bellamy Futrell remembered the holidays and weekends at Atlantic Beach: "Oh, Atlantic Beach was where blacks gathered on holidays and weekends. There was hardly walking room at holidays, and people just came and danced and had a glorious time. And those who could swim and those who couldn't, everybody was on the beach and in the water."[35]

The season usually opened on Easter Monday, with school buses bringing children for the annual school picnic from Conway, Loris, Georgetown, Charleston, Dillon, and Wilmington. The next big holiday was July 6, not July 4, because most people had to work on Independence Day. Every Thursday was "Maids Day" when white employers would bring their workers to Atlantic Beach for a holiday. An orange rope was anchored out in the ocean "dividing" Atlantic Beach from adjacent beaches because Atlantic Beach bathers were not allowed across those boundaries. "I cannot understand how they thought if we were in water confined to one spot that they wouldn't be contaminated by our blackness just because they put up a rope. It's water and it's flowing. It makes no sense," Alice Graham said with a laugh.[35]

By the 1960s residents of Atlantic Beach had to decide whether to consolidate with North Myrtle Beach or remain independent. They chose the latter, and the town was incorporated in 1966, with Emory Gore elected as the first mayor. The municipality built a town hall between 1967 and 1969 and formed a fire department in the early 1970s. U.S. senator Strom Thurmond helped the town obtain a grant to build a community center, which was completed in 1975. "Atlantic Beach was the only place for us to go. We could not go to Myrtle Beach, Ocean Drive, or anyplace else. At the service station, there was a black fountain and a white fountain, right next door to us on Highway 17. If you ordered food, you had to go to the back to take it out. So we were free [in Atlantic Beach]. Anyone in North Carolina, Virginia, all over the states was here in Atlantic Beach because they were free to do what they wanted to do and eat where they pleased and be served by waitresses and treated like human beings," said Earlene Woods, who has owned businesses in Atlantic Beach since the early 1950s. She remembered growing up in the 1930s in the Wampee community, when "there was just one little building right in front of the ocean called Black Hawk. I remember coming down, it wasn't paved, it was just a little trail where the cart wagon could come through. My grandfather would get all his children and his children's children back up [in] that wagon. The inland waterway wasn't there to divide us. We came over to do our fishing and whatever on those oxen carts. At that time, there wasn't any lights at all. So we had little candles and little lanterns on posts, sticking up near the end of the road so people would know where to turn. Lanterns sticking all in the buildings, that's what I remember." She also had warm memories of the Cotton Club: "It was an open building with just a top and a lot of piccolos [jukeboxes] all around. They had a cement floor out there and let me tell you, that cement floor ate up many, many soles of shoes. People were here all day and all night from all over the states." Other patios offered additional venues where people could dance all night. "What they called the Coliseum . . . we had Chubby Checker, Wilson Pickett, Al Green, Marvin Gaye. When they came to Myrtle Beach, they came here. And we housed them. Martha and the Vandellas, the Dixie Cups, what's that little woman who shakes a lot? Tina Turner! And Patti LaBelle. They performed in that arena. It's something to remember and I thank God for the portion that I remember," Woods said. Atlantic Beach was hurt dramatically by Hurricane Hazel in 1954 because it destroyed businesses, homes, and hotels, and many of the owners did not have insurance to rebuild. However, Woods said, "Integration was worse. Because the hurricane took the businesses, but integration took the people."[37]

In the early 1970s the influx of vacationers began to drop off because of the desegregation of other resort locations. Development largely stagnated, and businesses found more profitable locations. In a bid to attract visitors and raise money for the town, John Skeeters and three other residents had the idea in 1980 of inviting black motorcycle clubs from New York to Texas to a rally at Atlantic Beach over Memorial Day weekend. The Carolina Knight Riders motorcycle club hosted the event, which in its first years was relatively quiet. However, it quickly became an annual event that attracted tens of thousands, bringing much needed income and life back to the Black Pearl.[38]

Notes

Chapter One—From Earliest Inhabitants to the Dawn of the Twentieth Century

1. Reinhold Engelmayer, "The History of Early Man in the Grand Strand Area," *On the Beach* ([Summer 1979] n.d.), n.p., found in Horry County Vertical Files, South Caroliniana Library, University of South Carolina, Columbia.

2. Carl Steen, *Archaeological Investigations at Heron Pond/Diamond Back Development, Horry County, South Carolina* (Columbia, S.C.: Diachronic Research Foundation, 2000), n.p., site report on file at the S.C. Department of Archives and History, Columbia.

3. Ibid., 11.

4. Ibid., 15.

5. Ibid., 26.

6. A. Goff Bedford, *The Independent Republic—A Survey History of Horry County*, 2nd ed. (Conway, S.C.: Horry County Historical Society, 1989), 6; Walter Edgar, *South Carolina: A History* (Columbia: University of South Carolina Press, 1998), 21, 22, 24.

7. Edgar, *South Carolina*, 62.

8. J. W. Joseph, "Building to Grow: Agrarian Adaptations to South Carolina's Historical Landscapes," in *Carolina's Historical Landscapes: Archaeological Perspectives*, ed. Linda F. Stine et al. (Knoxville: University of Tennessee Press, 1997), 45.

9. Edgar, *South Carolina*, 58.

10. B. Keeling, "Geography Made Horry Different," *Myrtle Beach Sun-News*, March 31, 1990.

11. James Henry Rice, "Paladins of South Carolina," *State* (Columbia, S.C.), September 21, 1924, n.p.

12. Edgar, *South Carolina*, 149, 266. See also Jean West, "The Devil's Blue Dye: Indigo and Slavery," from *Slavery in America* multimedia project, available at http://www.slaveryinamerica.org/history/hs_es_indigo.htm (accessed August 20, 2005). The source for statistics noted are William James Hagy, *This Happy Land: The Jews of Colonial and Antebellum South Carolina* (Tuscaloosa: University of Alabama Press, 1993); and Marc Egnal, *New World Economies: The Growth of the Thirteen Colonies and Early Canada* (New York: Oxford University Press, 1998).

13. Heyward Cuckon Bellamy, "Vaught, South Carolina," *Independent Republic Quarterly* 19, no. 3 (Summer 1985): 19.

14. Connelly Burgin Berry, "What Has Happened to Gause's Swash?," *Independent Republic Quarterly* 30, no. 4 (Fall 1996): 7.

15. Connelly Burgin Berry, "The Horry County Vereens," *Independent Republic Quarterly* 6, no. 1 (January 1972): 6.

16. Connelly Burgin Berry, "Colonial Period in Horry County," *Independent Republic Quarterly* 9, no. 1 (January 1975): 13–15.

17. Bruno Gujer, "A Social History of Horry County before the Civil War," *Independent Republic Quarterly* 14, no. 4 (Fall 1980): 37–43.

18. C. Foster Smith, "Jeremiah Smith and the Confederate War," *Independent Republic Quarterly* 25, no. 3 (Summer 1991): 6–25.

19. U.S. Navy War Records Office, *Official Records of the Union and Confederate Navies in the War of the Rebellion*, series 1, vol. 15, 409–11, South Carolina Department of Archives and History, Columbia, S.C.

20. Connelly Burgin Berry, "Myrtle Beach Salt Industry," *Independent Republic Quarterly* 2, no. 3 (July 1968): 18–20.

21. Helen Milliken, *From the Beginning: A History of the Burroughs & Chapin Company* (Myrtle Beach, S.C.: Sheriar Press, 2004), 11. A more complete description of Burroughs & Collins Company's operations follows in chap. 2.

22. Charles Joyner, "The Far Side of the Forest: Timber and Naval Stores in the Waccamaw Region," *Independent Republic Quarterly* 18, no. 4 (Fall 1984): 13–17; Edgar, *South Carolina*, 138–39; Michael Harmon and Rodney Snedeker, "The Archaeological Record of Tar and Pitch Production in Coastal Carolina," in *Carolina's Historical Landscapes: Archaeological Perspectives*, ed. Linda F. Stine et al. (Knoxville: University of Tennessee Press, 1997), 145–47.

23. Roy Talbert Jr., *So Much to Be Thankful For: The Conway National Bank and the Economic History of Horry County* (Columbia, S.C.: Conway National Bank, 2003), 11.

Chapter Two—Transformation of the Sand

1. By 1906 Burroughs & Collins owned more than one hundred thousand acres of land in the area. This included the largest single tract of the former Withers estate, which extended on the north from where the Ocean Forest Hotel was built in 1929 to Spivey Beach on the south. See Edward E. Burroughs, "The Beginning of Myrtle Beach," *Independent Republic Quarterly* 5, no. 4 (October 1971): 17–18; C. B. Berry, "Towns and Communities in Horry County," *Independent Republic Quarterly* 29 (Winter 1982): 18; and Tom Fetters, "Loggers of Conway and the Independent Republic," *Independent Republic Quarterly* 20, no. 1 (Winter 1986): 6.

2. In 1904 the rail line from Conway to Myrtle Beach was renamed the Conway, Coast & Western, with the objective of crossing the Little Pee Dee River and reaching Mullins and Marion. The following year the line was sold to James H. Chadbourn.

3. Esther Nance Gray, "The Best of Many Worlds," *Independent Republic Quarterly* 18, no. 3 (Summer 1984): 11–14.

4. E. Horry Benton, interview by Barbara Stokes, April 27, 2004, Myrtle Beach Oral History Project, Chapin Memorial Library, Myrtle Beach, S.C.

5. *Horry Herald*, November 1, 1900, n.p. Oral tradition holds that a contest was held to name the town and Adeline Burroughs, widow of Franklin G. Burroughs, chose the winning name.

6. Edward E. Burroughs, "In My Time," *Independent Republic Quarterly* 28, no. 4 (Fall 1994): 26.

7. Their occupations, according to the 1910 U.S. census for Horry County, were hardware merchant, physician in drugstore practice, and bank cashier, respectively.

8. Nita Malom, "E. E. Burroughs Recalls 'It Took One Year to Build First Hotel,'" *North Myrtle Beach Times,* July 1, 1976, 19.

9. Milliken, *From the Beginning,* 42.

10. "Big Company at Myrtle Beach," *Horry Herald,* March 23, 1905, n.p.

11. Alfred Runte, *National Parks: The American Experience,* 3rd ed. (Lincoln: University of Nebraska Press, 1987), 44, 94.

12. The hotel was called the Myrtle Beach Hotel on postcards and in later newspaper articles, but Sea Side Inn is the most commonly used name, in addition to what is used in newspaper ads.

13. Michael Karl Witzel, *The American Gas Station* (Osceola, Wis.: Motorbooks International, 1992), 15, 29.

14. Talbert, *So Much to Be Thankful For,* 93.

15. "Locals and Personals" column, *Horry Herald,* June 19, 1924, n.p.

16. Malom, "E. E. Burroughs Recalls 'It Took One Year to Build First Hotel,'" 19. Born in 1900, Edward Egerton Burroughs was the son of Franklin Augustus and Iola Buck Burroughs. He died in 1979.

17. "Suffered Accident While Out Riding," *Horry Herald,* June 21, 1917, 3.

18. Lena Lencek and Gideon Bosker, *The Beach: The History of Paradise on Earth* (New York: Viking Press, 1998), 139–40.

19. Ibid., 147–48.

20. *The Progressive Railway of the South, Winter Golf Courses, Hotels and Boarding Houses, 1915,* Seaboard Air Line Railway brochure.

21. Milliken, *From the Beginning,* 60.

22. In 1906 Benjamin Collins sold his interest in Burroughs & Collins to the Burroughs brothers. The company retained his name, however.

23. Florence Epps, "Mr. Chapin Meets Myrtle Beach," *Independent Republic Quarterly* 1, no. 3 (July 1967): 78.

24. "Stock Changes Hands," *Horry Herald,* October 9, 1919, n.p.

25. It is believed that the lumber from the commissary was used to build the Myrtle Beach Colored School, which opened in 1932.

26. Bedford, *Independent Republic,* 133.

27. Edgar, *South Carolina,* 485.

28. "Seaside Resort Opens Tuesday" and "Seaside Lots Now Offered," *Horry Herald,* June 2, 1921, 1 and 5, respectively.

29. Adeline Godfrey Pringle Merrill, ed., "Personal History of the F. G. Burroughs Family," unpublished manuscript, 2003, 205, Chapin Memorial Library, Myrtle Beach, S.C.

30. "Myrtle Beach Club Building," *Horry Herald,* March 2, 1922, 2; Register of Deeds, Horry County, S.C., Book B-5, 63, September 23, 1922. The pier was built but was only 250 feet long initially.

31. Bernard S. Solomon, ed., *Myrtle Beach Today and Tomorrow* (August 16, 1935): 3. This promotional magazine was "published in the interest of a rapidly growing beach metropolis."

32. "Whole Coast Making Move," *Horry Herald,* May 14, 1925, 1.

33. "South Carolina Coast Section More Beautiful than Florida," *Beaufort Gazette,* June 18, 1925, 1.

34. According to the late Catherine Lewis, local historian and retired director of the Horry County Library system, Burroughs broke with Singleton because he learned that Singleton hired another man to serve in his place in the Confederate army.

Chapter Three—Depression-Era Developments

1. Archie Vernon Huff, *Greenville: The History of the City and County in the South Carolina Piedmont* (Columbia: University of South Carolina Press, 1995), 292; Edgar, *South Carolina,* 485, 499; U.S. Bureau of the Census, Fourteenth Census (1920) and Fifteenth Census (1930), Horry County, Dogwood Neck Township (Myrtle Beach), S.C. For an analysis of the populations of South Carolina counties, see http://www.sciway.net/data/county-population/index.html.

2. Talbert, *So Much to Be Thankful For,* 100.

3. David L. Carlton, "Unbalanced Growth and Industrialization: The Case of South Carolina," in *Developing Dixie: Modernization in a Traditional Society,* ed. Winfred B. Moore Jr., Joseph F. Tripp, and Lyon G. Tyler Jr. (Westport, Conn.: Greenwood Press, 1988), 117; "How the Wheels Got Turning: A Historical Perspective on American Roads," http://www.inventors.about.com/library/inventors/blcar3.html (accessed March 3, 2005).

4. Carlton, "Unbalanced Growth," 122.

5. 1929 Atlantic Coastal Highway map, http://www.sc.edu/library/socar/images/im00spr/map3.jpg (accessed March 5, 2005). In 1929 the Atlantic Coastal Highway was U.S. Interstate 17. Myrtle Beach was connected to this highway via Highway 38 (modern-day U.S. Highway 501) through Conway and Marion.

6. Milliken, *From the Beginning,* 71.

7. Huff, *Greenville,* 296.

8. James D. Grist, "How Springs and Rice Did It," dateline Columbia, *Horry Herald,* March 4, 1926, 1.

9. James Henry Rice, *Glories of the Carolina Coast,* 2nd ed. (Columbia, S.C.: R. L. Bryan Company, 1926), 58.

10. *Horry Herald* accounts differ on the number of acres sold to Woodside. One article dated February 25, 1926, said 66,505 acres, and another dated March 11, 1926, reported 64,488 acres.

11. "Myrtle Beach Declared Sold," *Horry Herald,* February 25, 1926, 1.

12. "Begin Sales on June 5," *Horry Herald,* April 22, 1926, 1.

13. The administration building would later be named Lafayette Manor, and the original Sea Side Inn would reclaim its name.

14. In reality, the "airport" was more of an airstrip and is believed to have been near present-day Mr. Joe White Boulevard (formerly Eleventh Avenue North) and Seaboard Street.

15. "Myrtle Beach, South Carolina, America's Finest Strand," *National Real Estate Journal,* June 10, 1929, n.p.; James A. Dunlap III, "Victims of Neglect: The Career and Creations of John T. Woodside, 1865–1986" (master's thesis, University of South Carolina, 1986), 48.

16. "New Building for Myrtle," *Horry Herald,* December 16, 1926, 1.

17. E. Horry Benton, interview by Catherine Lewis, December 4, 1992, Horry County Oral History Project, Kimbel Library, Coastal Carolina University, Conway, S.C.

18. E. Horry Benton, interview by Barbara Stokes, April 27, 2004.

19. Dunlap, "Victims of Neglect," 54.

20. *Arcady,* oversized prospectus, hardbound, published by Arcady Executives, New York, for limited distribution, dated February 5, 1929, and found at Chapin Memorial Library, Myrtle Beach, S.C. No records have been located to date of how many memberships were sold. The project was never developed.

21. Richard M. Hussey Jr., interview by Sarah Bryan, November 17, 2004, Myrtle Beach Oral History Project. Richard Hussey's brother was Robert Hussey Jr., who owned Ocean Motors and served on the first Myrtle Beach City Council in 1938.

22. Howell V. Bellamy Jr., interview by Sarah Bryan, April 28, 2005, Myrtle Beach Oral History Project.

23. "Floral Beach Plans Go Out," *Horry Herald,* May 13, 1926, n.p.

24. Genevieve Chandler Peterkin, interview by Jenifer Powers and Barbara Stokes, October 31, 2002, Myrtle Beach Oral History Project.

25. Dunlap, "Victims of Neglect," 59, 60.

26. Ibid., 57.

27. E. Horry Benton, interview by Catherine Lewis, December 4, 1992.

28. "Excerpts from the Burroughs Family," *Independent Republic Quarterly* 4, no. 3 (July 1970): 10; Dunlap, "Victims of Neglect," 62.

29. Henry Trezevant Willcox, "Growing Up with Myrtle Beach," in *Musings of a Hermit,* ed. Clarke A. Willcox, 4th ed. (Murrells Inlet, S.C.: The Hermitage, 1973), 146.

30. "International" was added to the golf club's name in the 1970s.

31. Bernard Baruch, *The Public Years: My Own Story* (New York: Holt, Rinehart and Winston, 1960), 230.

32. Jack Irby Hayes Jr., *South Carolina and the New Deal* (Columbia: University of South Carolina Press, 2001), 8, 39. The national average for citizens on relief was 10 percent.

33. *Horry Herald,* May 29, 1930, 2.

34. Register of Deeds, Horry County, S.C., Deed Index, Grantor (Myrtle Beach Farms Company), 1925 and 1926.

35. U.S. Bureau of the Census, Fifteenth Census (1930), Horry County, Dogwood Neck Township (Myrtle Beach), S.C.

36. Roger Biles, *The South and the New Deal* (Lexington: University Press of Kentucky, 1994), 58; Edgar, *South Carolina,* 501.

37. Philip Gray, "The Gray Family," unpublished family manuscript, printed ca. 1970, 59–61. Gray married Esther Nance in 1940, served on Myrtle Beach City Council from 1947 to 1954, and was a community leader.

38. S.C. State Park Service History, http://www.discoversouthcarolina.com/stateparks/1942.asp.

39. J. B. Eudy and Lloyce V. Nelson, "From the Depression Years, a Great Need Gave Birth to the 3-Cs," unpublished manuscript, Thomas Cooper Library, University of South Carolina, Columbia, 6–7.

40. Edna Kennerly, "The Civilian Conservation Corps as a Social Resource in South Carolina" (master's thesis, University of South Carolina, 1940), 14.

41. Homer A. Smith to Holmes B. Springs, June 14, 1934, State Commission of Forestry, Civilian Conservation Corps, "Myrtle Beach State Park, 1934–1942." All letters referred to in this section, unless otherwise noted, are located in this collection.

42. Springs to Smith, June 1, 1934.

43. Smith to Springs, June 14, 1934.

44. Smith to Orin M. Bullock, July 31, 1935.

45. Project estimate folders, State Forestry Commission, Civilian Conservation Corps, "Myrtle Beach State Park, 1934–1942."

46. S.C. State Department of Parks, Recreation and Tourism, historical files, Columbia, S.C.

47. "State Park Dedicated," *Horry Herald*, June 24, 1937, 1.

48. Some discrepancy exists about exactly how many guest rooms were originally designed for the hotel.

49. Slave Narrative Collection, Manuscripts and Prints and Photographs Division, Library of Congress, http://www.memory.loc.gov/ammem/snhtml/. Genevieve Chandler was also a noted painter of South Carolina low-country life.

50. Genevieve Chandler Peterkin, interview by Jenifer Powers and Barbara Stokes, October 31, 2002.

Chapter Four—War Comes to the Beach

1. Edgar, *South Carolina*, 456.

2. U.S. Bureau of the Census, Thirteenth Census (1910), Fourteenth Census (1920), and Fifteenth Census (1930), Horry County, Dogwood Neck Township (Myrtle Beach), S.C. This census population total does not include seasonal residents or visitors. The censuses were enumerated in April, before the summer season began.

3. Talbert, *So Much to Be Thankful For,* 137.

4. Edgar, *South Carolina*, 477.

5. "Ready for Opening at Myrtle Beach," *Horry Herald,* June 14, 1917, 1; "Locals and Personals" column, *Horry Herald*, June 21, 1917, 3; "Festivities at Myrtle Beach," *Horry Herald*, June 28, 1917, 4; "Myrtle Beach Has Good Season," *Horry Herald*, August 23, 1917, 1.

6. "Locals and Personals" column, *Horry Herald,* July 26, 1917, 3.

7. "Myrtle Beach Council of Defense," *Horry Herald*, June 20, 1918, 3.

8. David R. Coker, letter to S.C. County Council of Defense chairmen, June 27, 1917, Miscellaneous Correspondence, State Council of Defense 1917–18, Box 10, S192069, S.C. Department of Archives and History, Columbia.

9. "To Officers of All Community Councils," *Horry Herald,* June 6, 1918, 1; "War Savings Campaign Is on in Earnest," *Horry Herald*, June 20, 1918, 1; Edgar, *South Carolina*, 477. In announcing the six-hundred-thousand-dollar goal, Burroughs added that "the state organization is making a tremendous effort to try to get our quota in line," leading the reader to believe that the state council knew it was an unrealistic goal.

10. Emma J. Bryan Epps, interview by Sarah Bryan, March 9, 2004, Myrtle Beach Oral History Project.

11. Biles, *The South and the New Deal,* 2.

12. Edgar, *South Carolina,* 477; John Hammond Moore, "Nazi Troopers in South Carolina, 1944–1946," *South Carolina Historical Magazine* 81 (1980): 306–15.

13. Lawrence D. Magrath, letter to H. Reed Smith, October 13, 1917, Military Department, National Council on Defense, S192 069. Magrath served as mayor of Conway four times, 1915–16, 1919–22, 1925–34, and 1945–46.

14. "Fourth of July Celebration," *Horry Herald,* July 4, 1918, 1; Edgar, *South Carolina,* 477.

15. Emma J. Bryan Epps, interview by Sarah Luisa Bryan, March 9, 2004.

16. S.C. State Council of Defense, *Historical Account of the Activities of the South Carolina State Council of Defense, August 1, 1940–June 30, 1944* (Columbia, S.C., 1944).

17. Ibid., 288.

18. Springs was an appropriate ally in this pursuit as he was head of South Carolina's selective service program, a member of the Governor's Advisory Council on National Defense, and a dedicated supporter of Myrtle Beach development.

19. The U.S. Army Air Corps became the U.S. Army Air Force in 1941 and the U.S. Air Force in 1947.

20. U.S. Eastern District of South Carolina, District Court, Florence Division, Civil Action No. 657, Order for Possession, dated December 16, 1941, filed December 18, 1941.

21. U.S. Air Force Historical Division, "Brief History of Myrtle Beach Air Force Base, 1940–56," *Independent Republic Quarterly* 13, no. 2 (Spring 1979): 8–10; Mary Emily Platt Jackson, "Memories of the Beach—Before Development," *Independent Republic Quarterly* 24, no. 2 (Spring 1990): 5.

22. Complete Presidential Transcripts of Franklin D. Roosevelt, Da Capo Press, 1972, U.S. National Archives and Records Administration, Washington, D.C. For an account of President Roosevelt's stay at Hobcaw Barony, read Merriman Smith, *Thank You, Mr. President: A White House Notebook* (New York: Harper & Brothers, 1946), 133–44.

23. Sigmund Abeles, interview by Sarah Bryan, May 22, 2004, Myrtle Beach Oral History Project.

24. Athalia Stalvey Ramsey, interview by Sarah Bryan, January 21, 2005, Myrtle Beach Oral History Project. The U.S. Air Force Historical Office confirms that several of the men on the Doolittle mission, which occurred in April 1942, trained at Myrtle Beach Army Air Base, but the author is unable to confirm what dates they were at the base.

25. Blanche Floyd, "World War II," in her *Tales along the Grand Strand of South Carolina* (Winston-Salem, N.C.: Bandit Books, 1996), 119.

26. Eleanor C. Bishop, *Prints in the Sand: The U.S. Coast Guard Beach Patrol during World War II* (Missoula, Mont.: Pictorial Histories Publishing Co., Inc., 1989), 36.

27. Genevieve C. Peterkin, with William Baldwin, *Heaven Is a Beautiful Place* (Columbia: University of South Carolina Press, 2000), 69.

28. Archer and Anna Hyatt Huntington eventually amassed a total of nine thousand acres, which today largely comprises Brookgreen Gardens and Huntington Beach State Park. See Rick Simmons, "Did German U-Boats Patrol the Grand Strand during World War II?," *Alternatives News Magazine* (Myrtle Beach, S.C.), July 9–26, 1987.

29. Fritz Hamer, *The Homefront and the Beginning of Change: World War II and South Carolina, 1941–1945* (Columbia, S.C.: Palmetto Conservation Foundation, 1997), 7; Holmes B. Springs, Brig. Gen., *Selective Service in South Carolina, 1940–1947: An Historical Report* (Columbia, S.C., 1948), 40–41, 84, 112, 157.

30. Judy Ledford Wyatt, "United States Policy toward German Prisoners of War and Its Application in South Carolina" (master's thesis, University of South Carolina, 1985), 34, 77–80.

31. June Hora, interview by S.C. Education TV for *Myrtle Beach Memories,* spring/summer 2003, unedited videotape 13.

32. Sigmund Abeles, interview by Sarah Bryan, May 22, 2004.

33. Moore, "Nazi Troopers in South Carolina, 1944–1946"; Blanche Floyd, "When the POWs Came," *Myrtle Beach Magazine,* n.d., 24.

34. Harold Clardy, interview by S.C. Educational TV for *Myrtle Beach Memories,* spring/summer 2003, unedited videotape 15.

35. Hamer, *Homefront,* 16.

36. Sigmund Abeles, "My Yes-Tiddies," unpublished manuscript, Box 7 of 8, Folder 258, Sigmund Abeles Collection, South Caroliniana Library, University of South Carolina, Columbia.

37. Numan Bartley, *The New South, 1945–1980: The Story of the South's Modernization,* vol. 11 of *The History of the South,* ed. Wendell Holmes Stephenson and E. Merton Coulter (Baton Rouge: Louisiana State University Press and the Littlefield Foundation for Southern History of the University of Texas, 1995), 11.

38. David Halberstam, *The Fifties* (New York: Fawcett Books, 1993), 27.

39. Ibid, 704.

40. "Facilities of Air Base May Be Used for Pilot Training," *Myrtle Beach Sun,* January 26, 1951, 1.

41. "Anthony Says Unity of Purpose within Myrtle Beach Is Key to User of Base for Pilot Training," *Myrtle Beach Sun,* February 16, 1951, 1.

42. "Air Force Hopes to Use Base," *Myrtle Beach Sun,* January 18, 1951, 1.

43. During the first week of December 1943, the 354th provided escort for the Eighth Air Force's crippling bombing raids over Germany.

44. "World War II Fighter Group Will Be Reactivated Here," *Myrtle Beach Sun and Ocean Beach News,* December 5, 1956, 3.

45. Discussion of the international missions came from "About the Base, Myrtle Beach Air Force Base History," http://www.myrtlebeachonline.com (accessed August 21, 2003), which is the on-line version of the *Myrtle Beach Sun-News;* and "354 Fighter Wing," http://www.maxwell.af.mil/au/afhra/wwwroot/rso/wings_groups/pages (accessed August 11, 2005), from the Air Force Historical Research Division.

Chapter Five—Natural and Environmental History of the Grand Strand

1. Rhode Island encompasses 1,214 square miles, and Horry County has 1,134 square miles. The beach of Padre Island, Texas, is the longest in the United States, with 130 miles continuous sand beach. Horry County was one of the one hundred fastest growing counties in the United States between July 2004 and July 2005, according to *Money* magazine.

2. Edgar, *South Carolina,* 6.

3. City of Myrtle Beach, Comprehensive Plan, adopted April 13, 1999, amended September 2000, "Existing Conditions—Natural Resources," C.23–71; Bruce G. Thom, *Coastal and Fluvial Landforms: Horry and Marion Counties, South Carolina* (Baton Rouge: Louisiana State University Press, 1967), 6, 47.

4. Engelmayer, "History of Early Man in the Grand Strand Area," n.p.; Steen, *Archaeological Investigations,* 5.

5. Thom, *Coastal and Fluvial Landforms,* 17, 30.

6. "Lewis Ocean Bay Heritage Preserve," Heritage Trust Program Preserve Guide, S.C. Department of Natural Resources, http://www.dnr.state.sc.us/wild/heritage/hp/lewisob/default.htm (accessed March 21, 2005); Myrtle Beach Comprehensive Plan, adopted 1999, amended 2000, C.27.

7. George A. Howard, "Carolina Bays," electronically published paper, written 1997, http://www.georgehoward.net/cbays.htm (accessed March 21, 2005). According to his Web site, Howard is on staff at Restoration Systems, LLC, Raleigh, N.C.

8. Thom, *Coastal and Fluvial Landforms,* 17.

9. James R. Fussell, "Some Aspects of the Geography of Recreation in Coastal South Carolina" (master's thesis, University of South Carolina, 1966), 45.

10. Tempe Oehler, interview by Jenifer Powers, August 6, 2003, Myrtle Beach Oral History Project.

11. Fussell, "Some Aspects of the Geography of Recreation," 46.

12. City of Myrtle Beach, Comprehensive Plan, adopted 1999, amended 2000, C.54–C.64.

13. Hayes, *South Carolina and the New Deal,* 54.

14. S.C. State Parks, Recreation and Tourism, Annual Reports, 1970–71 and 1975–76.

15. Ann Wilson, Paul McCormack, and Scott Enter, "History of Myrtle Beach State Park" (unpublished manuscript, n.d.).

16. Robert Turner, "Myrtle Beach State Park," Superintendents' Report, meeting of the S.C. State Parks Superintendents, 1984; Robert Turner and Ann Wilson, interview by Jenifer Powers, February 25, 2004, Myrtle Beach Oral History Project. In November 2002 the entire pool structure, including basin and pipes, was removed for safety reasons.

17. Robert Turner and Ann Wilson, interview by Jenifer Powers, February 25, 2004; Wilson et al., "History of Myrtle Beach State Park."

18. Walton Rawls, ed., *A Century of American Sculpture: Treasures from Brookgreen Gardens* (New York: Abbeville Press, 1981), 13–14.

19. Ray Sigmon, Mike Foley, and Irvin Pitts, *Huntington Beach State Park Visitor's Guide* (Columbia: S.C. State Department of Parks, Recreation and Tourism, 2001), 1, 19.

Chapter Six—The Ties That Bind Us Together— Religion and Education

1. Lewis P. Jones, "Religion in South Carolina: An Overview," in *Religion in South Carolina,* ed. Charles Lippy (Columbia: University of South Carolina Press, 1993), 14–15.

2. Tempe Oehler, interview by Barbara Stokes, March 5, 2004, Myrtle Beach Oral History Project. Oehler's father was Nicholas Collins Hughes Jr. (1883–1956), who

surveyed the original Myrtle Beach municipal plat in 1935, in addition to drawing many other maps of the area.

3. "Great Chance Fronts Horry," *Horry Herald,* March 11, 1926, 2.

4. Mrs. J. J. Able Jr., "Baptists Started First Church in Myrtle Beach, Others Soon Followed with Local Growth," *Myrtle Beach Sun and Ocean Beach News,* March 28, 1956, n.p. The percentages of affiliations were likely higher than reported, especially in the African American community.

5. Lewis P. Jones, "History of Public Education in South Carolina," in *Public Education in South Carolina: Historical, Political and Legal Perspective,* ed. Thomas R. McDaniel (Spartanburg, S.C.: Bookstore, Converse College, 1984), 1; Catherine H. Lewis, *Horry County, South Carolina 1730–1993* (Columbia: University of South Carolina Press, 1998), 140–50.

6. Eva Claire Riggs, "'We Hardly Ever Went to Beach, Never Ventured Far into Ocean,'" *Myrtle Beach Sun-News,* October 29, 1964, C8.

7. The *Horry Herald* for October 13, 1910, listed all school districts and trustee names in the county. The land on which the school sat is described in Horry County Register of Deeds, Conway, S.C., March 9, 1911, Book LLL, 277. This deed indicates that Burroughs & Collins Co. sold the Myrtle Beach School District No. 13 two acres for sixty dollars. This land was in Conway Township and was known as the Old Schoolhouse near Myrtle Beach. The deed said that it was bound on the north and east by lands formerly owned by Burroughs & Collins and deeded to Henry Lamb, Richard Randall, and Caesar Lewis, on the south by the lands of Henry Hardee, and on the west by the road leading from Pine Island to the Socastee Road.

8. Edgar, *South Carolina,* 464, 489–90, 490n23; U.S. Office of Education, *Biennial Survey of Education in the United States, 1928–1930* (Washington, D.C.: Government Printing Office, 1932), 2:28–29.

9. "Horry Divided for Districts," *Horry Herald,* May 26, 1927, 1. Prior to the opening of its high school in 1928, Myrtle Beach District No. 13 was part of Socastee High School District No. 6. See Gladys Ferguson, "School System Has Shown Amazing Growth in Myrtle Beach," *Myrtle Beach Sun,* December 10, 1958, n.p.; "Plans for New School," *Horry Herald,* May 12, 1927, n.p.; and "To Dedicate School," *Horry Herald,* February 16, 1928, n.p.

10. Carol L. Lewis, "Myrtle Beach's Class of 1933 Reminisces," *Myrtle Beach Sun-News,* June 12, 1983.

11. Tempe Oehler, interview by Barbara Stokes, March 5, 2004.

12. Sigmund Abeles, interview by Sarah Bryan, May 22, 2004; Billy Roberts, discussion with Barbara Stokes, May 20, 2005.

13. Joseph, Roosevelt, and Jim Bellamy, interview by Sarah Bryan and Barbara Stokes, February 15, 2004, Myrtle Beach Oral History Project.

14. James C. Benton, interview by Barbara Stokes, July 8, 2003.

15. This school remained in use until a new high school complex opened on Robert Grissom Parkway in the early 1990s.

16. Jones, "History of Public Education in South Carolina," 24.

17. "To Officers of All Community Councils," *Horry Herald,* June 6, 1918, 4.

18. Alumni, Myrtle Beach Colored School, transcripts of unedited group interviews by Time Warner, Myrtle Beach, June 19, 2001, Myrtle Beach Oral History Project.

19. Division of Surveys and Field Service, *Horry County Schools: A Survey Report* (Nashville, Tenn.: George Peabody College for Teachers, 1946), 9–28; "An Horry County Life," *Independent Republic Quarterly* 26 no. 2 (Spring 1992): 35–36.

20. James F. Byrnes, *All in One Lifetime* (New York: Harper & Brothers, 1958), 408.

21. Jones, "History of Public Education in South Carolina," 25; Edgar, *South Carolina,* 522–23; Byrnes, *All in One Lifetime,* 408.

22. Alumni, Myrtle Beach Colored School, transcripts of unedited group interviews by Time Warner, Myrtle Beach, June 19, 2001, Myrtle Beach Oral History Project.

23. Gladys Ferguson, "School System Has Shown Amazing Growth in Myrtle Beach," *Myrtle Beach Sun,* December 10, 1958, n.p. Carver Training School had several different names over the next twenty-five years: it was changed to Carver Elementary in 1970, then to Central Elementary in 1974, and then to Lakewood Elementary in 1975. It closed as a school in 1983 and was demolished in the 1990s.

24. Division of Surveys and Field Service, *Horry County Schools,* 72, 83.

25. Myrtle Beach High School Yearbook, 1959, 40.

26. "School Seeks Federal Funds," *Myrtle Beach News,* May 19, 1955, 1.

27. Alumni, Myrtle Beach Colored School, transcripts of unedited group interviews by Time Warner, Myrtle Beach, June 19, 2001, Myrtle Beach Oral History Project.

28. Keith Cribb, interview by Sarah Bryan, November 16, 2004, Myrtle Beach Oral History Project.

29. Louise Springs Crews, interview by Sarah Bryan, October 16, 2004, Myrtle Beach Oral History Project.

30. "2,685 Students Enter Myrtle Beach Schools," *Myrtle Beach Sun-News,* September 2, 1965, 1.

31. The GI Bill, officially called the Servicemen's Readjustment Act of 1944, provided, among other things, stipends covering college tuition and living expenses for veterans.

32. "Horry Junior College Accepting Registrants," *Myrtle Beach Sun,* July 28, 1954, 1. In 1993 Coastal Carolina University became an independent public institution, separate from the University of South Carolina. By 2003 more than six thousand students were enrolled at CCU, representing all fifty states.

33. Gray, "Gray Family," 106–7; Horry-Georgetown Technical College Mission Statement, http://www.hgtc.edu/welcome/mission.htm. In 2005 more than four thousand students were enrolled at the college.

34. Etrulia Dozier, interview by Sarah Bryan, April 27, 2005, Myrtle Beach Oral History Project. Dozier retired from the Horry County School District in 1998. See also Lewis, *Horry County, South Carolina,* 154; Mary Laird Whitmire, "The WPA and Development of the Public Library System in South Carolina," unpublished manuscript, Connie Schulz File, South Caroliniana Library, University of South Carolina, Columbia; and Paul Quattlebaum, "History of the Library Movement," originally published July 1, 1949, reprinted in *Independent Republic Quarterly* 8, no. 3 (July 1974): 4, 5.

35. "Chapin's Librarian Boone to Retire," *Lowcountry Review,* May 2–23, 1990, n.p.

Chapter Seven—The Pavilion: A Monument to Community,
Tourism, and Memory

1. Will Moredock, *Banana Republic: A Year in the Heart of Myrtle Beach* (Charleston, S.C.: Frontline Press, Ltd., 2003), 28.

2. Merrill, "Personal History of the F. G. Burroughs Family," 203.

3. Susan Hoffer McMillan, *Myrtle Beach and Conway in Vintage Postcards* (Charleston, S.C.: Arcadia, 2001), 10, 20; Talbert, *So Much to Be Thankful For,* 103.

4. Annette Epps Reesor, "Sand, Surf and Shells—A Child's Eye View," *Independent Republic Quarterly* 1, no. 3 (July 1967): 8, 9.

5. The hotel Pavilion continued to exist as late as 1927. When the Sea Side Inn was physically moved closer to the waterfront in 1927 and connected to the 1920 annex, the hotel Pavilion was dismantled. Its parts may have been used in building Myrtle Lodge.

6. Susan Hoffer McMillan, *Myrtle Beach and the Grand Strand* (Charleston, S.C.: Arcadia, 2004), 23.

7. John Kenrick, "A History of the Musical Minstrel Shows," http://www.musicals 101.com/minstrel (accessed May 3, 2005).

8. Susan and Marshall McMillan, discussion with Barbara Stokes, July 29 and August 3, 2005.

9. Milliken, *From the Beginning,* 83, 164.

10. Census of Classic Wood Carousels, National Carousel Association, http://www.nca-usa.org/census/census-CLA (accessed May 3, 2005); Susan McMillan, "Myrtle Beach Melodies," *Sandlapper,* July 1977, 25.

11. U.S. Department of the Interior, National Park Service, National Register of Historic Places Registration Form for German Band Organ, Horry County, S.C.

12. Frank Beacham, *Whitewash: A Southern Journey through Music, Mayhem and Murder* (New York: the author, 2002), 27.

13. Disagreements continue as to how and where the dance was born. Frank Beacham's interviews about the background of the dance were with some of its earliest and best-known practitioners.

14. Milliken, *From the Beginning,* 87.

15. Harold Clardy, discussion with Barbara Stokes, February 7, 2003.

16. Charles Joyner, interview by Sarah Bryan, May 20, 2004, Myrtle Beach Oral History Project.

17. Sigmund Abeles, interview by Sarah Bryan, May 22, 2004.

18. Howell Bellamy Jr., interview by Sarah Bryan, April 28, 2005.

19. Jack Thompson, interview by Barbara Stokes, June 23, 2004.

Chapter Eight—Family-Owned and -Operated

1. Sea Side Inn underwent several name changes and spellings in its short lifetime (1901–49). I have chosen to spell it as it was presented in its first advertisements in the *Horry Herald* in 1901. It was also referred to as the Myrtle Beach Hotel. After 1926 it was renamed The Strand and The Carolina when the newly constructed Myrtle Beach Estates' Administration Building was named the Sea Side Inn. In the 1930s the latter property was renamed Lafayette Manor and the original Sea Side Inn got its name back.

2. Myrtle Beach Farms Company was spun off from Burroughs & Collins and incorporated on October 1, 1912. The charter said that it would conduct a mercantile

business; manage the hotel, amusement park, and grounds; buy, improve, and develop real estate; and conduct a general farming business.

3. Nita Malom, "E. E. Burroughs Recalls 'It Took One Year to Build First Hotel,'" *North Myrtle Beach Times,* July 1, 1976, 19.

4. McMillan, *Myrtle Beach and the Grand Strand,* 7.

5. A hard clay road was completed from Conway to Myrtle Beach via Socastee in 1914 and was replaced by a paved road in 1923.

6. "Myrtle Beach Declared Sold," *Horry Herald,* February 25, 1926, 1. There is some question as to whether the annex mentioned in this article is the Myrtle Lodge or the Bath House.

7. The newer hotel was heated, while the original Sea Side Inn was not.

8. Janis Stewart Smith, interview by Sarah Bryan, August 24, 2003, Myrtle Beach Oral History Project.

9. "Puts in Radio," *Horry Herald,* September 30, 1926, 3; "Big Fox Hunt at the Beach," *Horry Herald,* October 7, 1926, 2; "A Red Letter Day for Myrtle Beach," *Horry Herald,* September 2, 1926, n.p.; "Big Day at Myrtle Beach," *Horry Herald,* November 25, 1926, 1.

10. Its popularity as a hotel also waned because of its close proximity to the noise of the amusement park.

11. "Yacht Club Full," *Horry Herald,* July 3, 1924, 1.

12. "Horry Women Register to Vote," *Horry Herald,* October 14, 1920, n.p.; Edgar, *South Carolina,* 471.

13. Register of Deeds, Horry County, S.C., mortgage to Annie and Leila [*sic*] Burney from Myrtle Beach Farms Co., August 21, 1923, for Lot 5, Block 1; deed filed January 3, 1924, Book B-5, No. 256, $300; U.S. Bureau of the Census, Fourteenth Census (1920), Williamsburg County, Johnson Township, Hemingway, S.C.; *Myrtle Beach News,* April 30, 1939, n.p

14. Harold Clardy, interview by Barbara Stokes, February 7, 2003, Myrtle Beach Oral History Project; Julia Macklen, interview by Catherine Lewis, March 25, 1998, Horry County Oral History Project.

15. Gray, "Gray Family"; Register of Deeds, Horry County, S.C., mortgage from Myrtle Beach Farms to Myrtle Gause, August 19, 1935, Book 94, p. 253.

16. Register of Deeds, Horry County, S.C., mortgage from Myrtle Beach Farms to Pat Rousseau Ivey, March 26, 1934, Book 94, p. 54, lot 233. Some confusion arises as to the names of each of the buildings that were part of the Patricia complex. However, dates are consistent in all accounts.

17. Sigmund Abeles, interview by Sarah Bryan, May 22, 2004; Sigmund Abeles, Commencement Address, Coastal Carolina University, May 6, 2000, Box 8, File 277, Sigmund Abeles Collection, South Caroliniana Library, University of South Carolina, Columbia.

18. Abeles, Commencement Address, Coastal Carolina University. President Franklin Roosevelt visited the Myrtle Beach Army Air Force Base on April 23, 1944, during a month-long stay at Bernard Baruch's Hobcaw Barony in Georgetown County. While Churchill visited Baruch on separate occasions, a joint visit of the two has only been rumored and no primary-source documentation can confirm it.

19. Sigmund Abeles, "My Yes-Tiddies," unpublished memoir, Box 7 of 8, Folder 258, 31, Sigmund Abeles Collection, South Caroliniana Library, University of South Carolina, Columbia.

20. Horry County Council, Petitions for Licenses to Operate Tourist Courts, 1938–40, L26087, S.C. Department of Archives and History, Columbia. The dates of these licenses reflect an annual licensing process. The record did not include previous or later years of licensing and so should not be read as start-up dates for the operations.

21. U.S. Department of the Interior, National Parks Service, National Register of Historic Places Registration Form for the Chesterfield Inn, ca. 1995. The hotel was placed on the National Register in 1996.

22. John A. Jakle, Keith A. Sculle, and Jefferson S. Rogers, *The Motel in America* (Baltimore: Johns Hopkins University Press, 1996), 18.

23. City of Myrtle Beach, S.C., Zoning Ordinance, adopted September 17, 1947.

24. Jakle et al., *Motel in America,* 16.

25. South Carolina State Chamber of Commerce, *Dollars in Flight: A Manual Showing Why and How South Carolina Should Promote Tourist Trade* (Columbia, S.C., January 1951).

26. Jakle et al., *Motel in America,* 45.

27. Ibid, 79, 82.

28. Norma Whisnant, discussion with Barbara Stokes, August 3, 2004; E. Horry Benton, interview by Barbara Stokes, April 27, 2004.

29. Greater Myrtle Beach Chamber of Commerce, Myrtle Beach, S.C., *The Role of Advertising & Travel Promotion in the Economic Development of Myrtle Beach, S.C.: A Decade of Progress, 1954–1964,* brochure (1964), 39. The $40 million in new construction did not include the construction at the Myrtle Beach Air Force Base.

30. Katherine Fuller, "Populuxe Motels: Preservation in Myrtle Beach, South Carolina", and The Wildwoods, New Jersey" (master's thesis, Goucher College, 2002), n.p.

31. Jakle et al., *Motel in America,* 79.

32. The chain hotel billed its restaurant as a Holiday Inn restaurant. It was called the Black Angus and was operated by Tony and Angie Thompson from 1956 to 1971. The Thompsons also operated the Kozy Korner beginning in 1949.

33. Ed Archer, e-mail to Barbara Stokes, August 9, 2005. Archer is vice president and associate general counsel for InterContinental Hotels Group, which owns the Holiday Inn chain.

Chapter Nine—Tourism

1. Cindy S. Aron, *Working at Play: A History of Vacations in the United States* (New York: Oxford University Press, 1999), 4–5, 16–18, 33, 49.

2. Solomon, *Myrtle Beach Today and Tomorrow,* July 31, 1935.

3. Lencek and Bosker, *The Beach,* 139–40, 147–48, 164.

4. Talbert, *So Much to Be Thankful For,* 168–70; "Newspaper Men Select Myrtle Beach," *Horry Herald,* March 13, 1922, n.p.; "Plans Making about Editors," *Horry Herald,* May 11, 1922, n.p.; "Chamber Plans Are a Success," *Horry Herald,* June 22, 1922, n.p.

5. Aron, *Working at Play,* 241n21; Julius Weinberger, "Economic Aspects of Recreation," *Harvard Business Review* 15 (Summer 1937): 448–63.

6. Horace A. Carter, *Jimmy D'Angelo and Myrtle Beach Golf* (Tabor City, N.C.: Atlantic Publishing Co., 1991), 56.

7. The term "Grand Strand" originated in 1949 with Claude and Harry Dunnagan's Grand Strand News Bureau in Ocean Drive Beach. They used the name in press releases and brochures to describe ten miles of coast from Little River through Windy Hill Beach. In 1957 the organization changed its name to Greater Myrtle Beach Chamber of Commerce, and in 1979 the name was changed to Myrtle Beach Area Chamber of Commerce. In 1959 the Greater Myrtle Beach Chamber of Commerce successfully petitioned its members in the "original" Grand Strand area to adopt the name to cover the South Carolina coastal area from the North Carolina line to Pawleys Island. See "Grand Strand Tagged to Describe 50-mile Area of Carolina Coast," *Myrtle Beach Sun and Ocean Beach News,* March 25, 1959, 1.

8. In 1950 Mark Garner and Horace Carter founded the *Myrtle Beach Sun.* They purchased the *Ocean Beach News* in 1953 and merged it with the *Sun* in 1954. Garner purchased the *Myrtle Beach News* in 1961 and merged it with the *Sun and Ocean Beach News,* forming the *Myrtle Beach Sun-News.* The latter was sold to the State-Record in 1973. Garner served as mayor of Myrtle Beach from 1966 until 1974.

9. Tom Hamrick, "My Myrtle, How You've Grown," *Sandlapper,* June 1973, 33–37.

10. Carter, *Jimmy D'Angelo,* 70, 158.

11. Greater Myrtle Beach Chamber of Commerce, Myrtle Beach, S.C., *Myrtle Beach and the Grand Strand: Our Potential as a Trade Center,* brochure, ca. 1963, Mark Garner Collection, Chapin Memorial Library, Myrtle Beach, S.C.

12. Henrietta Abeles to Sigmund Abeles, Sigmund Abeles Collection, South Caroliniana Library, University of South Carolina, Columbia.

13. The leases were not resolved until January 1990. The former Magic Harbor property was turned into a storage area for recreational vehicles in 1998.

14. "Myrtle Beach News," *Horry Herald,* June 5, 1930, n.p.; John Margolies, with Nina Garfinkel and Maria Reidelbach, *Miniature Golf* (New York: Abbeville Press, 1987), 72, 83.

15. Elvin Drew Tirrell, interview by Sarah Bryan, September 14, 2004, Myrtle Beach Oral History Project.

16. Talbert, *So Much to Be Thankful For,* 215–17.

17. Aron, *Working at Play,* 238.

18. U.S. Bureau of the Census, Thirteenth Census (1910) and Twentieth Census (1980), Horry County, Conway Township and Dogwood Neck Township (Myrtle Beach), S.C.

19. James R. Fussell and Richard G. Silvernail, "The Impact of Recreation on Coastal South Carolina," *Business and Economic Review* 13 (October 1966): 1.

20. U.S. Bureau of the Census, 1964 Census of Agriculture, Horry County, S.C., June 1966.

21. Greater Myrtle Beach Chamber of Commerce, Myrtle Beach, S.C., *The Grand Strand and Its Tourist Industry: What They Mean to Horry County* (white paper by Grand Strand–County Relations Committee, ca. 1962).

22. Greater Myrtle Beach Chamber of Commerce news release, dated February 10, 1961.

23. S.C. State Department of Parks, Recreation and Tourism, *South Carolina Travel and Tourism Data, 1972–1978* (Columbia, S.C., 1978).

24. Talbert, *So Much to Be Thankful For,* 241.

Chapter Ten—Myrtle Beach, the City, 1937–1980

1. U.S. Bureau of the Census, Fifteenth Census (1930) and Sixteenth Census (1940), Horry County, Dogwood Neck Township (Myrtle Beach), S.C.

2. "Myrtle Beach Incorporates in 1937," *Myrtle Beach Sun-News,* Strand '65 Historical-Progress Special Edition, n.d., n.p. The discussion in the following paragraphs about incorporation is from this article, unless otherwise noted.

3. "Resort Act Not Liked," *Horry Herald,* June 3, 1937, n.p.; "Election at Myrtle Beach," *Horry Herald,* May 13, 1937, 1.

4. Myrtle Beach Committee for Incorporation, "Notice for Election," August 2, 1937.

5. Athalia Stalvey Ramsey, interview by Sarah Bryan, January 21, 2005.

6. From the candidates in the earlier election, Ramsey had switched to the mayoral race, and Hughes, Nance, Pearson, and Jones dropped out of the race.

7. Myrtle Beach Committee for Incorporation, "Notice of Election," August 2, 1937.

8. "Fire Dept. Has Shown Rapid Growth," *Myrtle Beach Sun,* June 25, 1954, 1.

9. E. Horry Benton, interview by Barbara Stokes, April 27, 2004.

10. Paul Quattlebaum formed Quattlebaum Ice Company in the early 1900s, and in 1912 he merged the power company and the ice company.

11. "Company Gets Another Plant," *Horry Herald,* June 19, 1930, 1; J. A. Zeigler, "Area Has Plentiful Supply of Electricity," *Myrtle Beach News,* June 2, 1955, 6; Paul Quattlebaum, Letter to the Editor, *Myrtle Beach News,* September 7, 1951, n.p.

12. Gray, "Gray Family," 90. Gray was reelected to the city council in 1949.

13. Piedmont would begin service to Myrtle Beach in 1950.

14. "City Council Demands Letts Prove Charges," *Myrtle Beach News,* October 15, 1949, 1.

15. "Ramsey Wins by Big Vote," *Myrtle Beach News,* November 12, 1949, 1.

16. J. Marcus Smith, "Recalling Old School Days," *Myrtle Beach Sun-News,* October 18, 1997, n.p.

17. U.S. Department of the Interior, National Park Service, National Register of Historic Places Registration Forms, C1955, Multiple Property Documentation Form —Historic Resources of Myrtle Beach.

18. U.S. Air Force Historical Division, "Brief History of the Myrtle Beach Air Force Base, 1940–1956," *Independent Republic Quarterly* 13, no. 2 (Spring 1979): 10.

19. E. A. Anthony, "Self-Sufficient Myrtle Beach," in *Aero Digest, Aviation Engineering* (New York: Aeronautical Digest Publishing Corporation, April 1950); "Crescent Air Strip Underwent Name Change," *Myrtle Beach Sun and Ocean Beach News,* February 15, 1956, Sec. 2, 4.

20. Delta Airport Consultants, Horry County Department of Airports, "Myrtle Beach International Airport Master Plan," update to Final Report, November 2001, Horry County Dept. of Airports, Myrtle Beach, S.C.

21. Edgar, *South Carolina,* 518.

22. "Lone Myrtle Beach Negro Voters Requested That Names Be Removed," *State* (Columbia, S.C.), August 11, 1948, A7.

23. Tempe Oehler, interview by Barbara Stokes, March 5, 2004. Rae Farrington, a local realtor, was the first woman to be elected to the Myrtle Beach City Council in

1947. The second woman was L'Nora Misenheimer, owner of the Driftwood guest house, in 1954. The third was Marjorie Stonebrook, a civic leader, who was elected to the council in 1977.

24. "500 Hear Candidates," *Myrtle Beach News*, November 2, 1951, 1; "Know Your City," *Myrtle Beach News*, September 21, 1951, 1.

25. "Workers Celebrate as Drive Reaches Summit," *Myrtle Beach Sun and Ocean Beach News*, November 23, 1956, n.p.; *Life Sounds*, Grand Strand General Hospital newsletter, 6, no. 2 (March/April 1993); "Money Raised for Ocean View over Nine Year Period," *Myrtle Beach Sun-News*, Strand '65—30 Years of Vigorous Growth Special Issue, n.d., n.p.

26. U.S. Bureau of the Census, Sixteenth Census (1940) and Nineteenth Census (1970), Horry County, Dogwood Neck Township (Myrtle Beach), S.C.; South Carolina Budget and Control Board, Office of Research and Statistics, *South Carolina Statistical Abstract 1972;* "Retail Sales by Category in City of Myrtle Beach, 1963–1979," City of Myrtle Beach, S.C., Central Business District Master Plan Study, 1979, table 4.

27. City of Myrtle Beach, S.C., Comprehensive Plan, adopted March 1979.

Chapter Eleven—Grand Strand Leisure

1. Franklin G. Burroughs, "Duck Hunting on the Grand Strand," *Independent Republic Quarterly* 27, no. 1 (Winter 1993): 6–10.

2. E. Horry Benton, interview by Barbara Stokes, April 27, 2004.

3. Dorothy Filius Green, *Prolongation of a Vision: A History of Briarcliffe Acres, South Carolina* (N.p.: the author, 1988), 5–6; Darwin Shaw, *As Only God Can Love: A Lifetime of Companionship with Meher Baba* (Myrtle Beach, S.C.: Sheriar Press, 2003), n.p.

4. Annie Louise Chestnut Squires, "How I Remember It, Written August 1980," *Independent Republic Quarterly* 24, no. 2 (Spring 1990): 13–17.

5. Annette Epps Reesor, "A Myrtle Beach Album," *Sandlapper,* July 1975, 15–20; Alumni, Myrtle Beach Colored School, transcripts of unedited group interviews by Time Warner, Myrtle Beach, June 19, 2001, Myrtle Beach Oral History Project; Mary Sarkis Hobeika, "Big Joe Sarkis, First Foreign Born Citizen," *Independent Republic Quarterly* 2, no. 3 (July 1968): 10.

6. C. Burgin Berry, interview by Barbara Stokes and Jenifer Powers, June 26, 2003, Myrtle Beach Oral History Project.

7. "Netting Opposed," *Myrtle Beach Sun-News*, November 1, 1961, 1.

8. Blackfish is the familiar name for black sea bass.

9. Victor G. Burrell, *The Recreational Fisheries in South Carolina: The Little River Story,* S.C. Department of Natural Resources, Marine Resource Division, Charleston, S.C., June 2000, Educational Report 19, 4–29.

10. Marcus Smith, "Horse Races Were Popular on Strand," *Myrtle Beach Sun-News,* March 4, 1995, n.p.; "Washington Park Race Track 'Where the Turf Met the Surf,'" *Myrtle Beach Sun-News,* Strand '65 Historical-Progress Special Edition, June 1965, n.p.

11. Myrtle Beach City Council Minutes, May 8 and May 12, 1956.

12. An article written by E. A. Anthony, Myrtle Beach Airport manager, in April 1950 said that the U.S. War Assets Administration transferred the base in October

1948. An article by the U.S. Air Force Historical Division said that November 1, 1947, was the date that the base was deactivated, with the runways and tower transferred to the city for a municipal airport.

13. "Boston Braves Renew Contract for 1950," *Myrtle Beach News,* October 22, 1949, n.p.; "City Lists Accomplishments," *Myrtle Beach News,* October 1, 1949, n.p.

14. *The Progressive Railway of the South, Winter Golf Courses, Hotels and Boarding Houses, 1915,* Seaboard Air Line Railway brochure.

15. Frederick Miles purchased the Ocean Forest Country Club in 1944 and renamed it Pine Lakes Golf Club. It is also called "The Grandaddy" of Myrtle Beach golf courses.

16. Carter, *Jimmy D'Angelo,* 6, 57, 62; The Dunes Golf and Beach Club history, http://www.dunesgolfandbeachclub.com/history (accessed January 6, 2003).

17. Carter, *Jimmy D'Angelo,* 158.

18. Ibid., 70; Jim Pettit, "Cecil Brandon, Myrtle Beach Golf Forever Linked," *Triad Golf Today Magazine,* March–April 2002, http://www.triadgolf.com/mar-apr2002/majorplayersCecil (accessed June 4, 2005); "Golf Boom: A Snowstorm, the Package Deal, Publicity Put Grand Strand Golfing on the Map," *State* (Columbia, S.C.), September 26, 1976, E1.

Chapter Twelve—Hurricane Hazel and Its Transformation of the Grand Strand

1. Formed in 1938, the chamber of commerce was disbanded about 1941 because of World War II.

2. South Carolina State Chamber of Commerce, *Dollars in Flight.*

3. Sources for information on the progress of the storm and the city's action leading up to and after it were from several sources, including the *Myrtle Beach Sun* and the *Myrtle Beach News:* Walter R. Davis, "Hurricanes of 1954," Monthly Weather Review, National Weather Bureau, December 1954; "Horry County, South Carolina Hurricanes, 1900–1996," Atlantic Oceanographic and Meteorological Laboratory, National Oceanic and Atmospheric Administration, U.S. Department of Commerce; and Military Department, Disaster Preparedness Agency, General Administration Files, S19120, S.C. Department of Archives and History, Columbia.

4. Lloyd A. Ward, "Helping Hands," unpublished article, dated July 9, 1956, courtesy of Ann Ward.

5. Merlin Bellamy, interview by Barbara Stokes, March 23, 2004, Myrtle Beach Oral History Project.

6. Donald and Wickie Moore, interview by Barbara Stokes, September 1, 2004, Myrtle Beach Oral History Project.

7. Harry Hyman was the WMYB station manager in October 1954. Ernest W. Williams was mayor of Myrtle Beach at that time.

8. Hoyt Bellamy, interview by Barbara Stokes, February 13, 2004, Myrtle Beach Oral History Project.

9. Dino Thompson, interview by Barbara Stokes, April 7, 2004, Myrtle Beach Oral History Project.

10. U.S. Air Force, *History of the 727th Air Craft and Warning Squadron,* Microfilm Reel MO 196, Air Force Historical Agency, Washington, D.C.

11. Billy Roberts, interview by Barbara Stokes, April 14, 2004, Myrtle Beach Oral History Project.

12. Donald and Wickie Moore, interview by Barbara Stokes, September 1, 2004.

13. J. Marcus Smith, "Fickle Hazel Struck Here in Myrtle Beach," *Myrtle Beach Sun-News*, October 14, 1995, C1.

14. Merlin Bellamy, interview by Barbara Stokes, March 23, 2004.

15. Eatofel Vereen Thompson Arehart, interview by Catherine Lewis, April 16, 1993, Horry County Oral History Project.

16. Donald and Wickie Moore, interview by Barbara Stokes, September 1, 2004.

17. Frank Davis, interview by Barbara Stokes, February 12, 2004.

18. Lloyd A. Ward, "Helping Hands," unpublished article, dated July 9, 1956, courtesy of Ann Ward.

19. Dino Thompson, interview by Barbara Stokes, April 7, 2004.

20. Eatofel Vereen Thompson Arehart, interview by Catherine Lewis, April 16, 1993.

21. Donald and Wickie Moore, interview by Barbara Stokes, September 1, 2004.

22. C. Burgin Berry, interview by Catherine Lewis, March 18, 1991, Horry County Oral History Project.

23. Hoyt Bellamy, interview by Barbara Stokes, February 13, 2004.

24. Merlin Bellamy, interview by Barbara Stokes, March 23, 2004.

25. David Michaux, interview by Barbara Stokes, February 10, 2004.

26. Merlin Bellamy, interview by Barbara Stokes, March 23, 2004.

27. Clarence Gramling, interview by Barbara Stokes, February 11, 2004, Myrtle Beach Oral History Project.

28. Jack Thompson, interview by Barbara Stokes, June 23, 2004.

29. Ashley Ward, "Helping Hands," unpublished article, dated July 9, 1956, courtesy of Ann Ward.

30. Hoyt Bellamy, interview by Barbara Stokes, February 13, 2004.

31. Dino Thompson, interview by Barbara Stokes, April 7, 2004.

32. Billy Roberts, interview by Barbara Stokes, April 14, 2004.

33. Merlin Bellamy, interview by Barbara Stokes, March 23, 2004.

34. Eatofel Vereen Thompson Arehart, interview by Catherine Lewis, April 16, 1993.

35. Clarence Gramling, interview by Barbara Stokes, February 11, 2004.

36. Willie L. Isom, interview by Damon L. Fordham, October 29, 2002, Atlantic Beach Oral History Project, Atlantic Beach Historical Society.

37. Donald and Wickie Moore, interview by Barbara Stokes, September 1, 2004.

38. David Michaux, interview by Barbara Stokes, February 10, 2004.

39. Nelson and Emily Jackson, interview by Barbara Stokes, April 29, 2004, Myrtle Beach Oral History Project.

40. Orangeburg, S.C.: Sandlapper Publishing Inc., 1990.

Chapter Thirteen—African American Community

1. "Horry County, South Carolina, 1964 Statistical Data," Horry County Development Board, Conway, S.C.

2. Christine Brogdon, *The African American Family Farm, Post Bellum to 1999: A Manual for Freewoods* (Myrtle Beach, S.C.: Freewoods Foundation, 1991), 1–26.

3. Julian J. Petty, *The Growth and Distribution of Population in South Carolina*, Bulletin No. 11, State Council for Defense, Industrial Development Committee, Columbia, S.C., July 1943, produced for the S.C. State Planning Board. The increase

in the black birth rate may be due in part to the fact that more complete registration of black births occurred in these years.

4. Jennifer Amor, "His Memory Traces Town's History," *Myrtle Beach Sun-News,* April 24, 1975, C1.

5. Rubin Wineglass, interview by Sarah Bryan, June 15, 2005, Myrtle Beach Oral History Project.

6. Jake Abraham, interview by Sarah Bryan, June 16, 2005, Myrtle Beach Oral History Project.

7. U.S. Bureau of the Census, Fifteenth Annual Census (1930), Horry County, Dogwood Neck Township (Myrtle Beach), S.C.

8. Annette Epps Reesor, "De Angel of De Lawd,, More Memories of a Childhood at Myrtle Beach," *Independent Republic Quarterly* 5, no. 3 (July 1971): 23.

9. Wallace Evans, interview by Sarah Bryan, February 7, 2005, Myrtle Beach Oral History Project.

10. Julius W. "Joe" White shined shoes at Woody's Arcade Barber Shop for fifty years. He died in 1997.

11. Genevieve Chandler Peterkin, interview by Jenifer Powers and Barbara Stokes, October 31, 2002, Myrtle Beach Oral History Project.

12. Wallace Evans, interview by Sarah Bryan, February 7, 2005.

13. Wendy Conner, interview by Jenifer Powers, March 31, 2004, Myrtle Beach Oral History Project. Electricity was not available to many homes in the black communities until the 1950s.

14. Mary Canty, interview by Diane Stokes, May 2006, Myrtle Beach Oral History Project.

15. Howard H. Quint, *Profile in Black and White: A Frank Portrait of South Carolina* (Washington, D.C.: Public Affairs Press, 1958), 15.

16. Division of Surveys and Field Service, *Horry County Schools,* 53, 136.

17. Etrulia Dozier, interview by Sarah Bryan, April 27, 2005. Dozier retired from the Horry County School District in 1998.

18. Alumni, Myrtle Beach Colored School, transcripts of unedited group interviews by Time Warner, Myrtle Beach, June 19, 2001, Myrtle Beach Oral History Project.

19. Annie Bellamy Futrell, interview by Sarah Bryan, January 22, 2005.

20. Etrulia Dozier, interview by Sarah Bryan, April 27, 2005.

21. Unless otherwise noted, this and the following account of the KKK's Myrtle Beach activities were compiled from the following sources: *Myrtle Beach Sun* and *Myrtle Beach News,* September 1, September 8, and November 17, 1950; Catherine Lewis, "Klan Had a Long Reign of Terror," *Myrtle Beach Sun-News,* July 18, 1998, C1; and Beacham, *Whitewash,* 19–54.

22. Dino Thompson, *Greek Boy, Growing Up Southern* (Myrtle Beach, S.C.: Snug Press, 1999), 192.

23. Mary Canty, interview by Diane Stokes, May 2006. The party held by the Royal Courts of King Solomon on the night of August 26, 1950, was typical of the fund-raisers to help community members who were sick and had special needs, according to Canty.

24. "Grand Dragon Placed in Jail," *Myrtle Beach News,* September 1, 1950, 1. "Klan Leader Is under Arrest; Sheriff Makes Radio Address on Incident," *Myrtle Beach Sun,* September 1, 1950, 1.

25. Lewis, "Klan Had a Long Reign of Terror," C1.

26. "Lone Myrtle Beach Negro Voters Requested That Names Be Removed," *State* (Columbia, S.C.), August 11, 1948, A7.

27. S.C. State Commission of Forestry, Desegregation Files, Box 2, S.C. Department of Archives and History, S162024, Columbia, S.C.

28. "Negroes' Bid to Enter Park Fails," *Myrtle Beach Sun and Ocean Beach News,* August 31, 1960, 1; South Carolina State Park Service History, 1942–67, http://www.discoversouthcarolina.com (accessed March 6, 2005); S.C. State Commission of Forestry, Desegregation Files, Box 2. For more information on this topic, see Stephen Lewis Cox, "The History of Negro State Parks in South Carolina, 1940–1963" (master's thesis, University of South Carolina, 1992).

29. "Myrtle Beach Air Force Base Began at Town's Tiny Municipal Airport," *Myrtle Beach Sun-News,* Strand '65 Historical-Progress Special Edition, n.d., n.p. President Harry Truman desegregated the United States military by executive order in 1948.

30. Alumni, Myrtle Beach Colored School, transcripts of unedited group interviews by Time Warner, Myrtle Beach, June 19, 2001, Myrtle Beach Oral History Project.

31. Dr. Leroy Upperman, interview by Randall Wells, August 11, 1995, Horry County Oral History Project.

32. *Atlantic Beach Newsletter,* November 1985; "Her History," Town of Atlantic Beach Web site, http://www.atlanticbeachsc.com/asps/history.asp.

33. "The Atlantic Beach Story," http://www.chazznet.net/mday984.html (accessed September 19, 2003).

34. Willie L. Isom, interview by Damon L. Fordham, October 29, 2002.

35. Annie Bellamy Futrell, interview by Sarah Bryan, January 22, 2005, Myrtle Beach Oral History Project.

36. Alice Graham, interview by Damon L. Fordham, October 10, 2002, Atlantic Beach Oral History Project.

37. Earlene Woods, interview by Damon L. Fordham, October 10, 2002, Atlantic Beach Oral History Project.

38. Moredock, *Banana Republic,* 66.

Bibliography

Primary Sources

Letters, Books, Manuscripts, Journals, Government Records, and Brochures

Abeles, Sigmund. Collection. South Caroliniana Library, University of South Carolina, Columbia.

Arcady. Oversized prospectus, hardbound. Published by Arcady Executives, New York, for limited distribution. Dated February 5, 1929. Found at Chapin Memorial Library, Myrtle Beach, S.C.

Baruch, Bernard. *The Public Years: My Own Story*. New York: Holt, Rinehart and Winston, 1960.

Byrnes, James F. *All in One Lifetime*. New York: Harper & Brothers, 1958.

City of Myrtle Beach, S.C. Central Business District Master Plan Study, 1979.

———. City Council Minutes, May 8 and May 12, 1956. Minute Book #6, January 18, 1956–December 1, 1959.

———. Comprehensive Plan, adopted April 13, 1999, amended September 2000.

———. Comprehensive Plan, adopted March 1979.

———. Zoning Ordinance, adopted September 17, 1947.

Davis, Walter R. "Hurricanes of 1954, Monthly Weather Review." National Weather Bureau, December 1954.

Delta Airport Consultants. Horry County Department of Airports, "Myrtle Beach International Airport Master Plan." Update to Final Report, November 2001. Horry County Department of Airports, Myrtle Beach, S.C.

Gray, Esther Nance. "The Best of Many Worlds." Unpublished family manuscript, n.d.

Gray, Philip. "The Gray Family." Unpublished family manuscript, printed ca. 1970.

Greater Myrtle Beach Chamber of Commerce, Myrtle Beach, S.C. *The Grand Strand and Its Tourist Industry: What They Mean to Horry County*. White paper by Grand Strand–County Relations Committee, ca. 1962.

———. *Myrtle Beach and the Grand Strand: Our Potential as a Trade Center*. Brochure. Mark Garner Collection, Chapin Memorial Library, Myrtle Beach, S.C.

———. News Release, February 10, 1961.

———. *The Role of Advertising & Travel Promotion in the Economic Development of Myrtle Beach, S.C.: A Decade of Progress, 1954–1964*. 1964.

Horry County Council. Petitions for Licenses to Operate Tourist Courts, 1938–40. L26087, S.C. Department of Archives and History, Columbia.

Horry County Register of Deeds. Conway, S.C., Mortgage and Deed Records, 1900–1980.

"Horry County, South Carolina, 1964 Statistical Data." Horry County Development Board, Conway, S.C.

The Independent Republic Quarterly. Vols. 1–35. Conway, S.C.: Horry County Historical Society.

Merrill, Adeline Godfrey Pringle. "A Personal History of the F. G. Burroughs Family." Unpublished manuscript. 2003. Chapin Memorial Library, Myrtle Beach, S.C.

Military Department. Disaster Preparedness Agency. General Administration Files, S19120, S.C. Department of Archives and History, Columbia.

Myrtle Beach Committee for Incorporation. "Notice for Election," August 2, 1937.

Myrtle Beach High School Yearbook, 1959.

Peterkin, Genevieve Chandler. As told to William P. Baldwin. *Heaven Is a Beautiful Place.* Columbia: University of South Carolina Press, 2000.

Petty, Julian J. *The Growth and Distribution of Population in South Carolina.* Bulletin No. 11, State Council for Defense, Industrial Development Committee, Columbia, S.C., July 1943. Produced for the S.C. State Planning Board.

The Progressive Railway of the South, Winter Golf Courses, Hotels and Boarding Houses, 1915. Seaboard Air Line Railway brochure. South Caroliniana Library, University of South Carolina, Columbia, S.C.

Roosevelt, Franklin D. Complete Presidential Transcripts of Da Capo Press, 1972. U.S. National Archives and Records Administration, Washington, D.C.

Solomon, Bernard S., ed. *Myrtle Beach Today and Tomorrow.* Wilmington, N.C.: Wilmington Stamp and Printing, August 16, 1935.

South Carolina Budget and Control Board. Office of Research and Statistics. *South Carolina Statistical Abstract 1972.*

South Carolina State Chamber of Commerce. *Dollars in Flight: A Manual Showing Why and How South Carolina Should Promote Tourist Trade.* Columbia, S.C., January 1951.

South Carolina State Commission of Forestry. Civilian Conservation Corps. "Myrtle Beach State Park, 1934–42." S.C. Department of Archives and History, S162004, Columbia, S.C.

————. Desegregation Files, Box 2. S.C. Department of Archives and History, S162024, Columbia, S.C.

South Carolina State Council of Defense. *Historical Account of the Activities of the South Carolina State Council of Defense, August 1, 1940–June 30, 1944.* Columbia, S.C., 1944.

————. Miscellaneous Correspondence, 1917–18. Box 10, S.C. Department of Archives and History, S192069, Columbia, S.C.

South Carolina State Department of Parks, Recreation and Tourism. Annual Reports, 1970–71, 1975–76. Columbia, S.C.

————. Selected archival materials on the history of Myrtle Beach State Park.

————. *South Carolina Travel and Tourism Data, 1972–1978.* 1978.

Springs, Brig. Gen. Holmes B. *Selective Service in South Carolina, 1940–1947: An Historical Report.* Columbia, S.C., 1948.

Steen, Carl. *Archaeological Investigations at Heron Pond/Diamond Back Development, Horry County, South Carolina.* Columbia, S.C.: Diachronic Research Foundation,

2000. Site report on file at the S.C. Department of Archives and History, Columbia.

Thompson, Dino. *Greek Boy, Growing Up Southern.* Myrtle Beach, S.C.: Snug Press, 1999.

Turner, Robert. "Myrtle Beach State Park." Superintendents' Report, S.C. State Parks Superintendents, meeting, 1984.

U.S. Air Force. *History of the 727th Air Craft and Warning Squadron.* Microfilm Reel MO 196, Air Force Historical Agency, Washington, D.C.

U.S. Bureau of the Census. Twelfth through Twentieth Censuses (1900–1980), Horry County, Dogwood Neck Township, Myrtle Beach, S.C..

U.S. Department of Commerce. National Oceanic and Atmospheric Administration. Atlantic Oceanographic and Meteorological Laboratory. *Horry County, South Carolina, Hurricanes, 1900–1996.*

U.S. Department of the Interior. Chesterfield Inn, Horry County, S.C.

———. German Band Organ, Horry County, S.C.

———. Historic Resources of Myrtle Beach, Horry County, S.C.

———. National Park Service. National Register of Historic Places Registration Forms, C1995.

———. The Periscope, Horry County, S.C.

———. Pleasant Inn, Horry County, S.C.

U.S. Eastern District of South Carolina, District Court, Florence Division. Civil Action No. 657, filed December 18, 1941.

U.S. Navy War Records Office. *Official Records of the Union and Confederate Navies in the War of the Rebellion.* Series 1, vol. 15, 409–11.

Ward, Lloyd A. "Helping Hands." Unpublished article, dated July 9, 1956. Courtesy of Ann Ward.

Interviews, Oral Histories

Atlantic Beach Oral History Project, Atlantic Beach Historical Society, S.C.
Graham, Alice. Interview by Damon L. Fordham. October 10, 2002.
Isom, Willie L. Interview by Damon L. Fordham. October 29, 2002.
Woods, Earlene. Interview by Damon L. Fordham. October 10, 2002.

Horry County Oral History Project, Kimbel Library, Coastal Carolina University, Conway, S.C.
Arehart, Eatofel Vereen Thompson. Interview by Catherine Lewis. April 16, 1993.
Benton, E. Horry. Interview by Catherine Lewis. December 4, 1992.
Berry, C. Burgin. Interview by Catherine Lewis. March 18, 1991.
Macklen, Julia. Interview by Catherine Lewis. March 25, 1998.
Upperman, Dr. Leroy. Interview by Randall Wells. August 11, 1995.

Myrtle Beach Memories. S.C. Educational Television, Spring/Summer 2003.
Clardy, Harold. Unedited videotape 15.
Hora, June. Unedited videotape 13.

Myrtle Beach Oral History Project, Chapin Memorial Library, Myrtle Beach, S.C.
Abeles, Sigmund. Interview by Sarah Bryan. May 22, 2004.
Abraham, Jake. Interview by Sarah Bryan. June 16, 2005.
Alumni, Myrtle Beach Colored School. Transcripts of unedited group interviews by Time Warner, Myrtle Beach. June 19, 2001.

Bellamy, Howell V. Jr. Interview by Sarah Bryan. April 28, 2005.

Bellamy, Joseph, Roosevelt, and James. Interview by Sarah Bryan and Barbara Stokes. February 15, 2004.

Bellamy, Merlin. Interview by Barbara Stokes. March 23, 2004.

Benton, E. Horry. Interview by Barbara Stokes. April 27, 2004.

Berry, C. Burgin. Interview by Barbara Stokes and Jenifer Powers. June 26, 2003.

Canty, Mary. Interview by Diane Stokes. May 2006.

Clardy, Harold. Interview by Barbara Stokes. February 7, 2003.

Conner, Wendy. Interview by Jenifer Powers. March 31, 2004.

Crews, Louise Springs. Interview by Sarah Bryan. October 16, 2004.

Cribb, Keith. Interview by Sarah Bryan. November 16, 2004.

Dozier, Etrulia. Interview by Sarah Bryan. April 27, 2005.

Epps, Emma J. Bryan. Interview by Sarah Bryan. March 9, 2004.

Evans, Wallace. Interview by Sarah Bryan. February 7, 2005.

Futrell, Annie Bellamy. Interview by Sarah Bryan. January 22, 2005.

Gramling, Clarence. Interview by Barbara Stokes. February 11, 2004.

Hartshorne, Harold. Interview by Jenifer Powers. December 19, 2002.

Hussey, Richard M. Jr. Interview by Sarah Bryan. November 17, 2004.

Jackson, Nelson and Emily. Interview by Barbara Stokes. April 29, 2004.

Joyner, Charles. Interview by Sarah Bryan. March 20, 2004.

Moore, Donald and Wickie. Interview by Barbara Stokes. September 1, 2004.

Oehler, Tempe. Interview by Jenifer Powers. August 6, 2003. Interview by Barbara Stokes. March 5, 2004.

Peterkin, Genevieve Chandler. Interview by Jenifer Powers and Barbara Stokes. October 31, 2002.

Ramsey, Athalia Stalvey. Interview by Sarah Bryan. January 21, 2005.

Roberts, Billy. Interview by Barbara Stokes. April 14, 2004.

Smith, Janis Stewart. Interview by Sarah Bryan. August 24, 2003.

Thompson, Dino. Interview by Barbara Stokes. April 7, 2004.

Tirrell, Elvin Drew. Interview by Sarah Bryan. September 14, 2004.

Turner, Robert and Ann Wilson. Interview by Jenifer Powers. February 25, 2004.

Wineglass, Rubin. Interview by Sarah Bryan. June 15, 2005.

Other Interviews, Discussions

Archer, Ed. E-mail to Barbara Stokes. August 9, 2005.

Benton, James C. Interview with Barbara Stokes. July 8, 2003.

Bellamy, Hoyt. Interview by Barbara Stokes. February 13, 2004.

Davis, Frank. Interview by Barbara Stokes. February 12, 2004.

McMillan, Susan and Marshall. Discussion with Barbara Stokes. July 29 and August 3, 2005.

Michaux, David. Interview by Barbara Stokes. February 10, 2004.

Roberts, Billy. Discussion with Barbara Stokes. May 20, 2005.

Thompson, Jack. Interview with Barbara Stokes. June 23, 2004.

Whisnant, Norma. Discussion with Barbara Stokes. August 3, 2004.

Newspapers

Beaufort Gazette. Beaufort, S.C. June 18, 1925.

Horry Herald. Conway, S.C. Selected issues, 1900–1937.

Lowcountry Review. May 2–23, 1990.

Myrtle Beach News. Selected issues, 1938–1958.

Myrtle Beach Sun-News. History columns, 1990–1997. Selected issues, 1954–1990.

Myrtle Beach Sun and Ocean Beach News. Selected issues, 1951–1958.

North Myrtle Beach Times. July 1, 1976.

State. Columbia, S.C. Selected issues, 1924, 1948, 1976.

Secondary Sources

Aron, Cindy S. *Working at Play: A History of Vacations in the United States.* New York: Oxford University Press, 1999.

Bartley, Numan. *The New South, 1945–1980: The Story of the South's Modernization.* Vol. 11 of *The History of the South,* ed. Wendell Holmes Stephenson and E. Merton Coulter. Baton Rouge: Louisiana State University Press and The Littlefield Foundation for Southern History of The University of Texas, 1995.

Beacham, Frank. *Whitewash: A Southern Journey through Music, Mayhem and Murder.* New York: the author, 2002.

Bedford, A. Goff. *The Independent Republic—A Survey History of Horry County.* 2nd ed. Conway, S.C.: Horry County Historical Society, 1989.

Biles, Roger. *The South and the New Deal.* Lexington: University Press of Kentucky, 1994.

Bishop, Eleanor C. *Prints in the Sand: The U.S. Coast Guard Beach Patrol during World War II.* Missoula, Mont.: Pictorial Histories Publishing Co., Inc., 1989.

Brogdon, Christine. *The African American Family Farm, Post Bellum to 1999: A Manual for Freewoods.* Myrtle Beach, S.C.: Freewoods Foundation, 1991.

Brunson, Costella. *Revisiting Our Past, Focusing on Our Present, While Envisioning Our Future: 100th Anniversary of Sandy Grove Baptist Church.* Brochure. Myrtle Beach, S.C.: Sandy Grove Baptist Church, 2002.

Burrell, Victor G. *The Recreational Fisheries in South Carolina: The Little River Story.* Educational Report 19. S.C. Department of Natural Resources. Marine Resource Division. Charleston, S.C., June 2000.

Carlton, David L. "Unbalanced Growth and Industrialization: The Case of South Carolina." In *Developing Dixie: Modernization in a Traditional Society,* ed. Winfred B. Moore Jr., Joseph F. Tripp, and Lyon G. Tyler Jr. Westport, Conn.: Greenwood Press, 1988.

Carter, Horace A. *Jimmy D'Angelo and Myrtle Beach Golf.* Tabor City, N.C.: Atlantic Publishing Co., 1991.

Davey, Kitty. *Love Alone Prevails: A Story of Life with Meher Baba.* North Myrtle Beach, S.C.: Sheriar Press, 1981.

Division of Surveys and Field Service. *Horry County Schools: A Survey Report.* Nashville: George Peabody College for Teachers, 1946.

Edgar, Walter. *South Carolina: A History.* Columbia: University of South Carolina Press, 1998.

Eudy, J. B., and Lloyce V. Nelson. "From the Depression Years, a Great Need Gave Birth to the 3-Cs." Unpublished manuscript. Thomas Cooper Library, University of South Carolina, Columbia.

Federal Writers Project of the WPA. *First United Methodist Church History, Myrtle Beach, South Carolina, 1919–2000.* Myrtle Beach, S.C.: Fernandez Press, Inc., n.d.

————. *The History of First United Methodist Church, Myrtle Beach, South Carolina, 1938–1988.* Myrtle Beach, S.C.: Kwik Printing, n.d.

————. "Mount Olive AME Church." Unpublished article. Horry County Vertical Files, South Caroliniana Library, University of South Carolina, Columbia. Gift to the library on May 30, 1992.

————. *The Ocean Highway—New Brunswick, New Jersey to Jacksonville, Florida.* American Guide Series. New York: Modern Age Books, Inc., 1938.

————. *Tales along the Grand Strand of South Carolina.* Winston-Salem, N.C.: Bandit Books, 1996.

Green, Dorothy Filius. *Prolongation of a Vision: A History of Briarcliffe Acres, South Carolina.* N.p.: the author, 1988.

Halberstam, David. *The Fifties.* New York: Fawcett Books, 1993.

Hamer, Fritz. *The Homefront and the Beginning of Change: World War II and South Carolina, 1941–1945.* Columbia, S.C.: Palmetto Conservation Foundation, 1997.

Harmon, Michael, and Rodney Snedeker. "The Archaeological Record of Tar and Pitch Production in Coastal Carolina." In *Carolina's Historical Landscapes: Archaeological Perspectives,* ed. Linda F. Stine et al. Knoxville: University of Tennessee Press, 1997.

Hayes, Jack Irby Jr. *South Carolina and the New Deal.* Columbia: University of South Carolina Press, 2001.

"History of St. Andrew Catholic Church." In *St. Andrew Catholic Church Parish Directory, 2000–2001.*

Huff, Archie Vernon. *Greenville: The History of the City and County in the South Carolina Piedmont.* Columbia: University of South Carolina Press, 1995.

The Independent Republic Quarterly. Vols. 1–35. Conway, S.C.: Horry County Historical Society.

Jakle, John A., Keith A. Sculle, and Jefferson S. Rogers. *The Motel in America.* Baltimore: Johns Hopkins University Press, 1996.

James, Frederick C. *African Methodist Episcopal Church in South Carolina, A Bicentennial Focus.* N.p.: Seventh Episcopal District, 1987.

Jones, Lewis P. "History of Public Education in South Carolina." In *Public Education in South Carolina: Historical, Political and Legal Perspective,* ed. Thomas R. McDaniel. Spartanburg, S.C.: Bookstore, Converse College, 1984.

————. "Religion in South Carolina: An Overview." In *Religion in South Carolina,* ed. Charles Lippy. Columbia: University of South Carolina Press, 1993.

Joseph, J. W. "Building to Grow: Agrarian Adaptations to South Carolina's Historical Landscapes." In *Carolina's Historical Landscapes: Archaeological Perspectives,* ed. Linda F. Stine et al. Knoxville: University of Tennessee Press, 1997.

Lencek, Lena, and Gideon Bosker. *The Beach: The History of Paradise on Earth.* New York: Viking Press, 1998.

Lewis, Catherine H. *Horry County, South Carolina 1730–1993.* Columbia: University of South Carolina Press, 1998.

Life Sounds. Grand Strand General Hospital newsletter, vol. 6, no. 2, March/April 1993.

Margolies, John, with Nina Garfinkel and Maria Reidelbach. *Miniature Golf.* New York: Abbeville Press, 1987.

McGovern, James R. *And a Time for Hope: America in the Great Depression.* Westport, Conn.: Praeger, 2000.

McMillan, Susan Hoffer. *Myrtle Beach and Conway in Vintage Postcards.* Charleston, S.C.: Arcadia, 2001.

————. *Myrtle Beach and the Grand Strand.* Charleston, S.C.: Arcadia, 2004.

Milliken, Helen. *From the Beginning: A History of the Burroughs & Chapin Company.* Myrtle Beach, S.C.: Sheriar Press, 2004.

Moredock, Will. *Banana Republic: A Year in the Heart of Myrtle Beach.* Charleston, S.C.: Frontline Press, Ltd., 2003.

Nash, Gerald D. *The Crucial Era: The Great Depression and World War II, 1929–1945.* 2nd ed. New York: St. Martin's Press, 1992.

Parker, Randall E. *Reflections on the Great Depression.* Northhampton, Mass.: Edward Elgar, 2002.

Quint, Howard H. *Profile in Black and White: A Frank Portrait of South Carolina.* Washington, D.C.: Public Affairs Press, 1958.

Rawls, Walton, ed. *A Century of American Sculpture: Treasures from Brookgreen Gardens.* New York: Abbeville Press, 1981.

Runte, Alfred. *National Parks: The American Experience.* 3rd ed. Lincoln: University of Nebraska Press, 1987.

Sass, Herbert Ravenel. *The Story of the South Carolina Lowcountry.* 3 vols. West Columbia, S.C.: J. F. Hyer, 1956.

Shaw, Darwin. *As Only God Can Love: A Lifetime of Companionship with Meher Baba.* Myrtle Beach, S.C.: Sheriar Press, 2003.

Sigmon, Ray, Mike Foley, and Irvin Pitts. *Huntington Beach State Park Visitor's Guide.* Columbia: S.C. State Department of Parks, Recreation and Tourism, 2001.

Talbert, Roy, Jr. *So Much To Be Thankful For: The Conway National Bank and the Economic History of Horry County.* Columbia, S.C.: Conway National Bank, 2003.

Thom, Bruce G. *Coastal and Fluvial Landforms: Horry and Marion Counties, South Carolina.* Baton Rouge: Louisiana State University Press, 1967.

Whitmire, Mary Laird. "The WPA and Development of the Public Library System in South Carolina." Unpublished manuscript. Connie Schulz File, South Caroliniana Library, University of South Carolina, Columbia.

Willcox, Henry Trezevant. "Growing Up with Myrtle Beach." In *Musings of a Hermit,* ed. Clarke A. Willcox. 4th ed. Murrells Inlet, S.C.: The Hermitage, 1973.

Wilson, Ann, Paul McCormack, and Scott Enter. "History of Myrtle Beach State Park." Unpublished manuscript. n.d.

Witzel, Michael Karl. *The American Gas Station.* Osceola, Wis.: Motorbooks International, 1992.

Woodrum, Tommy, ed. *Sandy Presbyterians: One Man's View of the Presbyterian Churches on the Grand Strand.* Albans, W.Va.: the author, 1989.

Magazine and Journal Articles

Anthony, E. A. "Self-Sufficient Myrtle Beach." *Aero Digest, Aviation Engineering.* New York: Aeronautical Digest Publishing Corporation, April 1950.

Engelmayer, Reinhold. "The History of Early Man in the Grand Strand Area." *On the Beach* (n.d.). Found in Horry County Vertical Files, South Caroliniana Library, University of South Carolina, Columbia.

Floyd, Blanche. "When the POWs Came." *Myrtle Beach Magazine.* N.d., 24–25.

Hamrick, Tom. "My Myrtle, How You've Grown." *Sandlapper: The Magazine of South Carolina.* June 1973, 33–37.

McMillan, Susan. "Myrtle Beach Melodies." *Sandlapper: The Magazine of South Carolina.* July 1977, 25.

Moore, John Hammond. "Nazi Troopers in South Carolina, 1944–1946." *South Carolina Historical Magazine* 81 (1980): 306–15.

"Myrtle Beach, South Carolina: America's Finest Strand." *National Real Estate Journal.* June 10, 1929.

Reesor, Annette E. "A Myrtle Beach Album." *Sandlapper: The Magazine of South Carolina.* July 1975, 15–20.

Rhyne, Nancy. "The Arcady Dream, Part I." *Pee Dee Magazine* 2, no. 5 (March 1989).

———. "The Arcady Dream, Part II." *Pee Dee Magazine* 2, no. 6 (April 1989).

Simmons, Rick. "Did German U-Boats Patrol the Grand Strand during World War II?" *Alternatives News Magazine,* Myrtle Beach, S.C. July 9–26, 1987.

Theses, Dissertations

Craigie, Janel. "The Ocean Forest Hotel." Senior Thesis Project, Memphis State University, May 1987.

Dunlap, James A. III. "Victims of Neglect: The Career and Creations of John T. Woodside, 1865–1986." Master's thesis, University of South Carolina, 1986.

Fuller, Katherine. "Populuxe Motels: Preservation in Myrtle Beach, South Carolina, and The Wildwoods, New Jersey." Master's thesis, Goucher College, 2002.

Fussell, James R. "Some Aspects of the Geography of Recreation in Coastal South Carolina." Master's thesis, University of South Carolina, 1966. Also published as article in *Business and Economic Review,* October 1966.

Kennerly, Edna. "The Civilian Conservation Corps as a Social Resource in South Carolina." Master's thesis, University of South Carolina, 1940.

Lofton, Paul Stroman. "A Social and Economic History of Columbia, South Carolina, during the Great Depression, 1929–1940." Ph.D. diss., University of Texas at Austin, 1977.

Stokes, Barbara F. "The Evolution of a Historic Preservation Ethic in Myrtle Beach, S.C." Master's thesis, University of South Carolina, 2003.

Wyatt, Judy Ledford. "United States Policy toward German Prisoners of War and Its Application in South Carolina." Master's thesis, University of South Carolina, 1985.

Electronic Sources

"About the Base: Myrtle Beach Air Force Base History." http://www.myrtlebeachon line.com (accessed August 21, 2005).

"The Atlantic Beach Story." www.chazznet.net/mday984.html (accessed September 29, 2003).

"A Brief History of FPC." First Presbyterian Church Myrtle Beach. http://www .mbfpc.org (accessed January 15, 2004).

Census of Classic Wood Carousels. National Carousel Association. http://www.nca usa.org/census/census-CLA (accessed May 3, 2005).

Dunes Golf and Beach Club history. http://www.dunesgolfandbeachclub.com/ history (accessed January 6, 2003).

"Her History." Town of Atlantic Beach Web site. http://www.atlanticbeachsc.com/ asps/history.asp (accessed June 6, 2005).

Horry-Georgetown Technical College Mission Statement. http://www.hgtc.edu/welcome/mission.htm (accessed June 25, 2005).

"How the Wheels Got Turning: A Historical Perspective on American Roads." http://www.inventors.about.com/library/inventors/blcar3.html (accessed March 3, 2005).

Howard, George A. "Carolina Bays." Electronically published paper, written 1997. http://www.georgehoward.net/cbays.htm (accessed March 21, 2005).

Kenrick, John. "A History of the Musical Minstrel Shows." http://www.musicals101.com/minstrel (accessed May 3, 2005).

"Lewis Ocean Bay Heritage Preserve." Heritage Trust Program Preserve Guide. South Carolina Department of Natural Resources. http://www.dnr.state.sc.us/wild/heritage/hp.lewisob/default.htm (accessed March 21, 2005).

"Meher Baba." Religious Movements home page. http://www.religiousmovements.lib.virginia.edu/nrms/baba.com (accessed June 21, 2003).

1929 Atlantic Coastal Highway map. http://www.sc.edu/library/socar/images/im00spr/map3.jpg (accessed March 5, 2005).

Pettit, Jim. "Cecil Brandon, Myrtle Beach Golf Forever Linked." *Triad Golf Today Magazine*. March–April 2002. http://www.triadgolf.com/mar-apr2002/major playersCecil (accessed June 4, 2005).

Slave Narrative Collection. Manuscript and Prints and Photographs Division, Library of Congress. http://www.memory.loc.gov/ammem/snhtml/

South Carolina State Park Service History. http://www.discoversouthcarolina.com/stateparks/1942.asp (accessed March 6, 2005).

"354 Fighter Wing." Air Force Historical Research Division. http://www.maxwell.af.mil/au/afrha/wwwroot/rso/wings_groups/pages (accessed August 11, 2005).

West, Jean. "The Devil's Blue Dye: Indigo and Slavery." From *Slavery in America* multimedia project. http://www.slaveryinamerica.org/history/hs_es_indigo.htm (accessed August 20, 2005).

Index

Page references given in *italics* indicate illustrations or material contained in their captions.